South W
Family Histories

CORNWALL · DEVON · DORSET
GLOUCESTERSHIRE · SOMERSET
WILTSHIRE

Stuart A. Raymond

Published by the
Federation of Family History Societies (Publications) Ltd.,
The Benson Room, Birmingham & Midlands Institute,
Margaret Street, Birmingham, B3 3BS, U.K.

Copies also obtainable from:

S.A. and M.J. Raymond
P.O. Box 35
Exeter EX1 3YZ

First published 1998

ISBN: 1-86006-073-0

ISSN: 1033-2065

Printed and bound at the Alden Press, Oxford

Introduction

Genealogy is a never ending pursuit. The genealogist who says he has traced all his ancestors is a person to doubt. Nevertheless, many genealogists have undertaken an enormous amount of research, and have discovered much interesting information concerning their families. Some of this information has been published, and is readily available to researchers in libraries throughout the English-speaking world. The purpose of this book is to list all published histories and pedigrees relating to families which were resident in the historic counties of Cornwall, Devon, Dorset, Bristol, Gloucestershire, Somerset and Wiltshire. This listing includes published books and journal articles; however, it excludes numerous notes and queries published in family history society journals, except where the content is important. It also excludes pedigrees published in works primarily devoted to other topics, or in pedigree collections. Many such works are listed in other bibliographies in the *British genealogical bibliographies* series. Works dealing with specific genealogical sources, such as wills or monumental inscriptions, and relating to specific families, are also listed separately in the county volumes of this series. Biographies are not included. Numerous family histories also exist in a handful of copies deposited in one or two libraries; such works are excluded from this listing as being unpublished - although it has not always been easy to draw the line between published and unpublished material. Although it is as comprehensive a listing as possible, I am well aware that there are likely to be works that have been missed. If you are an assiduous researcher, you may well come across such items. If you do, please let me know, so that they can be included in the next edition.

Be warned — just because information has been published, it does not necessarily follow that it is accurate. I have not made any judgement on the accuracy of the works cited; that is up to you.

This book is based on the 'family histories' sections of the relevant county volumes in the *British genealogical bibliographies* series, which it supersedes. Many other titles have also been included; I am grateful to those who have written in with corrections to my previous volumes, and also to the librarians of the institutions where I have identified new titles — especially to Ian Maxted of the West Country Studies library in Exeter. Other libraries used for this book include the Devon Family History Society, the Somerset Local Studies Library, the Somerset Archaeological and Natural History Society, the Society of Genealogists and the British Library, amongst others. I am also grateful to Mark Gant, Claire Barraclough and Judy Morris, who all assisted with typing, to Brian Christmas for proof-reading, and to Bob Boyd who saw this book through the press. My thanks too to the officers of the Federation of Family History Societies, and to my family, whose support is vital for the continuation of this series.

Stuart A. Raymond.

Abbreviations

B.G.A.S.T.	Bristol and Gloucestershire Archaeological Society transactions
C.F.H.S.J.	Cornwall Family History Society journal
C.K.L.H.S.B.	Charlton Kings Local History Society bulletin
D.A.Tr.	Devonshire Association ... transactions
D.C.N.Q.	Devon and Cornwall notes and queries
D.F.H.	Devon family historian
D.N.	Proceedings of the Dorset Natural History and Archaeological Society
D.N.Q.	Devon notes and queries
E.D.A.A.S.Tr.	Exeter Diocesan Architectural and Archaeological Society transactions
E.D.A.S.Tr.	Exeter Diocesan Architectural Society transactions
F.F.	Forest fotsteps: journal of the Royal Forest of Dean Family History Society
G.N.Q.	Gloucestershire notes and queries
G.T.	The Greenwood tree: newsletter of the Somerset and Dorset Family History Society
J.B.A.	Journal of the Bristol and Avon Family History Society
J.D.F.H.S.	Journal of the Dorset Family History Society
J.G.F.H.S.	Journal of the Gloucestershire Family History Society
J.R.I.C.	Journal of the Royal Institution of Cornwall
M.G.H.	Miscellanea genealogica et heraldica
N.E.H.G.R.	New England historical and genealogical register
N.G.D.C.	Notes and gleanings ... Devon and Cornwall
N.Q.S.D.	Notes and queries for Somerset and Dorset
N.S.	New series
S.A.N.H.S.	Somerset Archaeological and Natural History Society proceedings
W.A.	Western antiquary
W.A.M.	Wiltshire archaeological and natural history magazine
W.F.H.S.	Wiltshire Family Society [journal]
W.N.Q.	Wiltshire notes and queries

Bibliographic Presentation

Authors' names are in SMALL CAPITALS. Book and journal titles are in *italics.* Articles appearing in journals, and essays, *etc.,* which form only part of a book, are in inverted commas and textface type. Volume numbers are in **bold** and the individual number of the journal may be shown in parentheses. These are normally followed by the place of publication (except where this is London, which is omitted), the name of the publisher and the date of publication. In the case of articles, further figures indicate page numbers.

Abbot
See Raymond

Abington
See Goodden

Acland
ACLAND, ANNE. *A Devon family: the story of the Aclands.* Chichester: Phillimore, 1981.

ACLAND, ANNE. *Killerton, Devon.* National Trust, 1997. Guidebook; virtually a history of the Acland family, including pedigree, 12-20th c.

ACLAND, J.A. *Aclands — and the Sea.* Dorchester: Dorset Press, 1976. Includes pedigree of Acland of Columb John, 12-17th c., and of Killerton, 12-20th c.

ACLAND, R., SIR. 'Six generations of change', *D.A.Tr.* **106**, 1974, 1-16.

AUTHERS, W. 'Devon memorials in Lichfield Cathedral - (Acland and Taylor)', *D.C.N.Q.* **33**, 1974-7, 225.

BESWETHERICK, KATHLEEN. *The Aclands and Bude Haven: the story of a Devon family and a Cornish town.* Bude: the author, 1995. 19th c., but includes pedigree, 12-20th c.

REYNOLDS, H.F. 'Acland of Fremington, Devon', *D.C.N.Q.* **17**, 1932-3, 360-2. 16-18th c.

Adams
BARTLETT, J.GARDNER. *Henry Adams of Somersetshire, England and Braintree, Mass: his English ancestry and some of his descendants.* New York: privately printed, 1927.

FAIRBANKS, HIRAM FRANCIS. 'English ancestry of Henry Adams of Braintree', *N.E.H.G.R.* **59**, 1906, 320-22. Of Somerset and Devon.

TOY, H. SPENCER. *The Adamses of Lidcot, at Laneast, Launceston.* Launceston: Wordens of Cornwall, 1969. 19th c.

Addington
BELFIELD, E.M.G. *The annals of the Addington family.* Winchester: Wykeham Press, 1959. Of Devon, Northamptonshire, Staffordshire, etc., Viscounts Sidmouth. Includes folded pedigree, 14-20th c.

Adeane
See Dene

Agg
'Hewletts and the Agg family', *Cheltenham Local History Society journal* **5**, 1987, 11-22. 19th c.

Alford
ALFORD, JOSIAH GEORGE. *Alford family notes, ancient and modern.* Phillimore, 1908. Dorset family.

STANDERWICK, JOHN WM. 'Alford family of Co. Somerset', *N.Q.S.D.* **5**, 1897-8, 69-70. See also 190 & 219.

Allen
ALLEN, FRANCIS OLCOTT. 'Allen family', *N.E.H.G.R.* **51**, 1897, 212-4. Extracts from Braunton parish register, 1581-1626.

EVANS, H.R. 'A Cornish family of tin-founders', *D.C.N.Q.* **28**, 1959-61, 209-10 & 229-33. Allen family, 18th c.

ROWE, JOSEPH HAMBLEY. 'The parentage and ancestry of Ralph Allen, the man of Bath', *J.R.I.C.* **18**(57), 1911, 365-73. 17-18th c.

Allin
ALLIN, GEORGE R. *Allin families of North Devonshire; with allied families Banbury, Detwiler, Hamm and Pontius.* Baltimore: Gateway Press, 1988. 18-20th c., includes pedigrees.

Alye
'The family of Alye', *Herald & genealogist* **6**, 1871, 223-31. Of Tewkesbury; includes pedigrees, 17th c.

Ames
AMES, REGINALD. 'Pedigree of Ames', *Genealogist* **2**, 1878, 273-81. Of Somerset, Gloucestershire, Hertfordshire and London; 17-19th c.

Amiel
See Merryweather

Amory
MEREDITH, GERTRUDE EUPHEMIA. *The descendants of Hugh Amory, 1605-1805.* Chiswick Press, 1901. Of Wrington, Bristol, the United States, *etc.,* 17-18th c. Includes pedigrees.

Andrew
SKINNER, A.J. 'Courtenay and Barnett families: issue of John Andrew, M.D.', *D.C.N.Q.* **14**, 1926-7, 163-4. Despite the title, primarily concerned with the 18th c. Andrew family.
See also Pitman

Andrews
'Dorset Bible entries', *N.Q.S.D.* **21**, 1935, 138.

Angove
ANGOVE, WENDY. 'The Angoves of Trevenson', *C.F.H.S.J.* **53**, 1989, 24 & 27. 17-18th c.

Angwin
ANGWIN, DONALD A., & BURNS, SHIRLEY G. *A history of the George Angwin family: Cornwall, England, 1490-1852; America, 1852-1855; Australia, 1855-1988.* Medina, Western Australia: S.G. Burns, 1988.

Anketell
See Bingham

Annear
ANNEAR, ADRIAN E.T. 'Annear name theories', *C.F.H.S.J.* **65**, 1992, 36-7. On the origin of the surname.

Annesley
'Royal and baronial descents of the families of Annesley, Cotton, Booth, Tyndale, and others', *B.G.A.S.T.* **14**, 1889-90, 101-16.

Annett
ANNETTE, F.H. 'Annetts and Annett in the Wessex region', *W.F.H.S.* **6**, 1982, 4-6. In Wiltshire, Berkshire, Hampshire and Gloucestershire; 18th c.

Anstis
BEWES, DAVID. 'Cornish Garter kings of arms', *C.F.H.S.J.* **43**, 1987, 14-17. John Anstis and his son held the office of Garter king of arms between them from 1718 to 1754. Bewes' article includes a pedigree, 17-18th c.
WAGNER, ANTHONY, & ROWSE, A.L. *John Anstis: Garter King of Arms.* H.M.S.O., 1992. 18th c., of Cornwall.

Apsley
HANKEY, JULIA ALEXANDER. *History of the Apsley and Bathurst families.* Cirencester: E.W. Savory, 1889. Includes pedigree, 14-17th c. Another edition, compiled by A.B. Bathurst, was published Cirencester: G.H. Harmer, 1903.

Arbalister
BENSON, J. 'Arbalister, Arblaster or Alabaster', *D.C.N.Q.* **24**, 1950-51, 112-6. See also 161-6. Medieval, of Bicton; also includes notes on Crawthorne, Stockhay, and Hache.

Archard
LINDLEY, E.S. 'William Archard: an unrecognised Gloucestershire worthy', *B.G.A.S.Tr.* **68**, 1949, 190-7. Includes pedigree, 16-17th c.

Archdeacon
SEARLEY, A.W. 'Haccombe, part II & III (1330-1440)', *D.A.Tr.* **51**, 1919, 181-210, & 52, 1920, 310-26. Concerned primarily with the Archdeacon family; includes pedigree.

Armstrong
HOLCROFT, H. *The Armstrongs of the Great Western: their times, surroundings & contemporaries.* Railway World, 1950.

Arnold
MERCER, R.V.F. *John Arnold and Son, chronometer makers, 1762-1843.* Antiquarian Horological Society, 1972. Of Bodmin and Saint Winnow, Cornwall and London. Includes wills.

Arrowsmith
FLETCHER, W.G.DIMOCK. 'The family of Arrowsmith', *G.N.Q.* **5**, 1894, 432-7. 17-18th c. pedigree.

Arthur(s)
ARTHUR, ROBERT WARREN. *Four centuries of Arthurs: history and genealogy of the descendants of John Arthur of Gloucestershire and the families of Elizabeth and John Arthur, emigrants to America.* [ ], [c.1988]
AWDAS, JEAN 'Mary Arthurs: who was she?' *J.G.F.H.S.* **64**, 1995, 14-15. 18th c., of Hawkesbury, *etc.*
SAWYER, F.E. *Genealogy and history of the descendants and ancestry of Richard Henry Arthur (born about 1824) of Cornwall Co., England, who immigrated to America 1847, and settled in Iowa Co., Wisconsin.* 2nd ed. America Falls, Idaho: the author, 1978.

Arundel(1)
ALEXANDER, J.J. 'The early Arundells', *D.C.N.Q.* **20**, 1938-9, 111-18 & 154-63. Medieval; includes list of family M.P's.
ARUNDELL, EDWARD. 'The Arundells of Gloucestershire,' *B.G.A.S.Tr.* **66**, 1947, 208-18. 15-16th c.
ARUNDELL, LORD. *Notes ... on the family history,* ed. Edward Doran Webb. Longmans, Green & Co., 1916. Arundell of Wardour, 16-20th c.

BASSET, BERNARD. 'The Arundells of Wardour,' *Month* **182**(954), 1946, 422-9. 16-20th c.

O., G. 'Arundelliana', *Collectanea topographica et genealogica* **3**, 1836, 389-95. Medieval; includes will of Sir John Arundell, 1433.

PADEL, O.J. 'The Arundells of Lanherne and their archive', *Cornwall Association of Local Historians journal* **29**, 1995, 8-23. Includes pedigree, 13-16th c.

STAMP, B. DUDLEY. 'Arundels of Trerice', *D.C.N.Q.* **31**, 1968, 89-90. 16th c.

STAMP, B. DUDLEY. 'The Cornish Arundells', *Old Cornwall* **7**, 1967-72, 351-6. 15-19th c.

SAYER, M.J. 'Pedigrees of county families, [1]', *Genealogists' magazine* **19**(8), 1978, 282-3.

WALSH, V. HUSSEY. 'The Arundells of Wardour', in DRYDEN, ALICE, ed. *Memorials of old Wiltshire.* Bemrose and Sons, 1906, 95-106. 16-19th c.

W., B.D. *Wardour and the Arundells not so long ago.* [ ]: [ ], 1982. 19-20th c.

YEATMAN, JOHN PYM. *The early genealogical history of the house of Arundell, being an account of the origin of the families of Montgomery, Albini, Fitzalan, and Howard, from the time of the conquest of Normandy by Rollo the Great.* Mitchell & Hughes, 1882.

'Pedigree of Arundell, Lord Arundell of Wardour', in HOWARD, J. JACKSON, & BURKE, H. FARNHAM, eds. *Genealogical collections illustrating the history of Roman Catholic families of England.* [Privately printed], 1887-92, 151-241.

See also Rundle

Ashburton
See Dunning

Ashe
JENNERS, A.J. 'Pedigrees of Ashe of Batcombe and Bond of Lutton', *M.G.H.* 5th series **1**, 1916, 12-14. Of Batcombe, Somerset and Lutton, Isle of Purbeck, pedigrees, 16-17th centuries.

Ashwood
ASHWOOD, PETER F. 'Which Ann went to Shropshire?' *J.G.F.H.S.* **63**, 1994, 11-12. Ashwood of Winchcombe, early 19th c.

Astley
See Barnes

Astry
See Chester

Atkyns
AUSTIN, ROLAND. 'Some account of Sir Robert Atkyns the Younger and other members of the Atkyns family', *B.G.A.S.T.* **35**, 1912, 69-92. 17-18th c.

Audley
DRAKE, W. R., SIR. 'Note as to the parentage of Blanche Audley, the wife of Robert Hatch of Wolley, Co. Devon', *Genealogist* **4**, 1880, 69-73. Includes pedigree of Audley, 14th c.

Avenell(l)
MACLEAN, JOHN, SIR. 'Family of Avenel', *B.G.A.S.T.* **4**, 1879-80, 313-9. Includes pedigree, 12-14th c.

WHITMARSH, J. 'Avenell family', *W.A.* **4**, 1885, 139-40. Medieval.

Avery
AVERY, ELROY McKENDREE, & AVERY, CATHARINE HITCHCOCK. *The Groton Avery clan.* 2 vols. Cleveland: [ ], 1912. Primarily concerned with the North American branch, but includes a chapter on the Averys in S.W.England, 16-17th c.

Ayer
SKINNER, A.J. 'Ayer of Fen Ottery', *D.C.N.Q.* **9**, 1916, 37-43. See also 93-5. Includes pedigree, monumental inscriptions, wills, etc., 17-18th c.

See also Eyre

Ayleway
COCKAYNE, G.E. 'Memoranda concerning the family of Ayleway of Gloucestershire', *M.G.H.* 2nd series **2**, 1886, 313-5. 17th c.

Ayliffe
JACKSON, J.E. 'The Ayliffes of Grittenham', *W.A.M.* **21**(62), 1884, 194-210. 17-18th c.

Bacon
FOGGITT, GERTRUDE. 'The Bacon pedigree', *Baconiana* 3rd series **21**, 1932-4, 217-20. Medieval origins of a Somerset family.

BARTLETT, R.G. 'Bacon family of Somerset', *N.Q.S.D.* **3**, 1893, 16. See also 53. Includes pedigree, 17-18th c.

BOND, T. 'On the family of Roger Bacon', *S.A.N.H.S.* **25**(2), 1879, 29-32. Medieval.

Badcock
TYLER, J.C. 'Badcock of Devon and Somerset', *M.G.H.* 5th series **6**, 1926-8, 301-9. Pedigree, 17-20th c., with wills etc.

Bailey
PEPPERELL, A. 'Capt. James Bailey, 1742-1810', *D.C.N.Q.* **29**(11), 1964, 301-2. Includes list of descendants.
See also French

Baker
BAKER, GORDON. *Of Somerset stock: the fortunes of a country family.* Williton: the author, 1980. Baker family; includes pedigrees, 14-20th c.
See also De Boteville

Balch
BALCH, GALUSHA B. *Genealogy of the Balch families in America.* Salem, Mass: Eben Putnam, 1897. Originally a Somerset family.
BALCH, J. 'Husbands and wives: Balch spouses', *G.T.* **13**(3), 1988, 88-9. List of spouses, with dates of marriage.
BALCH, THOMAS WILING. *Balch genealogica.* Philadelphia: Allen, Lane & Scott, 1907. Somerset and U.S. family.

Ball
BALL, MICHAEL D. *The Ball team: a family history.* Oshawa, Ontario: the author, [1982]
BALL, MARION. *The chronicles of the Ball family.* Torquay: Devonshire Press, [1928?] Of Daccombe, Exeter, *etc.* 17-20th c.
BALL, NAN S. *Ball family of Stokeinteignhead, Devon, England.* Charleston, North Carolina: [the author], 1944. Includes pedigrees, 17-19th c.
WRIGHT, WILLIAM BALL. *Ball family records: genealogical memoirs of some Ball families of Great Britain, Ireland and America.* York: Yorkshire Printing Co., 1908. Primarily concerned with the Irish family, but includes chapter on 'the Ball family of Bampton, Co. Devon, and Youghal, Co.Cork', 16-19th c.

Balston
LINDSAY, JOHN F. *The Balstons: Dorset yeomen and Hunter Valley settlers: a family history, 1500-1982.* Kincumber, N.S.W.: the author, c.1984. For a list of associated names, see review in *G.T.* **9**(2), 1984, 49.

Bamfylde/Bampfield
BENSON, J. 'Bampfylde House', *D.C.N.Q.* **22**(17), 1946, 301-3. Bampfield family, 14-16th c.

DRAKE, WILFRED. 'Stained glass in Bamfylde House, Exeter', *D.C.N.Q.* **6**, 1910-11, 225-8.
DYMOND, ROBERT. 'Bampfylde House, Exeter', *Archaeological journal* **31**, 1874, 95-7. Includes a pedigree of Bampfylde of Poltimore, 13-19th c.
HYLTON, LORD. 'The manor houses of Hardington and Vallis', *S.A.N.H.S.* **74**, 1928, 78-86.
'Colenel Hugh Bampfield's relict: Kings Teignton registers', *D.N.Q.* **2**, 1902-3, 234-6. 17th c.
'Excerpta e cartis familiae de Bamfylde de Poltimore, Devon', *Topographer* **5**, 1821, 59-60. Pedigree, medieval.

Banbury
See Allin

Banckes
ATTWOOD, J.S. 'Banckes family of Exeter and Heavitree', *W.A.* **11**, 1892, 151-5. See also 196.

Banger
NEVIL, EDMUND. 'Dorsetshire freeholders: Banger-Russell', *N.Q.S.D.* **90**, 1905, 222-6. See also 274-5. Includes monumental inscriptions and parish register extracts.

Bankes
BANKES, VIOLA. *A Dorset heritage: the story of Kingston Lacy.* Richards Press, 1953.
Catalogue of a Dorset family: an exhibition from the Bankes of Kingston Lacy & Corfe Castle archive to celebrate the centenary of the National Trust. [Dorchester]: Dorset County Archives Service, 1995.
Kingston Lacy, Dorset. Rev. ed. National Trust, 1991. Includes pedigree of Bankes, 16-20th c.

Baragwanath
HILL, TREVOR, & HILL, MARGARET. 'The Baragwanaths of Towednack', *C.F.H.S.J.* **65**, 1992, 21-2. 19th c.

Barbor
R., H. 'Barbor of Barnstaple', *N.Q.S.D.* **4**, 1894-5, 376-8. See also **5**, 1897-8, 31.
REYNOLDS, HY. FITZGERALD. 'Barbor of Fremington, Co. Devon', *D.C.N.Q.* **13**, 1924-5, 139-42. See also 303-5. 17-19th c.

Barclay

BARCLAY, CHARLES W., et al. *History of the Barclay family with full pedigree from 1066 to [1933].* 3 vols. St Catherine Press, 1924-34. Contents: Pt.1. [Gloucestershire family, by Charles W. Barclay.] Pt.2. The Barclays in Scotland from 1067 to 1660, by Hubert F. Barclay. Pt.3. The Barclays in Scotland and England, by Hubert F. Barclay and Alice Wilson-Fox. Apart from Gloucestershire and Scotland, the family also had branches in London — where a member founded Barclays Bank — Walthamstow, Essex and Bury Hill, Dorking, Surrey.
See also Berkeley

Baring

ZIEGLER, PHILIP. *The sixth great power: Baring, 1762-1929.* Collins, 1988. Includes pedigree, 18-20th c.

Baring-Gould

MONK, S.GORDON. *Lew House, Lew Trenchard church, and Baring-Gould.* Plymouth: Clarke, Doble and Brendon, 1961. Includes pedigree of Gould, 13-20th c.

Barker

BARKER, A.L. *The Barkers of Aston.* Plymouth: Mayflower Press, W. Brendon & Son, 1932.
The Barkers of Bath: Victoria Art Gallery, Bath, 17 May-28 June 1986. Bath: Phillips & Jollys 1986. Exhibition catalogue; includes pedigree, 18-19th c.

Barmondin

See Maynard

Barnard

ONIONS, K. 'A poor family from Mitcheldean', in SMITH, B.S., ed. *Studies in Dean history.* Bristol: University of Bristol Dept of Extra-Mural Studies, 1963. Barnard family, late 18th c. Includes pedigree.

Barnes

BARNES, ARTHUR HARMAN. *History of a family: Barnes.* [Ormskirk]: [the author?], 1967-8. Of Frome, Somerset, Bristol, Herefordshire, and Reading, Berkshire. Includes pedigree, 17-20th c.
See Tugwell

Barrett

BARRETT, DAN E. *Barrett: our family name.* Ontario: the author, c.1981. Wiltshire family.
See Andrew and Courtenay

Barnes

See Pitman

Baron

LLOYD, E.D. 'The Egloskerry Barons', *C.F.H.S.J.* **8**, 1978, 12-15.
'The Baron family of Egloskerry', *C.F.H.S.J.* **36**, 1985, 21. 17-18th c.
See also Russell

Barrow

CRAWLEY-BOEVEY, ARTHUR WILLIAM. 'Pedigree of Sir Charles Barrow, Bart., of Highgrove, Minsterworth, co. Gloucester', *Genealogist* N.S., **30**, 1914, 73-86.
See Poulett and Paulet

Bartelot

BARTELOT, R. GROSVENOR. *Our family surname.* Privately printed, 1944. Of various counties, including branches in Devon, Cornwall and Somerset.

Bartlett

B., R.G. 'Bartlett of Stourton Caundle', *N.Q.S.D.* **17**, 1923, 30-2. 17-18th c.
BARTLETT, WILLIAM. *Pedigree of the family of Bartlett of Marldon, Co. Devon.* 2 vols. [?]: privately printed, 1890-99.
BARTLETT, WILLIAM, comp. *Papers on the subject of St. Mary Church, in the county of Devon, read ... by Canon Brownlow ... together with pedigrees, wills and administrations of the family of Bartlett of St. Mary Church, and of Marldon and Teignmouth in the same county and notes on that and the Salter families, bookplates, &c.* [ ]: [the compiler?], 1899? Includes reprinted papers from *D.A.Tr.,* 1886-98, together with much other material on the Bartlett and Salter families.
BOWEN, ELIZABETH. 'The Bartlett family, Bristol wine merchants', *J.B.A.* **18**, 1979, 7-10. See also **19**, 1980, 31.
BARTLETT, WILLIAM. 'Families of the name of Bartlett: extracts from the parish registers of Paignton church, Devon', *M.G.H.* 3rd series **4**, 1902, 128-32. 16-19th c., also includes extracts from the register of St. David's, Exeter.
'Families of the name of Bartlett', *M.G.H.* 3rd series **3**, 1900, 137-9. Extracts from the parish registers of Charlton, Topsham and Exeter, 16-19th c.

Bathurst

'The Bathurst family of Lechlade', *G.N.Q.* **1**, 1881, 369-71.
See also Apsley

Bartow

BARTOW, EVELYN. *Bartow genealogy.* Baltimore: Innes & Co., 1878. Supplement 1879. Of France, Devon and the United States, 17-19th c.

CUMYN, ANNA KEY BARTOW. *The Bartow family: a genealogy.* Montreal: the author, 1984. Of France, Devon, and the United States, 16-20th c.

Baskerville

BASKERVILLE, S.R., & BASKERVILLE, D 'The Baskerville family', *D.F.H.* **32**, 1984, 12-14.

Basset

'[Account of the Bassett family of Tehidy]', *Annual report of the Royal Cornwall Polytechnic Society* **84**, 1917, 101-6. 13-19th c.

B[ARRON], OSWALD. 'Our oldest families, XII: the Bassetts', *Ancestor* **11**, 1904, 55-60. 12-19th c.

TANGYE, MICHAEL. *Tehidy and the Bassetts.* Redruth: Dyllansow Truran, 1984. 14-19th c.

SHAIRP, S T. *Family record, or, a genealogical account of the families which branch off from the Bassets and Courtenays from 1734 to the present time.* Totnes: Theodore Hannaford, 1856.

Bastard

ADAMS, JOHN. 'The Bastards of Blandford', *Architectural Review* **143**, 1968, 445-50. 18th c.

HENDERSON, K.D.D. 'The Bastards of Blandford Forum', *N.Q.S.D.* **28**, 1968, 149-51. See also 152.

Bat(e)man

GRACE, MARK A.S. 'Batman: the descendants of the 16th c. Batman / Battman / Bateman family in the Kingswood area', *J.B.A.* **70**, 1992, 8-9.

Bater

BOWERMAN, A.L. *The Bater book and allied families: Shore-Ensley, Granger-Thomas.* Baltimore: Gateway Press, 1987. Of Devon and Michigan.

Batt

LEA, J. HENRY 'The English ancestry of the families of Batt and Byley of Salisbury, Mass.', *N.E.H.G.R.* **51**, 1897, 181-8 & 348-57; **52**, 1898, 44-51. Of Salisbury, Wiltshire; includes parish register extracts, wills, marriage licences, with pedigrees, 16-17th c.

LEA, J. HENRY. *The English ancestry of the families of Batt and Biley.* Boston: David Clapp, 1897. Reprinted from *N.E.H.G.R.* Includes 17th c. pedigree, with wills and parish register extracts.

'The English ancestry of the families of Batt and Byley, of Salisbury, Massachusetts', *W.N.Q.* **2**, 1896-8, 577-83; **3**, 1899-1901, 35-40. Includes pedigree of Batt, 16-17th c., with wills, etc.

Batten

BATTEN, W.M. 'Batten family of Devon and Cornwall', *D.C.N.Q.* **7**(2), 1912, 78.

PAGET, M. 'The Knappings, and its occupiers', *C.K.L.H.S.B.* **23**, 1990, 20-25. Includes pedigrees of Batten, 17-18th c., and Currier, 16-17th c.

Battiscombe

BARROW, GEOFFREY BATTISCOMBE. *A history of the Battiscombe and Bascom families of England and America.* Research Publishing, 1976. Dorset family.

Battman

See Bat(e)man

Baugh

See De Boteville

Bave

POYNTON, F.J. 'Evidences from registers supporting the pedigree of Bave', *M.G.H.* 2nd series **1**, 1886, 216-8. Parish register extracts from Bath Abbey, St. James Bath, Tickenham, and St. James, Bristol.

POYNTON, F.J. 'The Baves of Bath and of Barrow Court, Tickenham, Co. Somerset, allied to the Haringtons, both of Kelston and Corston, in the same county', *M.G.H.* 2nd series **1**, 1886, 167-70. Includes monumental inscriptions from various churches.

POYNTON, F.J. 'Pedigree of Bave of Bath and of Barrow Court, Tickenham', *M.G.H.* 2nd series **1**, 1886, 189-92.

Bawden

See Rundle

Bayley

HORTON-SMITH, L. GRAHAM HORTON. 'The Bayley family of Dorset, Somerset, Oxon, and Berks', *N.Q.S.D.* **25**, 1950, 41-9.

Bayntun

BAYNTUN-COWARD, HILTON, ed. *Notes on the Bayntun family.* Bath: George Bayntun, 1977. Includes pedigrees, medieval-20th c.

Beach

See Sadler

Beadle

FRANKLIN, PETER. 'A glimpse of medieval family life', *Family tree magazine* **10**(12), 1994, 17-18. Beadle family of Kingston, Gloucestershire, 14th c.

Beale

BEALE, G.A. *The uses of genealogy.* [Cadenza], 1981. Includes the familial historian, and the Beales of Blandford.

Bealing

BEALING, N.C. 'Bealing: the name in London records', *N.Q.S.D.* **30**, 1974-9, 214-6. See also 295-6. Dorset family.
BEALING, N.C. 'The Bealings: a Dorset family in c.17-c.18 London', *G.T.* **7**(2), 1982, 33-4.

Beard

BEARD, T.F. 'Beard family', *D.C.N.Q.* **31**, 1968-70, 192. 18th c.

Beauchamp

BATTEN, JOHN. 'The barony of Beauchamp of Somerset', *S.A.N.H.S.* **36**(2), 1890, 20-59.
BENSON, J. 'The founder of Frithelstock Priory', *D.C.N.Q.* **23**(3), 1947, 73-8. Beauchamp family history, 11-14th c.
CARTER, W. F. 'The Beauchamps of Somerset', *Genealogist* N.S. **33**, 1916-17, 151-4.

Beaumont

'Beaumont', *D.C.N.Q.* **26**, 1954-5, 79-82. Medieval

Beckford

GREGORY, W. *The Beckford family: reminiscences of Fonthill Abbey and Lansdown Tower.* Simpkin Marshall Hamilton Kent & Co., 1898. 18-19th c.
MELVILLE, LEWIS. *The life and letters of William Beckford of Fonthill.* William Heineman, 1910. Includes notes on family, 16-18th c.

Bedford

M[URRAY], O.A.R. 'The Rev. Thomas Bedford and his descendants', *D.C.N.Q.* **10**, 1918-19, 50-55. See also **9**, 1916-17, 172-3 & 207; **10**, 1918-19, 223. Of Devon and Cornwall, 17-18th c.
See also Russell

Belet

HARFIELD, CLIVE. 'The Belets: notes on a medieval Dorsetshire family from the 11th to the 14th centuries', *D.N.* **106**, 1984, 43-9. Includes pedigree.

Bennet(t)

BENNETT, JOHN. *A memoir of the Bennett family of South Wilts.* Privately printed, 1952. Includes pedigrees, 16-20th c.
KERSWELL, R.G. *The Bennets of Tresillian.* Edinburgh: Pentland Press, 1994. 18-20th c.
KING, EDWARD. 'Bennett of Hexworthy, in the parish of Lawhitton, and county of Cornwall', *Genealogist* **4**, 1880, 144-50.
TABRETT, I. 'The Bennett-Keene papers', *Search: journal of the Banwell Society of Archaeology* **15**, 1979, 6-9. Includes pedigrees of Keene, 17-19th c. and Bennett, 18-20th c.
WARNER, JILL. *The Bennetts of Lyme Regis, 1762-1911.* Twickenham: G. Warner, 1997. Not seen.
'Bennett: genealogical memoranda relating to the Bennett family ...', *M.G.H.* **1**, 1868, 294-7. Of Devon and Cornwall.
See also Keene

Bere

SAYER, M.J. 'Pedigrees of county families, [1]', *Genealogists' magazine* **19**(8), 1978, 284-5. Of Morebath and Timewell

Berkeley

BARKLY, HENRY, SIR. 'The Berkeleys of Cobberley', *B.G.A.S.T.* **17**, 1892-3, 96-125. 12-15th c.
BARKLY, HENRY, SIR. 'The Berkeleys of Dursley', *B.G.A.S.T.* **13**, 1888-9, 188-95.
BARKLY, HENRY, SIR. 'The Berkeleys of Dursley during the 13th and 14th centuries', *B.G.A.S.T.* **9**, 1884-5, 2, 27-76. Includes pedigree, and list of tenants of Dodington sued in 1287.
BARKLY, HENRY, SIR. 'The earlier house of Berkeley', *B.G.A.S.Tr.* **8**, 1883-4, 193-223. Includes pedigree, 11-13th c.
BARKLY, HENRY, SIR. 'The earliest pipe roll', *Genealogist* N.S., **3**, 1886, 79. Berkeley family, 11th c.

BARRON, OSWALD. 'Our oldest families, X: the Berkeleys', *Ancestor* **8**, 1904, 73-81. 11-19th c.

CLAY, CHARLES, SIR. 'The marriages of Robert, Son of Robert, Son of Harding', *B.G.A.S.T.* **80**, 1961, 90-92. Berkeley forebears, medieval.

COOKE, JAMES HERBERT. 'The Berkeley manuscripts and their author, John Smyth', *B.G.A.S.T.* **5**, 1880-1, 212-21. Notes on Smyth's works, then in mss, i.e., *Lives of the Berkeleys, Description of the Hundred of Berkeley,* list of freeholders of Berkeley Hundred, etc.

FINBERG, H.P.R. 'Three studies in family history', in his *Gloucestershire studies.* Leicester: Leicester University Press, 1957, 145-83. Berkeley of Berkeley, Kingscote of Kingscote, and Holder of Taynton.

FOSBROOKE, THOMAS DUDLEY. *Berkeley manuscripts: abstracts and extracts of Smyth's lives of the Berkeleys ... including all the pedigrees in the ancient manuscript, to which are annexed a copious history of the castle and parish of Berkeley ... and biographical anecdotes of Dr Jenner.* J. Nichols & Son, 1821.

KENNEDY-SKIPTON, H.S. 'The Berkeleys at Yate', *B.G.A.S.T.* **21**, 1898, 25-31. 15-17th c.

LINDLEY, E.S. 'Some early Berkeley ladies', *B.G.A.S.T.* **84**, 1965, 31-43. Medieval.

MOORE, MATTEY. 'Berkeley Castle yesterday and today', *Connoisseur* **137**, 1956, 241-8. Berkeley family, brief summary.

SINCLAIR, ALEXANDRA. 'The great Berkeley lawsuit revisited, 1417-39', *Southern history* **9**, 1987, 34-50.

SMITH, WILLIAM JAMES. 'The rise of the Berkeleys: an account of the Berkeleys of Berkeley Castle, 1243-1361', *B.G.A.S.T.* **70**, 1951, 64-80; **71**, 1952, 101-21. Includes pedigree, 12-14th c.

SMYTH, JOHN. *The Berkeley manuscripts: the lives of the Berkeleys, lords of the Honour, castle and manor of Berkeley, in the County of Gloucester, from 1066 to 1618, with a description of the Hundred of Berkeley and of its inhabitants,* ed. Sir John Maclean. 3 vols. Gloucester: J. Bellows for B.G.A.S., 1883-5. Includes much documentary material.

'The Berkeleys of Uley', *G.N.Q.* **7**, 1900, 127-33, and 153-8. Includes outline pedigree, 11-16th c.

See also Barclay and Cancia

Berrett

BERRETT, LA MAR C. *Down Berrett Lane.* 2 vols. Orem, Utah: John Watts Family Organization, 1980. Steeple Ashton and U.S.A., 17-20th c.

Berryman

WALTERS, JUDITH ALLISON. *Berryman, Rodda and Williams records from Crowan, Cornwall, England, 1693-1849.* Bothell, Washington: the author, c.1984.

Besils

DUNLOP, J. RENTON. 'Pedigree of the Besils family of Gloucestershire, Wiltshire, Devonshire, Berkshire, and Somersetshire', *M.G.H.* 5th series **5**, 1923-5, 63-82. Medieval; includes many notes.

Bethel

BETHEL, DAVID. 'Painswick: Bethel family connections', *J.G.F.H.S* **66**, 1995, 15-17; **67**, 1995, 23-5. Includes pedigrees, 18-20th c.

Bettesthorne

COLLINS, S. M. 'A Wiltshire ancestor for Her Majesty the Queen', *W.A.M.* **50**(180), 1943, 375-8. Medieval pedigree of Bettesthorne.

Beville

BOVILL, W. 'Bevill family', *D.C.N.Q.* **23**, 1947-9, 107-12 & 129-30. See also 118-9. Medieval-16th c.

HENDERSON, C. 'Beville obituary', *D.C.N.Q.* **16**, 1930, 19-26. Medieval-16th c. genealogical notes.

TAYLOR, T. 'Bevile of Drennick and Woolston', *J.R.I.C.* **17**(2), 1908, 236-40. Includes pedigree, 14-16th c.

Bevyn

See Montagu

Biconylle

BICKNELL, A.S. *Excerpta Biconyllea: a forgotten chancellor and a forgotten knight: notes for a history of the Somerset family of Biconylle.* Rev. ed. Taunton: Barnicott and Pearce, 1900. Includes various *inquisitions post mortem,* folded pedigree, 13-16th c., *etc*

Bidgood

BRUSHFIELD, T.N. 'The apprentices' warning-piece', *D.N.Q.* **1**, 1900-1, 219-24. A 17th c. murder.

Bigland

GRAY, IRVINE. 'Ralph Bigland and his family', *B.G.A.S.T.* **75**, 1956, 116-33. Includes pedigree, 17-18th c.

Bilbie

BAILEY, R. 'Eccentric bell-founders of the Mendips', *Country life* **125**, 1959, 212-3. 18th c., Bilbie family.

Biley

See Batt

Billet

CLARKE, PHILIP J. 'The Billets of North Wraxall', *W.F.H.S.* **27**, 1987, 26-8. See also **39**, 1990, 223. Emigrants to Canada. Includes pedigree, 18-19th c.

Bingham

COLBY, DR., & $RYLANDS, J., eds. 'Pedigrees from the visitation of Dorset 1623', *M.G.H.* 2nd series **2**, 1888, 265-7. Includes Bingham and Anketell.

McCALMONT, ROSE E. *Memoirs of the Binghams*, ed. C.R.B. Barrett. Spottiswoode & Co., 1915. Dorset family. Includes pedigree, 13-18th c.

Birch

'Birch family in Somerset and Dorset', *N.Q.S.D.* **25**, 1950, 219-22. Includes pedigree, 17-18th c.

Bisse

GRIGSON, FRANCIS. *Genealogical memoranda relating to the family of Bisse*. Mitchell and Hughes, 1886. Includes probate records, Chancery proceedings, *etc.*, with pedigree, 16-18th c.

GRIGSON, F. 'Genealogical memoranda relating to the Bisse family', *M.G.H.* 2nd series **1**, 1886, 283-5, 322-4, 328-32, 342-5, 369-72 & 376-9; **2**, 1888, 12-15, 20-23, 62-4, 78-9, 93-4, 110-12 & 125-8. Somerset and Gloucestershire; includes pedigrees, 16-17th c., legal proceedings, etc., 16-18th c., extracts from Bristol burgess rolls and apprenticeship registers, parish registers of Maperton, Somerset, and Oldbury on the Hill, Gloucestershire, etc.

GRIGSON, F. 'Pedigree of Bisse', *M.G.H.* 2nd series **2**, 1888, 139-52. Includes extracts from Almsford, Martock, and other parish registers.

JEWERS, ARTHUR J. 'Bisse family', *N.Q.S.D.* **5**, 1897-8, 213-6. See also 310. Includes wills, monumental inscriptions and parish register extracts.

WIGAN, HERBERT. 'Bisse notes: being additions to genealogical memoranda relating to the Bisse family compiled by Mr. Francis Grigson', *M.G.H.* 3rd series **4**, 1902, 122-9.

Includes pedigree of Bisse of Almsford, Somerset, list of wills of Wiltshire Bisse family proved at Salisbury 16-18th c.; also wills of Thomas Ashe of Batcombe, 1558, and Mathewe Grene of Milton Clevedon, 1574 and extracts from parish registers of Almsford and Martock, Somerset, Bristol, etc.

'Bisse pedigree', *M.G.H.* 2nd series **1**, 1886, 283-5.

Blackaller

See Marwood

Blackburrow

BROMWICH, DAVID. 'The Blackburrow family in Banwell and Australia', *Search: journal of the Banwell Society of Archaology* **17**, 1983, 23-4. Includes pedigree, 18-19th c.

Blagden

See Hale

Blake

BLAKE, FRANCIS E. 'The Blake family in England', *N.E.H.G.R.* **45**, 1891, 35-8. Of Pitminster, Somerset, 16-17th c.

BLAKE, MARK. 'Some early Wiltshire emigrants to Australia', *Hatcher review* **2**(17), 1984, 328-34. Blake family; 19th c.

CURTIS, C.D. 'Blake, Robert, General-at-Sea (1598-1657)', *N.Q.S.D.* **29**, 1974, 141-3 & 166-170.

SAYER, M.J. 'Pedigrees of county families', *Genealogists' magazine* **19**(8), 1978, 285-6.

A record of the Blakes of Somersetshire, especially in the line of William Blake of Dorchester, Mass., the emigrant to New England, with one branch of his descendants. Boston: privately printed, 1881. 14-19th c.

Blathwayt

DOBBIE, B.M. WILLMOTT. *A nest of suffragettes in Somerset: Eagle House, Batheaston.* Bath: Batheaston Society, 1979. Partially a Blathwayt family history, early 20th c.

Blewett

LAWS, PETER. 'A Cornish family: Blewett of Colan', *Old Cornwall* **4**, 1943-50, 384-6. 15-19th c.

Blight

EVA, C.A. 'A Penzance schoolmaster (Thomas Blight) and his sons', *Old Cornwall* **2**(12), 1936, 18-9.

PRICE, SEYMOUR J. 'The Blight family', *Transactions of the Baptist Historical Society* **5**, 1931-3, 268-73. 18-20th c.

Blount
'Blount of Gynge Joyberd Laundry, Essex, Penkridge, Staffs., Kingston Blount, Oxon., Putteridge, Herts., and Beversbrook and Calston, Wilts.', *M.G.H.* 5th series **7**, 1929-31, 120-24. 12-15th c. pedigree.

Bloyou
TAYLOR, THOMAS. 'Blohin: his descendants and lands', *Ancestor* **9**, April 1904, 20-27. See also **10**, July 1904, 226. Descent through Bloyou and Carminow, medieval.

Bluett
ASHWORTH, EDWARD. 'The manor house of Holcombe Court and the church of Holcombe Rogus, Devon', *E.D.A.A.S.Tr.* 1st series **6**, 1861, 235-49. Includes much information on the Bluett family, 11-19th c.

Boase
BOASE, CHARLES WILLIAM, BOASE, GEORGE CLEMENT, & BOASE, FREDERIC. *An account of the families of Boase or Bowes, originally residing at Paul and Madron in Cornwall, and of other families connected with them by marriage.* 2nd ed. Truro: Netherton & Worth, 1893.

Bocland
MORIARTY, G.A. 'The ancestry of Isabel de Bocland', *M.G.H.* 5th series **5**, 1923-5, 149-68. 12th c., includes medieval pedigrees of Meurdrac and Bocland.

Bodley
PRESSWELL, PAUL T. 'A Devonian's gift to Oxford', *Coat of arms* N.S., **10**(164), 1993, 155-63. Bodley family, includes pedigree, 15-17th c.
TROUP, FRANCES B. 'The pedigree of Sir Thomas Bodley', *D.A.Tr.* **35**, 1903, 713-74. Includes folded pedigree, will and abstract of *inquisition post mortem.*

Bodrugan
WHETTER, JAMES. *The Bodrugans: a study of a Cornish medieval knightly family.* Gorran: Lyfrow Trelyspen, 1995.

Bolt
BOLT, BARBARA. *The Bolt pedigree.* 3rd ed. [ ]: the author, 1995. 17-20th c., of Devon, *etc.*

Bond
BOND, MARTIN. *A Dorset family: a brief history of the Bonds.* Wareham: the author, 1993. Includes pedigree, 16-20th c.

BOND, RAY. 'Bond family history: the Woolpack Inn, Slad, Painswick', *J.G.F.H.S.* **51**, 1991, 19. 19th c.
BOND, THOMAS. *Pedigree of the family of Bond of the Isle of Purbeck in the county of Dorset.* Frederick Pickton, 1858. 15-19th c.
MERRITT, JEANETTE. *The Bond family of Ruanlanihorne, Cornwall, England, 1737-1994.* Camborne: the author, 1995.
ROSE, JANET R. 'The Bonds of Bath (with notes on the Symes and Main Families', *J.B.A.* **35**, 1984, 27-31.
See also Ashe

Bonham
KIDSTON, GEORGE JARDINE. *The Bonham Of Wiltshire and Essex.* Devizes: C.H. Woodward, 1948. Includes pedigrees, 14-15th c.
KIDSTON, GEORGE. 'The Bonham family', *N.Q.S.D.* **19**, 1929, 185-90. Wiltshire family.

Bonville
BRIDIE, MARION FERGUSON. *The story of Shute: the Bonviles and Poles.* Axminster: Shute School, 1955.
D., J. 'Documents relating to the estate of Sir William Bonville, of Shute, Co. Devon, *temp* Edw. III', *Collectanea topographica et genealogica* **8**, 1843, 237-47. Includes deeds and his 1407 will.
PICKEN, W.M.M. 'The Cornish heritage of the Bonvilles, by descent from Champernon and Fitz Walter', *D.C.N.Q.* **24**, 1950-51, 227-30. Medieval.
ROGERS, W.H.H. 'The Dorset chapel and Knightstone; Bonville and Sherman; Ottery St. Mary', *N.Q.S.D.* **7**, 1901, 187-91 & 235-43. See also 322. Reprinted in his *Archaeological papers relating to the counties of Somerset, Wilts, Hants and Devon.* [ ]: the author, 1902.
See also Churchill, Fitzroger, Fox and Tailbos

Bonython
BONYTHON, ERIC GLENIE. *History of the families of Bonython of Bonython and Bonython of Cardew in the Duchy of Cornwall, to which is added, an account of the Bonythons who settled in South Australia, the small branch at Newlyn East and St.Columb Minor, Cornwall, and those who settled in what is now Maine, U.S.A., in 1630.* Netley, S.A.: Griffin Press, 1966. Medieval-20th c., includes folded pedigree.

BONYTHON, JOHN. 'The Bonython family of
Bonython and Cardew', *C.F.H.S.J.* **61,** 1991,
6-9. Medieval-20th c.
BONYTHON, JOHN LANGDON. 'The Bonython
family: Bonython of Bonython in Cornwall:
arms of Bonython', *W.A.* **1,** 1881-2, 77.
BONYTHON, J. LANGDON. 'The Bonythons of
Bonython in Cornwall', *D.C.N.Q.* **13,**
1924-5, 132-4. 14-15th c.
BURKE, HENRY FARNHAM, SIR. *History of the
family of Bonython of Bonython in the
County of Cornwall.* Harrison & Sons,
1926. 13-19th c.
'The Bonython family: Bonython of Bonython
in Cornwall', *W.A.* **1,** 1881-2, 200-14. See
also **2,** 1882-3, 34 & 129. Mainly 16-17th c.,
includes pedigree.

Booth
RAWLINS, D. 'The Devon connection', *D.F.H.*
10, 1979 12-13. Also relates to Tucker
family.
See also Annesley

Booty
BOOTY, HAROLD. *The Bootys of Norfolk,
Suffolk, Kent and Devonshire.* Privately
issued, 1983. 16-20th c., includes pedigrees.

Border
BLAIKIE, LYNETTE. *The Border family from
Devon to Durham.* Brisbane: the author,
1987. Includes pedigree, 18-20th c.

Borlase
BORLASE, W.C. *The descent, name, and arms of
Borlase of Borlase in the County of
Cornwall, with a chart pedigree ...* George
Bell & Sons, 1888. Medieval-19th c.
BORLASE, WILLIAM COPELAND. 'History of the
family of Taillefer *alias* Borlase, of Borlas
Frank Taillefer in the county of Cornwall',
Genealogist N.S. **2,** 1885, 1-14, 129-41, 225-
39 & 283-92; N.S. **3,** 1886, 53-63; N.S. **4,**
1887, 160-5; N.S. **5,** 1889, 29-35. See also **3,**
1886, 125. Includes folded pedigree,
12-19th c.
MURRIN, T.H. 'John and Walter Borlase, father
and son', *Old Cornwall* **8**(4), 1975, 191-8.
17-18th c.
'Borlase family', *W.A.* **1,** 1881-2, 151-2. See
also 152-3. Medieval.

Boteler
See Drake and Sudeley

Botfield
See De Boteville

Botreaux
GREENFIELD, B.W. 'Scheme shewing the
connection between the several families of
Botreaux, St. Loe, Drokensford, Cheverel,
Stafford of Hoke, Hungerford, Paveley of
Broke, Chidiok, Fitz Waryn, Bradston, De
La Pole, Ingoldsthorpe, St. Maur, Pever of
Toddington and De La Zouch of
Haryngworth', *M.G.H.* 2nd series **2,** 1888,
314-7. Medieval, of various counties,
including Hooke, Dorset, Toddington,
Bedfordshire and Brook, Wiltshire.
Haryngworth is unidentified.
See also Moeles

Bottrall
See Ridington

Boucher
BOUCHER, R. 'Boucher', *W.N.Q.* **5,** 1902-5,
142-4. 18th c., includes wills and parish
register extracts.
See also Cromwell

Boughton
BOUGHTON, ELSIE. 'Which John?' *F.F.* **17,** 1994,
30-31. Boughton family, 18th c. Brief.

Bourne
See Eyre

Bouveries
PLEYDELL-BOUVERIE, JACOB. 'Laurens Des
Bouveries (1536-1610), his descendents, and
the Huguenot connection', *Hatcher review*
2(19), 1985, 411-20. Includes pedigree, 16-
18th c.

Bowdage
SKINNER, A.J. 'Tristram Bowdage', *D.C.N.Q.*
10, 1918-19, 326-7. Pedigree, 17-18th c.

Bowden
See Cornish-Bowden

Bowditch
BOWDITCH, HAROLD. *The Bowditch family of
Salem, Massachusetts: a genealogical
sketch prepared for distribution on the
occasion of the 100th anniversary of the
family Christmas party, Christmas Day,
1936.* Boston: Recording Statistical
Corporation, 1937. Originally of Dorset.
MORIARTY, G. ANDREWS. 'Genealogical research
in England: Bowditch', *N.E.H.G.R.* **72,** 1918,
223-40. See also **78,** 1924, 144-6; **82,** 1928,
303-12. Thornecombe, Devon; includes
wills, parish register extracts; deeds, *etc.,*
16-18th c.

Bower

BOWER, H.B. 'Bower of Claremont,' *M.G.H.* 5th series 7, 1929-31, 125-9. Claremont, East Teignmouth; also of Dorset and Somerset, etc., 16-19th c.

BOWER, H.B. *Bower of Claremont, Donhead, Dorchester, Lostwithiel and Weymouth.* Fleet: E. Dwelly, 1929. Donhead, Wiltshire; Claremont, Devon; Dorchester and Weymouth, Dorset, and Lostwithiel, Cornwall.

BOWER, HUBERT. *Bower family of Gloucestershire.* Privately published, 1871.

Bowes

See Boase

Bowre

COLBY, DR., & RYLANDS, J.P. 'Pedigrees from the visitation of Dorset 1623', *M.G.H.* 2nd series 2, 1888, 204. Includes Bowre and Buckler.

Bowring

KEIR, DAVID. *The Bowring story.* Bodley Head, 1962.

WARDLE, ARTHUR C. *Benjamin Bowring and his descendants: a record of mercantile achievement.* Hodder & Stoughton, 1938. Includes folded pedigree, 14-19th c.

Box

FARRELL, BETTY. 'The Box family: seven generations', *D.C.N.Q.* 32, 1971-3, 244-51. 17-19th c.

See also Fowell

Boyt

BOYT, KEVIN. 'A carters life and times', *J.D.F.H.S.* 2(2), 1989, 59-61. Includes Boyt pedigree, 19-20th c.

Brad(e)ston

AUSTIN, ROLAND. 'Notes on the family of Bradeston', *B.G.A.S.T.* 47, 1925, 279-86. Medieval.

See also Botreaux

Bradley

See Spooner

Bragge

SQUIBB, G.D. 'The Bragge family of Sadborow and their muniments', *D.N.* 64, 1942, 58-68. Includes pedigree, 16-19th c.

Braithwaite

HANSFORD, F.E. 'With the Braithwaites in Dorset', *Dorset year book* 1955-6, 87-96.

Brannam

BRANNAM, PETER. *A family business: the story of a pottery.* Exeter: Devon Print Group, 1982. Brannam family business, mainly 20th c.

Branwell

HOLGATE, I. 'The Branwells at Penzance', *Bronte Society Transactions* 13, 1960, 425-32. Life of Elizabeth Branwell, foster-mother to the Brönte children.

RICHARDS, S., & OLDHAM, L. 'The Branwell home in Penzance: an account of no.25 Chapel Street, Penzance', *Old Cornwall* 8, 1973-9, 321-7. 18-19th c.

ROWE, J. HAMBLEY. *The maternal relatives of the Bröntes.* Shipley: Outhwaite Bros., 1923. Branwell family, 18-19th c.

ROWE, J. HAMBLEY. 'Branwell and Brönte', *D.C.N.Q.* 6, 1910-11, 111.

Braund

BRAUND, LEONARD W. *A race apart: the Braunds of Bucks and elsewhere.* Bideford: [the author], 1994. Of Bucks Mill, Devon; includes pedigrees, 17-19th c.

Bray

ADAMS, G.E. 'Genealogical memoranda relating to the family of Bray of Barrington, Co. Glos., and Berks', *M.G.H.* N.S., 1, 1874, 613. Pedigree, 16-17th c.

BROWNE, A.L. 'The Bray family in Gloucestershire', *B.G.A.S.Tr.* 55, 1933, 293-315. Includes pedigree, 15-17th c.

BROWNE, A.L. 'The Brays of Grand Barrington', *B.G.A.S.T.* 57, 1935, 158-75. 17-18th c.

Brendon

CURGENVEN, J. BRENDON. *The family of Brendon and Westcott in St.Dominick, Cornwall, and their descendants.* Hildenborough, Kent: privately printed, 1903. Medieval-19th c.

Braose

See Toriton

Brethers

See Goldesborough

Brent

See Harington

Brett

BROWN, FREDERICK. 'The Brett family', *S.A.N.H.S.* 28(2), 1882, 79-88. Somerset family.

Brewer

DEAKIN, MICHELLE. 'Joey Brewer's book', in CORNWALL RECORD OFFICE. *Review and accession list.* 1990-91, 32-3. Includes pedigree of Brewer, 18-19th c., of Bath and Cornwall.

HOBSON, R.B. 'The Brewer family,' *D.F.H.* **69**, 1994, 13-21. Of Bampton and London, 18-20th c.

See also Goddard and Tracy

Brian

ALEXANDER, J.J. 'The Brians of Torbryan', *D.C.N.Q.* 19(1), 1936, 6-11. Medieval.

ALEXANDER, J.J. 'Early owners of Torbryan manor', *D.A.Tr.* **68**, 1936, 197-214. Brian family.

STANES, R. G. F. 'Sir Guy de Brian', *D.A.Tr.* **92**, 1960, 249-78. Includes pedigree, 14th-15th c.

Bridgeman

LOVELOCK, SUE. 'Bridgeman trail', *W.F.H.S.* 31, 1988, 34-6. Includes pedigree, 17-19th c.

Brightley

MAACK, J.J. 'Brightley pedigree', *D.C.N.Q.* 36(2), 1987, 74. 14th c.

See also Stowford

Brionne

ROSE-TROUP, F. 'The Brionne and Redvers pedigrees', *D.C.N.Q.* 18(6), 1935, 246-51.

Britton

BRITTON, DENIS. *Family pursuit.* [ ]: the author, 1995. Of Devon, *etc.*, includes pedigrees, 16-20th c., of Britton *als* Bruton family.

STILSBURY, G. BRITTON. *The Brittons of Kingswood Chase and some Gloucestershire connections, 1498-1985.* Bristol: V. Britton, c.1985.

Briwer

HALSBURY, EARL OF. 'Presidential address: the pleasures of scale', *D.A.Tr.* **92**, 1960, 19-35.

WATKIN, H.R. 'A great Devonian: William Briwer', *D.A.Tr.* **50**, 1918, 69-169. Includes pedigree, 12th-13th c.

Briwes

GRIFFITH, L. 'Briwes of Staple, Somerset', *Notes & queries* 162, 1932, 3-5, 21-4, 39-42, 59-61, 78-80, 95-7, 132-4, 164-5, 218-20, 254-6, 276-9, 311-13, 402-3, 416-8, 434-7 & 455-8. 13-14th c.

Brönte

See Branwell

Brook

ROGERS, W.H. HAMILTON. *Brook of Somerset and Devon: barons of Cobham in the county of Kent, their local history and descent.* Taunton: Barnicott and Pearce, 1899-1901. Reprinted from *S.A.N.H.S.* 44(2), 1898, 1-78; 45(2), 1899, 1-24; 46(2), 1900, 109-24. Also published in Rogers's *Archaeological papers relating to the counties of Somerset, Wilts., Hants., and Devon.* [ ]: the author, [1902].

WERE, F. 'Brook family', *N.Q.S.D.* **6**, 1899, 263-4.

Brooke

BROOKE, GILBERT EDWARD. *Brooke of Horton in the Cotswolds, with notes on some other Brooke families.* Singapore: Methodist Publishing House, 1918. Includes pedigree, 14-19th c.

Brooking

The Brooking family historian. Hassocks, Sussex: Brooking Society, 1983- . Family originated in South Devon.

ALLEN, HELEN. 'The travels of a family bible', *D.F.H.* **69**, 1994, 25-8. Brooking family, 17-20th c.

Brotherhood

LELEUX, SYDNEY A. *Brotherhoods, engineers.* Dawlish: David & Charles, 1965. Includes pedigree of Brotherhood family, 19-20th c.

Broughton

WILKIN, W.H. 'Broughton of Warbrightesleigh', *D.C.N.Q.* **16**, 1930-31, 168-72. Includes extracts from Stoodleigh parish register, 17-18th c., etc.

Brown

BELLOWS, JOHN. *Browns of Bartonbury,* Gloucester: John Bellows, 1899. Reprinted from *Friends quarterly examiner* 7th month, 1899.

COWARD, EDWARD. 'Notes on farming families of the 19th century in Wiltshire', *W.A.M.* 45(154), 1931, 336-41. Notes on Brown, Stratton and a number of other families.

ENGLISH, E.T. *The Browns of Plymouth.* [Plymouth?]: the author, 1971.

FULLERTON, J. 'Hannah Cowleys descendants', *D.C.N.Q.* **26**, 1954-5, 106-8. Brown family.

HAINES, ROBERT J. 'Has anyone seen Charlie Brown?' *J.G.F.H.S.* **39**, 1988, 15-16. See also **40**, 1989, 12. Brown family, 18-19th c.

TILY, JANET. 'So who the hell was Walter Brown?' *J.B.A.* **79,** 1995, 38-41. 19-20th c.

Browne

BADDELEY, ST. CLAIR. 'The Brownes of Woodchester and the Roman Pavement', *Notes and queries* **151,** 19, 26, 94-5. 18th c.

MARSHALL, CHARLES W. *The Browne family of Bristol, London, etc., from the mid-seventeenth century.* Exeter: the author, 1979.

MORTON, EDWARD. *The Browne family of Kington St.Michael, Co. Wilts ...,* ed. Charles W.Marshall. Exeter: the author, 1.983. 16-20th c.

'Pedigrees from the visitation of Dorset, 1623: Browne', *M.G.H.* 2nd series **2,** 1888, 60-2.

Browning

BADDELEY, VINCENT, SIR. 'The ancestry of Robert Browning, the poet', *Genealogical magazine* 8(1), 1938, 1-6. Dorset; 18-19th c.

LANE, A.J. 'The Brownings of Woodyates', *Dorset year book* 1972-73, 27-32.

LANE, ANTHONY J. 'Thereby hangs a Dorset tale', *Dorset year book* 1990, 5-8. Browning family.

Browse

COWELL, PETER. 'Browse', *D.C.N.Q.* **28,** 1959-61, 253-61. 17-18th c.

Brune

See Prideaux

Bruton

That's B-R-U-T-O-N: journal of the Bruton one-name study. 1992- .
See also Britton

Brydges

BELTZ, GEO. FRED. *Review of the Chandos peerage case, adjudicated 1803, and of the pretensions of Sir Samuel Egerton, Brydges, bart., to designate himself per legem terrae Baron Chandos of Sudeley.* R. Bentley, 1834. Brydges and Knatchbull families.

Bubb

BUBB, G.W. 'Researching the Bubb family history', *J.G.F.H.S.* **6,** 1980, 10-14. 17-19th c.

PITHER, MAUREEN. 'The Bubb family', *J.G.F.H.S.* **36,** 1988, 13. Births, marriages and deaths, 19th c.

Buck

POULTER, MARY. 'O'er ancient Badon's mystic spring', *J.B.A.* **59,** 1890, 22-8. Buck and Norton families of Bath, 19th c.

Buckeridge

DYER, ANTHONY STEPHEN. 'Buckeridge family', *W.N.Q.* **6.** 1908-10, 571-2. 17-18th c.

Buckingham

BUCKINGHAM, RICHARD. *A history of the Buckingham family.* Looseleaf format. [Hook]: the author, 1994. Of North Hill, Cornwall, *etc.,* 16-20th c.

Buckland

NORGATE, MARTIN. 'Buckland *et al.,* pipemakers in Melksham', *W.A.M.* **78,** 1983, 125-7. Buckland family, 17-18th c.

Buckler

See Bowre

Budd

OSWALD, NEVILLE C. 'The Budds of North Tawton: a medical family of the 19th century', *D.A.Tr.* **117,** 1985, 139-50.

Budge

BUDGE, R. 'The Budges of Linkinhorne', *Old Cornwall* **7,** 1967-72, 405-10. 16-19th c.

Budgett

LINDEGAARD, PATRICIA. *The Budgetts of Kingswood Hill and their Bristol family.* Brislington: [the author?] 1988. Includes pedigree, 18-19th c.

Budgell

SKINNER, A.J. 'Budgell of St. Thomas, Exeter', *D.C.N.Q.* **10,** 1918-19, 206-7. 17-18th c.

Bull

See Clarke

Buller

The Buller papers: a series of historical documents selected from the family records of the Bullers of Shillingham and Morval in the county of Cornwall. Privately printed, 1895.

Bulley

WATKIN, H.R. 'Bulley and Jerrard (or Jellard) families', *D.C.N.Q.* **11,** 1921, 304-5. See also **12,** 1922, 16-17 & 68.

Bulteel

STAPLETON, E. 'Bulteel family', *British archivist* 1(14), 1914, 117. Devon family.
See also Pitman

Bunker

BUNKER, HENRY L. *Bunker family history.* [ ]: Bunker Family Association, 1984. Of Devon, Bedfordshire, and the United States. Mainly medieval-20th c.

Burall
MEAD, C.J.H. 'The Burral and Paull families', *Royal Cornwall Polytechnic Society report* **112**, 1945, 48-58. 18-19th c.

Burcie/y
FRY, EDW. ALEX. 'Burcy family', *N.Q.S.D.* **17**, 1923, 128-32 & 149-56. Dorset family deeds, 14-16th c., with pedigree.
LYTE, H.C. MAXWELL. 'Burcie, Falaise and Martin', *S.A.N.H.S.* **65**(2), 1919, 1-27.
See also Falaise

Burden
BUTLER, E.L. 'The Burdens of Purbeck', *G.T.* **3**(3), 1978, 41-3. Includes pedigree, 17-19th c.

Burgess
SMITH, ENID. *A family record.* [ ]: [195-?]. Burgess family, 18-20th c.

Burland
B., J.B.H. 'The Burlands of Steyning', *N.Q.S.D.* **3**, 1893, 269. Includes pedigree.

Burleston
See Chudderlegh

Burnell
See Cocktree

Burt
TERRY, GEORGE SKELTON. 'Genealogical research in England: Burt-March', *N.E.H.G.R.* **86**, 1932, 77-84, 216-20 and 247-52. Burt and March families of Halberton, Devon, *etc.,* 16-17th c. Includes wills, extracts from parish registers and court rolls, *etc.*

Burton
BERESFORD, JOHN. 'The Burtons of Sutton Montis, Co. Somerset', *Notes & queries* **150**, 1926, 404-5.
NAISH, SANDRA. 'Burton family of Tisbury', *W.F.H.S.* **28**, 1988, 12-15. Includes pedigree, 18-20th c.

Bury
JONES, W. 'John Bury, Canon-residentiary of Exeter Cathedral, and his sons-in-law and descendants', *N.G.D.C.* **4**, 1891, 65-71. See also 84.

Busby
STAPLETON, GUY. 'A family in transition: the weaving Busbys of Moreton, Gloucestershire', *Genealogist's magazine* **17**, 1972, 67-74. 18-19th c.

Bush
GOULSTONE, JOHN. 'Bishop Rush and some family connections', *J.B.A.* **70**, 1992, 34-9. Includes pedigrees of Bush, 15-16th c., and Purnell, 18th c.
'Paul Bush, the last rector of Edington and first bishop of Bristol', *W.N.Q.* **4**, 1902-4, 97-107 & 145-56. See also 426-7. Includes pedigree, 16th c., monumental inscription, and various Bush wills.

Bushell
LANGSTON, J.N. 'Old Catholic families of Gloucestershire: the Bushells of Broad Marston', *B.G.A.S.T.* **75**, 1956, 105-15 & 144(f). Includes pedigree, 13-17th c.

Bussel
ALEXANDER, J.J. 'Early owners of Bradley manor', *D.A.Tr.* **68**, 1936, 187-95. Bussel and Yarde families, 13th-15th c.

Butler
See Little

Byam
BYAM, EDWARD S. *Chronological memoir of the Reverends Henry, John and Edward Byam, sons of the Rev. Lawrence Byam, rector of Luckham, Somersetshire, during the reigns of Elizabeth and James I, from A.D. 1574 to A.D. 1614.* Tenby: R. Mason, 1862. Includes pedigree, medieval-19th.

Byfleet
WHITFIELD, I.M. 'A Somerset recusant family', *N.Q.S.D.* **29**, 1974, 215-20. Byfleet of Bratton Seymour, 16-17th c.

Bylee
See Batt

Byles
BYLES, HENRY NATHANIEL. *The Byles family.* Revised by John Beuzeville Byles. Weymouth: Sherren, 1959.

Byley
See Batt

Cabell
DJABRI, SUSAN CABELL. *The story of the Sepulchre: the Cabells of Buckfastleigh and the Conan Doyle connection.* Wimbledon: Shamrock Press, [1991?]. 16-17th c.

Cadbury
LANE, JOHN. 'The Cadbury family in Devon', *D.C.N.Q.* **11**, 1920-21, 365-6. 16-19th c.

WILLIAMS, IOLO A. *The firm of Cadbury 1831-1931.* Constable and Co., 1931. Of Birmingham – but originally of S.W.England.

Caddell
See Cary

Cadetrew
SOMERS COCKS, J.V. 'A Widecombe-in-the-Moor land boundary', *D.C.N.Q.* **30**, 1965-7, 180-3. Transcript of 14th c. deed, Thomas de Spicwyk to Gilbert de Kadetrew, with 15th c. pedigree of Cadetrew family (not transcribed).

Cadleigh
See Grenville

Callard
BLOTT, S. 'Callard connections', *D.F.H.* **24**, 1982, 26-7. Information from family bible.
'Callard of Ford in Stockland, Dorset, now in Devon', *N.Q.S.D.* **12**, 1911, 181-2. 17-18th c.

Calston
Littlecote. Hatchard, 1900. Partly a history of the Calston, Darrell and Popham families.

Camborne
See Paynter

Cambray
DUNBAR-DUNBAR, J.A. *Family of Cambray of Great Rissington and Icomb, Gloucestershire, with a note upon the medieval Cambrays.* Phillimore, 1898. Includes pedigrees, 16-20th c., with monumental inscriptions, wills, etc

Cancia
PRIDEAUX, F.B. 'De Cancia and De Berkeley-De Canta families', *D.C.N.Q.* **15**, 1928, 27-30.

Canning
N. 'The family of Canning', *Herald & genealogist* **1**, 1863, 273-7. Of Bristol, includes pedigree, 13th c.
WADLEY, T.P. 'The Cannings of Foxcott', *Genealogist* **4**, 1880, 157-65. Of Foxcott, Warwickshire, and Gloucestershire, includes extracts from parish registers.

Canynges
PRYCE, GEORGE. *Memorials of the Canynges family and their times: their claim to be regarded as the founder and restorers of Westbury College and Redcliffe church, critically examined, to which is added, inedited memoranda relating to Chatterton.* Bristol: the author, 1854.

Cardew
CARDEW, FREDERIC. *A war list: descendants of the late Rev. Cornelius Cardew D.D., (1747-1831), capital burgess of Truro (1775), chaplain in ordinary to the Prince of Wales and rector of Erme, Cornwall – who served in the British forces in the Great War (1914-1919).* Whitchurch, Oxon: privately printed, 1920. Gives records of service of many descendants.
CARDEW, MICHAEL. 'Rev. Dr. Cornelius Cardew and his family', *C.F.H.S.J.* **44**, 1987, 17. Late 18th c.

Carew
CAREW, PETER. *Combat and carnival.* Constable, 1954.
COVYON, DEN. 'A genealogical note', *Old Cornwall* **3**(12), 1942, 496. Descent of Richard Carew from Edward III.
GLENCROSS, REGINALD M. 'The Carews, Baronets of Antony, Co.Cornwall', *Genealogist* N.S. **24**, 1908, 22-5. See also **25**, 1909, 154-6. 17-18th c.
HALLIDAY, F.E. *A Cornish chronicle: the Carews of Antony from Armada to Civil War.* Newton Abbot: David & Charles, 1967.
MCMEEN, DAVID B. 'The Carew family and its connections', *Notes & queries* **208**, 1963, 54. Includes pedigree, 15-17th c.
'Antony House and the Carew and Pole families', *C.F.H.S.J.* **45**, 1987, 15-17. 16-20th c.
PHILLIPPS, THOMAS, SIR. *Carew quarterings, pedigree of Carewe of Carewe Castle, Co. Pembroke, and Mohun's Ottery, Co. Devon, and the branches of Haccombe, Antony, Bury, and Crowcombe.* Middle Hill: the author, 1830.
RICHARDSON, JOAN A. CAREW. 'The piratical Carews of Dorset and Hampshire', *Catholic ancestor* **51**, 1994, 31-7. 16-17th c.
RICHARDSON, JOAN A. CAREW. 'The Carew family shipshape and Bristol fashion', *Catholic ancestor* **3**(3), 1900, 101-6. 18-19th c.
ROUND, J. H. 'The origin of the Carews', *Ancestor* **5**, 1903, 19-53.
SEARLEY, A.W. 'Haccombe, part VIII: early Carew period', *D.A.Tr.* **56**, 1924, 309-26.
'Armorial bookplate', *M.G.H.* N.S., **4**, 1884, 154. Of Camerton.
See also Craucombe and Pole

Carkeet

BRYANT, E.E. 'Carkeet of St.Ewe, Pelynt and St.Martyns-by-Looe', *D.C.N.Q.* **13**, 1924-5, 349-51. See also 354-5. 17-18th c.

BRYANT, EDITH. 'Carkeet of St.Ewe, Pelynt and St.Martins-by-Looe', *D.C.N.Q.* **15**, 1928-9, 297-301. 16-17th c.

BRYANT, EDITH. 'Monk and Carkeke families', *D.C.N.Q.* **15**, 1928-9, 195-6. 16-17th c.

Carlyon

POTTS, RICHARD. 'A Leicestershire link', *D.C.N.Q.* **30**, 1965-7, 293-5. Notes on Winstanley of Braunstone, Leicestershire, and Carlyon of Truro, 18-19th c.

Carminow

ROGERS, JOHN JOPE. 'Carminow of Carminow', *J.R.I.C.* **5**, 1874-8, 220-38. Includes pedigree, medieval.
See also Bloyou and Fitzroger

Carne

KENT, ALAN. 'The Carnes of Wales, Cornwall, & Rome', *C.F.H.S.J.* **53**, 1989, 22-3.

JENKYN, A.W. *From here to antiquity: a Celtic lineage. Carne of Glamorgan and Tresilian of Cornwall.* Eastwood, N.S.W.: Roy A. Dunstan, 1994. Includes pedigrees, Medieval - 18th c., wills, *etc.*

Caruthers

See Little

Carwithen

See Cooke and Sherman

Cary

CARY, HENRY GROSVENOR. *The Cary family in England.* Boston: Seth Corley Cary, 1906. Medieval-19th c.

DYMOND, ROBERT. 'Sir George Cary of Cockington', *D.A.Tr.* **6**, 1873-4, 276-92. Includes genealogical information.

HARRISON, F. *The Devon Carys.* 2 vols. New York: De Vinne Press, 1920.

R., J.B. 'Cary of Follaton', *D.N.Q.* **1**, 1900-1, 117. Name change to Caddell.

WATKIN, HUGH R. *The House of Stuart and the Cary family: James II and Torre Abbey.* Exeter: J. G. Commin, 1920. Appendix to *D.C.N.Q.* **11**, 1920. See also **11**, 1921, 161-2.
See also Prust and Knight

Cassey

LANGSTON, J.N. 'Old Catholic families of Gloucestershire: the Casseys of Wightfield in Dearhurst.' *B.G.A.S.T.* **74**, 1955, 128-52. Includes pedigree, 14-17th c.

Casswell

See Spooner

Castle

MARTIN, MAUREEN, & ABBLITT, LINDA. *Castle day-dreams.* Launceston, Tasmania: the authors, 1992. Castle family of Banwell and Tasmania; includes pedigrees, 18-20th c.

S., T.W.W. 'Cranborne: a trade token', *N.Q.S.D.* **3**, 1893, 154-6. See also 182. Includes genealogical notes on the Castle family of Cranborne.

Catchmay

ALLEN, WILLIAM TAPNELL. 'The family of Catchmay', *B.G.A.S.T.* **24**, 1901, 142-55. 14-18th c., includes extracts from parish registers, monumental inscriptions, etc.

Caunter

CAUNTER, F. LYDE. *Caunter family records.* Solicitors Law Stationery Society, 1930. Includes folded pedigree, 17-20th c.

WILKINSON, FREDA. 'The Caunters of Ponsworthy,' *D.H.* **42**, 1991, 28-9. 19-20th c.

Cavenett

IRELAND, K.J. 'Cavenett family', *D.C.N.Q.* **31**, 1968, 90.

Cecil

See Vaughan

Chafe

CHAFY, W.K.W. *Gesta Chaforum, or, notes on, and diaries kept by, the Chafes or Chafys of Chafe-combe, Exeter, and Sherbourne.* Rous Lench Court: privately printed, 1910.

JONES, WINSLOW. 'Thomas Chafe of Doddescott, in St. Giles in the Wood', *D.A.Tr.* **20**, 1888, 398-9.

MANSEL-PLEYDELL, J.C. 'Chafe-Chaffyn', *N.Q.S.D.* **1**, 1890, 248-9. See also 249-51, giving extracts from Folke parish register.
See also Chape

Chaffin

DRAKE, PHYLLIS, & DRAKE, STELLA JUDY. *The Chaffin family: a study of one name.* Basingstoke: the author, 1986. Somerset family

Challoner

See Knight

Champerno(u)n
BENSON, J. 'Champernowne and Drake', *D.C.N.Q.* **19**, 1936-7, 118-22. 17th c.

BENSON, J. 'Early Champernowne history', *D.C.N.Q.* **18**, 1934-5, 3-7. See also 81-4, 108-11, & 319-21.

TUTTLE, CHAS. W. 'Captain Francis Champernowne', *N.E.H.G.R.* **28**, 1874, 75-82, 318-23 and 403-9. Medieval-17th c.

WILLIAMS, JAMES FREDERIC. *A short summary of Champernowne family records.* [ ]: Philip Champernowne, [1931?] Medieval.

'Abstracts of some ancient deeds and other documents relating to the family of Champernoun of the county of Devon', *Family history* **1**, 1962, 31-3.

'Champernons of Clyst St. George and Tywardreath,' *D.C.N.Q.* **16**, 1930-31, 86-7. 14-16th c.

See also Bonville, Courtenay, and Talbot

Champneys
'Pedigrees from the visitation of Dorset 1623: Champneys', *M.G.H.* 2nd series **2**, 1888, 169.

Chandler
GLENN, THOMAS ALLEN. *Chandler of Oare (county of Wilts): report of searches in relation to the ancestry of John and George Chandler who sailed from England to the province of Pennsylvania, in the year 1686.* W.K. Morton & Sons, 1913.

'The Chandlers of Wiltshire', *W.N.Q.* **1**, 1893-5, 352-4. See also 410-13 & 448. 17th c. Emigrants to America.

See also Merryweather

Chandos
See Brydges

Channon
HAYWARD, JOHN. 'The Channon family of Exeter and London, chair and cabinet-makers', *Victoria & Albert Museum bulletin* **1**(1), 1966, 64-70.

Chapin
CHAPIN, HOWARD MILLAR. 'The English ancestry of Dea. Samuel Chapin of Springfield, Mass.,' *N.E.H.G.R.* **83**, 1929, 351-7. Of Paignton, 16-17th c.

Chapman
K., A. 'Chapman of Tetbury', *W.N.Q.* **1**, 1893-5, 372-3. 17th c.

Chappell
See Crocker

Chard
'Chard', *G.T.* **12**(2), 1987, 61.

Chasey
CHASEY, HAROLD. 'The Chasey family of central Somerset', *N.Q.S.D.* **31**, 1980-85, 411-4.

Chatterton
New facts relating to the Chatterton family gathered from manuscript entries in a 'history of the Bible', which once belonged to the parents of Thomas Chatterton the poet, and from parish registers. Bristol: W George & Son, 1883. 18th c.

See also Canynges

Chave
MONDAY, A.J. 'Devonshire surnames: Chave', *W.A.* **3**, 1884, 8.

Chedder
GEORGE, W. 'The De Chedder family of Bristol and Cheddar', *S.A.N.H.S.* **34**(2), 1888, 114-6. 13-14th c.

Chedderleigh
See Chudleigh

Cheevers
CHEEVERS, R. THOMAS. 'Roger, the father of William Chievre and Ralf Pomeroy', *D.C.N.Q.* **29**, 1962-4, 193-6. 11-12th c., Cheevers and Pomeroy families.

Chegwidden
WORK, MAURINE E. *Constantine, Cornwall to Adelaide, South Australia: the Chegwidden family and Chegwidden Farm.* The author, 1986.

Cheney
BATTEN, JOHN. 'The lady of Poyntington', *S.A.N.H.S.* **42**(2), 1896, 1-5. Cheney family; includes pedigree, 13-15th c.

PRIDEAUX, F.B. 'Cheneys in Devon', *D.C.N.Q.* **15**, 1928-9, 55-7. Medieval.

PRIDEAUX, F.B. 'Roridge chapel and its Cheney owners', *D.C.N.Q.* **15**, 1928, 66-8.

Cheriton
CHRISTIE, PETER. 'The true story of the North Devon savages,' *D.A.Tr.* **124**, 1992, 59-85. Cheriton family, 18th c.

Chernocke
See St. Barbe

Chesney
CHESNEY, R.W.L. 'Some medieval sheriffs of Somerset and Dorset', *Genealogists' magazine* **17**, 1973, 315-20. Chesney family.

Chester

WATERS, ROBERT EDMOND CHESTER. *Genealogical memoirs of the families of Chester of Bristol, Barton Regis, London and Almondsbury, descended from Henry Chester, sheriff of Bristol 1470, and also of the families of Astry of London, Kent, Beds., Hunts., Oxon. and Gloucestershire descended from Sir Ralph Astry, Kt., Lord Mayor of London, 1493.* Reeves & Turner, 1881.

Chetwynd
See Harington

Chevalier
See Martin

Ceverel
See Botreaux

Chewte
See Chute

Cheyne
FANSHAWE, H., & PRIDEAUX, F.B. 'Cheyne of Dorset and Wilts', *Notes & queries* **153,** 1927, 463. See also 388, & **155,** 1928, 301, 336-7, & 371.

Chichester
CHICHESTER, ALEX PALMER BRUCE, SIR. *History of the family of Chichester, from A.D. 1086 to 1870, including the descents of the various branches settled at Raleigh, Youlston, Arlington, Widworthy, Calverleigh Hall, and elsewhere in Devonshire; also of the Chichesters, Marquesses of Donegal, and Barons Templemore.* John Camden Hotten, 1871.
DRAKE, WILLIAM RICHARD. *Notes genealogical, historical, and heraldic of the family of Chichester, of Youlston, Hall, and Arlington, Co. Devon.* Privately printed, 1886. Extract from Drake's *Devonshire notes and notelets.*

Chick
TOMLINSON, MARGARET. *Three generations in the Honiton lace trade.* Exeter: Devon Print Group, 1983.
See also Notley

Chidgey
GILMAN, J.M. 'Captain Thomas Chidgey and the port of Watchet', *Maritime history* **4,** 1974, 31-48.

Chidiok
See Botreaux

Chilcott
ROBINSON, C.J. 'Chilcott of Co. Dorset', *N.Q.S.D.* **3,** 1893, 279. See also 339.

Child
LIGHT, M.E. 'Heddington and the Child family', *W.N.Q.* **2,** 1896-8, 207-18 & 261-71. See also 301-2. 15-18th c.

Ching
KING, G. 'The Ching family of Launceston', *Old Cornwall* **8,** 1973-9, 433-5. 18-20th c.
MOSSONG, VERNA. *Richard Ching, of the genuine stamp: an account of Richard Ching and his family, in Cornwall, England, and New Zealand.* Auckland: V. & I. Mossong, 1992. Includes pedigree, 18-19th c.
MOSSONG, VERNA. 'Chin/Chinn/Ching, of St.Keverne, Cornwall', *C.F.H.S.J.* **2,** 1976, 11-13. 19th c.

Chiswell
CHISWELL, ANN. 'History of the Chiswell surname', *D.F.H.* **1,** 1977, 15-18.

Chivers
JONES, WIN. 'The story of John Chivers and his wife Mary Ann, nee Gardiner, their ancestors, descendants, and the families they married into', *W.F.H.S.* **7,** 1982, 12-17. 19th c., Wiltshire and Australia.

Chiverton
'A note on the Chiverton family', *Genealogical quarterly* **30(4),** 1964, 154-5.

Choke
ROSENTHAL, JOEL T. 'Sir Richard Choke (d.1483) of Long Ashton', *S.A.N.H.S.* **127,** 1982/3, 105-21. Includes genealogical information.

Cholwich
EVANS, CHARLES. 'Cholwich of Blackawton, Devon', *D.C.N.Q.* **28,** 1959-61, 85-8. See also 160.

Christmas
MURRAY, O.A.R. 'Christmas family,' *D.C.N.Q.* **6,** 1910-11, 210-12. See also 175. 17-18th c.

Chubb
COLBY, REV., & RYLANDS, J.P. 'Pedigrees from the visitation of Dorset, 1623', *M.G.H.* 2nd. series **2,** 1888, 188-91. Includes Chubb, Clavelshey, Coker, and Fillol or Filiol.

Chudderlegh
PRIDEAUX, F.B. 'Chudderlegh and Burleston families', *D.C.N.Q.* **14,** 1926-7, 219-21. Includes pedigree of Ferrers, 14-15th c.

Chudleigh

ADAMS, MAXWELL. 'A brief account of Ashton church and some of the Chudleighs of Ashton', *D.A.Tr.* **31**, 1899, 184-98.

PRIDEAUX, F.B. 'Chudleigh and Chedderleigh', *D.C.N.Q.* **14**, 1926-7, 218-9. See also 267. Surnames derived from place-names; medieval.

Chudleigh memorials. [ ]: privately printed, [1916]. Chudleigh family, 15-20th c.

See also Strode

Churchey

SWEETMAN, GEORGE. *The 'Dogs' and its owners, with particular reference to the Churchey family in Wincanton.* Yeovil: Western Printing & Publishing Co., for the Wincanton Field Club., 1900.

Churchill

CHOPE, R. 'The Churchill family', *D.C.N.Q.* **11**, 1920-21, 51-2. Note by Sir Winston Churchill, c.1620-1668.

DAWE, N. 'The Dorset Churchills', *N.Q.S.D.* **27**, 1961, 185-93. See also 213-5 & 261-3. Includes 16-17th c. pedigree.

ELLICOTT, WILLIAM M. *Families of Churchill, Croker, Fox, Coplestone, Bonvile, Ellicott, etc., of Devonshire, England, and some of their descendants in America ...* Baltimore: [ ], 1931. Reprinted from the *Maryland historical magazine* **26**, 1931. Medieval-18th c.

RAVENHILL, H.E. 'Minterne: its connection with the Churchills and Digbys', *D.N.* **10**, 1889, 89-96. 17-18th c.

ROWSE, A.L. *The early and the later Churchills.* Reprint Society, 1959. Originally published as *The early Churchills* and *The later Churchills.* Macmillan, 1956-8.

ROYAL, N.J. 'Churchill family', *N.Q.S.D.* **29**, 1974, 249-51. See also **30**, 1974-9, 150 & 211. 16-17th c.

SNELL, ELIZABETH. *The Churchills: pioneers and politicians, England-America-Canada.* Tiverton: West Country Books, 1994. 16-20th c.

See also Fox

Chute

DUDLEY, D. 'Pedigree of Chute or Chewte', *N.E.H.G.R.* **13**, 1859, 123-4. 14-17thc., of Somerset.

Chynoweth

CHYNOWETH, HOWARD. *The Chynoweth family of Greenland, Michigan, with material relating to Dawe family relatives, the Cornish in Cornwall, and U.S.A.* Michigan history. Detroit: [?], 1966.

See also Ridington

Clake

See Cleak

Clapp

CLAPP, JOHN. *In search of adventure: a family history of Clapps from Devon.* Brighton, Australia: the Author, 1984.

See also Kestell

Clare

ALTSCHUL, MICHAEL. *A baronial family in medieval England: the Clares 1217-1314.* Baltimore: John Hopkins Press, 1965.

MACLAGAN, M. 'The heraldry of the house of Clare', *Family history* **2**(85/6); N.S., **61/2**, 1981, 2-12. Includes pedigree, 10-14th c.

Clark(e)

CLARK, ROGER. *Somerset anthology: twenty-four pieces,* ed. Percy Lovell. York: William Sessions, 1975. Mainly concerning the Clarks of Street, 19-20th c.

KELLAND, W.H. 'Genealogical notes on the families of Clarke Creemer, Gater, Northcote, Partridge, Kelland, Mitchell, Saunder and others', *W.A.* **4**, 1885, 125-30. Includes extracts from parish registers. For Kelland, see also 152.

JEWERS, A.J. 'Clarke family', *N.Q.S.D.* **5**, 1897-8, 274-6. 16th c.

RICHARDSON, W.H. 'Pedigree of the family of Clarke of Yarnscombe, Co. Devon, and of Waste Court, Abingdon, Co. Berks., from the records of the College of Arms', *Genealogist* **2**, 1878, 169-72. See also 173-5.

SUTTON, GEORGE BARRY. *A history of shoe making in Street, Somerset: C. & J. Clark, 1833-1903.* York: William Sessions, 1979. Includes pedigree showing linkage of Clark, Sturge, Melford, Bull and Stephens families, 17-20th c.

Clayfield-Ireland

WILLIAMSON, B. *The Clayfield-Irelands of Brislington.* [ ], 1986.

Cleak

CLEAK, ROLAND, & PARKER, GRACE. *Records of the Cleak(e) — Clake and Click families.* Rev. ed. Cirencester: E. R. Cleak, 1991. Of Devon, Gloucestershire and many other counties; lists post 1837 births, marriages and deaths, and post 1796 wills.

Cleall

CLIST, JUNE. 'Cleall marriages', *J.D.F.H.S.* 3(1), 1989, 14-16; 3(2), 1990, 48-50; 3(4), 1990, 127-30; 4(2), 1991, 51-3; 4(3), 1991, 114-5. List, 18-19th c.

Cleaveland

SKINNER, A.J. 'Ezra Cleaveland', *D.C.N.Q.* 10, 1918-19, 313. Cleaveland family extracts from Honiton parish register, 17-18th c.

Cleaver

See Humphrey

Cleeve

JAMES, J. 'Cleeve memorial, Kentisbeare church', *D.C.N.Q.* 36(1), 1987, 37-9.

Cleeveley

PAGET, M. 'A family of craftsmen and husbandmen: the Cleeveleys of Charlton Kings,' *C.K.L.H.S.B.* 11, 1984, 29-43; 12, 1984, 36-42; 13, 1985, 35-47. See also 15, 1986, 53-4. Includes pedigree, 16-18th c.

Clements

GOULSTONE, JOHN. 'The Clements of Englishcombe', *J.B.A.* 51, 1988, 26-9. 16-17th c.

Clevedon

MACLEAN, JOHN, SIR. 'The Clevedon family', *S.A.N.H.S.* 41(2), 1895, 1-37. Includes pedigree, 11-15th c.
See also Courtenay

Click

See Cleak

Clifford

CLIFFORD, ARTHUR. *Collectanea Cliffordiana.* Skipton: Skipton Castle Ltd., 1980. Originally published: Paris: the author, 1817.
CLIFFORD, HUGH. *The house of Clifford from before the Conquest.* Chichester: Phillimore, 1987.
OLIVER, GEORGE. *Cliffordiana.* Exeter: T. Howe, 1828?
'Pedigree of Clifford of Frampton, Co. Gloucester, of Dublin, and of Castle Annesley, Co. Wexford.' *M.G.H.* 5th series 5, 1925, 313-25.

Clift

AUSTIN, FRANCES, ed. *The Clift family correspondence, 1792-1846.* Sheffield: University of Sheffield Centre for English Cultural Tradition and Language, 1991. Of Cornwall.

Climo

CLIMO, FREDERICK HEDLEY BARKER, & CLIMO, PERCY LLOYD. *Mabinogi an Clem: the story of the children of Clem.* St.Catherines, Ontario: P.L. Climo, 1975. Climo family, 16-20th c.
CLIMO, PERCY L. 'Surname Climo', *D.C.N.Q.* 30, 1965-7, 59-60.

Clutterbuck

WITCHELL, MARK EDWIN NORTHAM, & HUDLESTON, CHRISTOPHER ROY, eds. *An account of the principal branches of the family of Clutterbuck from the sixteenth century to the present, chiefly based upon the Heralds' visitations.* Gloucester: John Bellows, 1924. Includes pedigrees.
'Clutterbuck of Hardenhuish', *W.N.Q.* 1, 1893-5, 304-6. See also 517-8. 18-19th c.
'The Clutterbuck family, of Stanley St Leonards', *G.N.Q.* 3, 1887, 6-9.
'The family of Clutterbuck', *G.N.Q.* 5, 1894, 378-93, 426-7, 454-60, 511-13, 546-60; 6, 1896, 13-16. Includes pedigrees, 16-19th c.

Coade

AUTHERS, W. 'Coade and Sealy families', *D.C.N.Q.* 33(1), 1974, 26-8. See also 33(6), 1976, 226-7 & 32(7), 1973, 220-1.

Coates

See Russell

Cobham

See Brook

Cobleigh

GIFFARD, H.F. 'Cobleigh of Brightleigh', *D.N.Q.* 1, 1900-1, 210-4. See also 244-5.

Cobley

CHANTER, J.F. 'Uncle Tom Cobley', *D.C.N.Q.* 11, 1920, 7-9, 70, & 164.
See also Stowford

Cock

PACKER, GOLDA, MCDONALD, ROY, & JOHNS, DALE. *The tangled tela: 124 biographies of Cock/Langmead families, 1797-1892.* Moonta: the authors, 1986. Cock of Redruth, Langmead of Dartmouth, emigrants to Australia.

Cockington

BENSON, J. 'Cockington and Cokematon', *D.C.N.Q.* **22**(15), 1945, 273-4.

Cockram

HERTFORD, HENRY. 'A Cullompton worthy', *D.C.N.Q.* **19**, 1936, 132-6. Robert Cockram, 1553-1632, fellow of Oriel College, Oxford, and his ancestors.

HERTFORD, HENRY. 'Robert Cockram: a Cullompton worthy', *Notes & queries* **170**, 1936, 401-2.

Cocks

SOMERS COCKS, J.V. *A history of the Cocks family.* 4 parts. Teignmouth: Brunswick Press, 1963-7. Includes folded pedigrees, 17-18th c. with wills etc.

'Cocks pedigree', *M.G.H.* **1**, 1868, 238-41. Of Gloucestershire; 17-18th c.

Cocktree

LEGA-WEEKES, E. 'Cocktree', *D.N.Q.* **1**, 1900-1, 103-4. See also 151-2. Descent of Cocktree through Cocktree, Burnel and Wyke, 13-15th c.

Codner

HOPKINS, J.T. 'The Codners of Berry Pomeroy', *D.C.N.Q.* **34**(4), 1979, 133-9. 17-18th c.

Codrington

CODRINGTON, R.H. 'A family connexion of the Codrington family in the XVIIth century', *B.G.A.S.T.* **18**, 1893-4, 134-9.

CODRINGTON, R.H. *Memoirs of the family of Codrington of Codrington, Didmarton, Frampton-on-Severn and Dodington.* Letchworth: Arden Press, 1916.

CODRINGTON, R.H. 'Memoirs of the family of Codrington of Codrington, Didmarton, Frampton-on-Severn, and Dodington', *B.G.A.S.T.* **21**, 1898, 301-45. Includes pedigrees, 14-19th c.

LOWE, ROBSON. *The Codrington correspondence, 1743-1851.* Robson Lowe, 1951.

Coffin

BROWN, JOHN COFFIN JONES. 'The name and armorial bearings of the Coffin family', *N.E.H.G.R.* **35**, 1881, 376-81. 13-17th c. Of Alwington, Devon.

MUGFORD, W.E. 'Tristram Coffin of Brixton, Devon', *D.N.Q.* **2**, 1902-3, 142-4. 17th c. pedigree.

See also Rowe

Cogan

MCCRACKEN, GEORGE E. 'Early Cogans, English and American', *N.E.H.G.R.* **110**, 1956, 185-201, 258-76; **111**, 1957, 5-18, 81-91 & 168-87. Medieval-18th c. Of Somerset, Devon, *etc.*

See also Conway

Cogar

HARRISON, KEN. 'My Cogar ancestry', *C.F.H.S.J.* **59**, 1991, 35. See also **63**, 1992, 27-8. Medieval-20th c.

Coke

WARBURTON-COX, A.F. 'Coke of Thorne in Ottery St. Mary', *D.C.N.Q.* **22**(8), 1943, 191-2.

See also Coxe

Cokematon

See Cockington

Coker

WERE, F. 'Coker armorials', *N.Q.S.D.* **7**, 1901, 328-9. See also 347.

See also Pitman

Colby

COLBY, F.T. *Colby of Great Torrington, Devon: some account of that family and its alliances for five generations.* Exeter: privately printed, 1880.

COLBY, F.T. *An appendix to Colby of Great Torrington, containing an account of families of the same name in other counties, and additional notes to the former volume.* [Exeter?]: privately printed, 1880.

COLBY, F.T. *Pedigrees of five Devonshire families: Colby, Coplestone, Reynolds, Palmer and Johnson.* Exeter: privately printed, 1884. Appendices, additions and corrections published 1885 and 1894.

See also Coplestone

Colchester

DIGHTON, CONWAY. 'The Colchester family', *G.N.Q.* **5**, 1894, 251-2. Extracts from Ashelworth parish register.

Cole

COLE, C.H.B. *Descendants of John Cole of North Molton, Devonshire.* 2nd ed. Sandford St. Martin: C. H. B. Cole, 1987, 17-20th c.

COLE, CHARLES. *The Cole family of Ashreigny, Devonshire.* 4 vols. Crediton: the author, 1997. Not seen.

COLE, JAMES EDWIN. *The genealogy of the family of Cole, of the county of Devon, and of those of its branches which settled in Suffolk, Hampshire, Surrey, Lincolnshire and Ireland.* J.R. Smith, 1867. Medieval-19th c.

Coleraine
MELLOR, A. SHAW. 'The Coleraine family of Longford', *W.A.M.* **52**(189), 1948, 328-37. 17-18th c.

Coleridge
COLERIDGE, LORD. *The story of a Devonshire house.* 2nd ed. T. Fisher Unwin, 1906.

TOOHEY, TIMOTHY. *Piety and the professions: Sir John Coleridge and his sons.* Garland, 1987. 18-19th c.

See also Northcote

Collard
'A Collard family', *Family history* **2**(9), 1964 68-9. Pedigree, 17-19th c. Of Somerset.

Collet
CHADD, MARGARET. *The Collet sagas.* Norwich: Elvery Dowers, 1988. Gloucestershire, Suffolk and London family.

CHAMBERS, BARBARA J. 'The Collett family of Arlington Row', *J.G.F.H.S.* **69**, 1966, 9-10. Of Arlington, Gloucestershire, 18-19th c.

Collier
BENSON, R. *Memoirs of the life and writings of the Rev. Arthur Collier, M.A., rector of Langford Magna in the County of Wilts from A.D. 1704 to A.D. 1732, with some account of his family.* Edward Lumley, 1837.

MOBBS, A.M. *Notable local families: the Colliers.* Horrabridge & district, pt.4. [Horrabridge: the author, 1988].

See also Dodington

Combes
COMBES, LAWRENCE. 'The Wiltshire Combes family', *W.F.H.S.* **6**, 1982, 13-15. Medieval-20th c.

VON ROEMER, MARY. 'Notes on the descendants of Edward Combe of Bridsor in Tisbury', *W.N.Q.* **8**, 1914-16, 63-73 & 100-9. 16-18th c.

VON ROEMER, MARY. 'Notes on the lineage of Richard de Combe, lord of Fitelton, Combe and Todeworth, sheriff of Wilts, 18 Edward 1', *W.N.Q.* **7**, 1911-13, 433-44 & 499-511. 13-16th c.

Compton
'Comptons of Wigborough: baptisms of the Comptons of Wigborough and their connections in the registers of South Petherton, co. Somerset', *M.G.H.* N.S., 4, 1884, 334-5.

Conant
CONANT, FREDERICK ORDELL. *A history and genealogy of the Conant family in England and America: thirteen generations, 1520-1857, containing also some genealogical notes on the Connet, Connett and Connit families.* Portland: Privately printed, 1887. Of Devon, the U.S.A., etc. Includes numerous extracts from original records.

Conway
NORRIS, H. 'King Charles II at Coaxden Hall', *N.Q.S.D.* **3**, 1893, 306-13. Includes pedigree of Conway, and notes on Cogan family.

Conybeare
CONYBEARE, FREDERICK CORNWALLIS, ed. *Letters and exercises of the Elizabethan schoolmaster, John Conybeare, schoolmaster at Molton, Devon, 1580, and at Swimbridge, 1594, with notes and a fragment of autobiography by William Daniel Conybeare.* Henry Frowde, 1905. Includes pedigrees of Conybeare and Olivier.

Coode
PICKEN, W.M.M. 'The descent of Coode of Morval from Prouz, Moeles, and Daumarle', *D.C.N.Q.* **29**(5), 1963, 142-5. See also **32**(1), 1971, 22-3. Mainly medieval.

Cook
'Cook of Halberton and Tiverton: the mystery of the Rixer alias', *D.F.H.* **73**, 1995, 17-19. 17-18th c.

Cooke
WORTHY, CHARLES. 'The families of Cooke and Carwithen', *W.A.* **9**, 1890, 132. See also 168-9 & 201-2, & **10**, 1891, 12-14.

See also Sherman

Coombe
COOMBE, JOAN. *Cornish connections: the Coombe family history.* Black Forest, South Australia: J. Coombe, 1993.

Cooper Dean

BRUCE, GEORGE. *A fortune and a family: Bournemouth and the Cooper Deans*. Bridport: Laverstock Books, 1987. Includes pedigree, 17-20th c.

Cope

COPE, E.E. 'Pedigree of the family of Cope', *M.G.H.* 3rd series **4**, 1902, 237-44 & 289-91.

Coplestone

ALEXANDER, J.J. 'The early Coplestones', *D.C.N.Q.* **20**(2), 1938, 51-5. 1240-1500.

COPLESTONE, F.W. 'Coplestone and Bradford families', *D.N.Q.* **2**, 1902-3, 144. See also 247-50.

DAY, FRED. 'Copleston family', *D.C.N.Q.* **9**, 1916-17, 254-6. See also **10**, 1918-19, 80-82.

RESON, MURIEL. 'Copleston of Copleston in Colebrooke, Devon.' *Family history* 15(126); N.S., **102**, 1992, 261-75. See also 15(127); N.S. **103**, 1992, 130-32.

RESON, MURIEL. '[Pedigree of Coplestone of Ley, Morwenstow, 16-17th c.]', *C.F.H.S.J.* **25**, 1982, 13.

SKINNER, A.J., & M[URRAY], O.A.R. 'Coplestone family', *D.C.N.Q.* **9**, 1917, 254-6; **10**, 1918, 23 & 80-2. Extracts from parish registers.

WILKIN, W.H. 'Copleston of Offwell', *D.A.Tr.* **63**, 1931, 241-54. 18th-19th c.

Coplestone Family Newsletter: Organ of the Coplestone Family History Society. London: the Society, 1979- . Includes many brief articles and notes not otherwise listed here.

'Table showing the descent of Coplestone of Woodland, and of Colby of Great Torrington, Devon, and of the origin of the quarterings borne by Coplestone of Coplestone', *M.G.H.* N.S., **2**, 1877, 73-6. Medieval-19th c.

See also Churchill, Colby, Fox and Litelcote

Corben

CHABOT, DIANA. *The Corbens of Purbeck.* Hove: Hemphill Publications, 1995. 17-19 c.

DAVIS, F.N. 'Corben family', *N.Q.S.D.* **18**, 1926, 139-40.

Corbyn

PRIDEAUX, F.B. 'Corbyn: Le Yreis', *D.C.N.Q.* **15**, 1928, 64-6.

Corker

'The Corkers of Cornwall', *Royal Cornwall Polytechnic Society Annual report* **105**, 1938, 71-95. 17-19th c.

Cornish

CORNISH, J.G. 'Keble and the Cornishes of Salcombe', *D.C.N.Q.* **18**(4), 1934, 159-61.

CORNISH, VAUGHAN. *A family of Devon: their homes, travels and occupations.* St. Leonards: King Bros. & Potts, 1942.

DU BOULAY, JAMES T. HOUSSEMAYNE. *Notes to accompany a pedigree of the family of Cornyshe of Thurlestone in the county of Devon.* Winchester: Warren and Son, 1903. Includes folded pedigree, 16-19th c.

JONES, W. 'The first Lord Teignmouth and the family of Cornish', *N.G.D.C.* **3**, 1890, 103-4.

The Choughs: the journal of the Society of Cornishes. 1992- .

See also Kestell

Cornish-Bowden

FOX, HUBERT CORNISH, ed. *Cornish-Bowdens of Newton Abbot: family letters.* Bridgwater: Whitby, Light & Lane, 1965. 19-20th c.

Corr

S., J. 'Corr of Aldbourne', *W.N.Q.* **4**, 1902-4, 410-14. 18thc.

Coryton

HULL, P.L. 'The Coryton muniments', *List of accessions [Cornwall Record Office]* 1981/2, 53-6.

Cosowarth

MARTIN, EDWARD. *The Cosowarth family of Coswarth in Colan, Cornwall.* Ipswich: the author, 1991. Includes pedigree, 15-18th c.

MARTIN, E.A. 'The family and name of Coswarth', *D.C.N.Q.* **32**, 1971-3, 184-5. See also **33**, 1974-7, 25-6. 16-17th c.

Cosserat

SKINNER, A.J. 'Cosserat family', *D.C.N.Q.* **11**, 1920-21, 338-9. 18-19th c. extracts from marriage licences.

Coster

HAMILTON-EDWARDS, GERALD KENNETH SAVERY. *Pedigree of the family of Coster of London, Witheridge, Devon, and of New Zealand.* [Plymouth?]: [the author?], 1944.

Coswarth

MARTIN, E.A. 'The family and name of Coswarth', *D.C.N.Q.* **32**(6), 1972, 184-5.

MARTIN, E.A. 'The name of Cosworth and surname derived first-names', *D.C.N.Q.* **33**(1), 1974, 256.

Cotgrave

See Turner

Cot(t)el(l)

COTTELL, WILLIAM HENRY. *A history of the Cotel, Cottell, or Cottle family, of the counties of Devon, Somerset, Cornwall and Wilts. Compiled from county histories, heralds visitations, etc.* Taylor & Co., 1871.

COTTELL, WILLIAM HENRY. *Pedigree of the family of Cotell, Cotele, Cottell, or Cottle of the counties of Devon, Somerset, Cornwall, and Wilts.* Mitchell & Hughes, [1891]

COTTELL, W. H. 'Cotel, Cottell, or Cottle family', *N.Q.S.D.* **1**, 1890, 105-6. Includes grant of free warren to Sir Edye Cotel, Knt., 1248, with names of witnesses.

TAPLEY-SOPER, H. 'Parish register inaccuracies', *D.C.N.Q.* **9**, 1916, 5-6. See also 53-4. Cottell family.

SKARDON, T.G. 'Cottell, Walters, Molford and Dolbeare families', *D.N.Q.* **1**, 1900-1, 152.

Cottey

BIZLEY, ALICE C. 'The Cottey family of Reenwartha in Perranzabuloe, 1615-1841', *Old Cornwall* 10(2), 1986, 66-9.

Cottington

WILLIAMS, J. ANTHONY. 'A Wiltshire recusant family: a malitious prosecution', *Wiseman review* **488**, 1961, 146-8. Cottington family, 17-18th c.

Cotton

CHOPE, R. 'Cotton and Savery families', *D.C.N.Q.* **12**, 1922, 175-7.
See also Annesley

Couch

MARTIN, E.A. 'The Couch family of Glasney College, Penryn', *Old Cornwall* **7**, 1973, 512-6.

Courtenay/Courtney

CHERRY, M. 'The Courtenay Earls of Devon: the formation and disintegration of a late medieval aristocratic affinity', *Southern history* **1**, 1979, 71-97.

CLEAVELAND, EZRA. *A genealogical history of the noble and illustrious family of Courtenay, in three parts. The first giveth an account of the Counts of Edessa, of that family. The second, of that branch which is in France. The third, of that branch which is in England.* Exeter: E. Farley, 1735.

COURTNEY, CHRISTOPHER L., SIR. *The Courtney family.* The author, 1967.

DRAKE, H.H. 'Courteney and Champernown families', *D.C.N.Q.* **9**, 1916, 28-9.

DURANT, HORATIO. *Sorrowful captives: the Tudor Earls of Devon.* Pontypool: Hughes & Son, 1970.

HORWOOD, ALFRED J. 'The manuscripts of the Right Honourable the Earl of Devon at Powderham Castle, Co. Devon', in HISTORICAL MANUSCRIPTS COMMISSION. *Third report ...* C.673. H.M.S.O., 1872, 216. Brief list including genealogical material.

HUTCHINSON, O. 'Pedigree and arms of the Courtenay family at their first settlement in England', *N.G.D.C.* **2**, 1889, 50-56, 89-93 & 97. See also 65-8.

IMBERT-TERRY, H.M. 'The royal Courtenays', in SNELL, F.J. *Memorials of old Devonshire.* Bemrose & Sons, 1904, 34-62.

LADD, JAMES. *Topsham saga: the Earls of Devon.* Topsham: Apsam Books, 1993. Courteney family, medieval.

LEPINE, DAVID N. 'The Courtenays and Exeter Cathedral in the later middle ages', *D.A.Tr.* **124**, 1992, 41-58.

NICOLAS, HARRY, SIR. *Report of proceedings on the claim to the Earldom of Devon in the House of Lords, with notes and appendix, containing copies of patents and cases illustrative of the claim.* J. & W. T. Clarke, 1832.

OLIVER, GEORGE, & JONES, PITMAN. 'Genealogy of the family of Courtenay, Barons of Okehampton and Earls of Devon', *Archaeological Journal* **10**, 1853, 53(f). Folded pedigree.

ROGERS, W.H. HAMILTON. 'Courtenay-Clyvedon, in Somerset', *N.Q.S.D.* **6**, 1899, 241-5. Reprinted in his *Archaeological papers relating to the counties of Somerset, Wilts., Hants., and Devon.* [ ]: reprinted for the author, 1902.

RUSPINI, FRANK ORDE. 'The family of Courtenay, Earls of Devon', *Reliquary* **17**, 1876-7, 17-22, 97-104, 135-40 & 213-4.

SEARLEY, A.W. 'Haccombe, pts. V-VI: the Courtenay period (c.1400-1426)', *D.A.Tr.* **54**, 1922, 271-82; **55**, 1923, 242-51.

THOMASON, J.A.F. 'The Courtenay family in the Yorkist period', *Bulletin of the Institute of Historical Research* **45**, 1972, 230-46.

VINCENT, J.A.C. 'The runaway match of Elizabeth Courtenay', *Genealogist* **6**, 1882, 193-9.
'The marriage settlement of Hugh de Courtenay and the daughter of the Fair Maid of Kent', *N.G.D.C.* **5**, 1892, 78-80. 1362.
See also Andrew, Basset, Engayne, Hamlyn, Martin, Rowe and Tracy.

Cove
COVE, MARY. 'Notes on the history of the Cove family', *Kingsbridge History Society recorder* **6**, 1991, 3-7. 17-20th c.

Cowes
DAVIS, WALTER GOODWIN. 'Genealogical research in England: Cowes of Ipswich, Mass.', *N.E.H.G.R.* **85**, 1931, 385-8. Cowes family of Stokeinteignhead, 17th c.

Cowiley
See Browin

Cowling
LYON, HEATHER I. *In the steps of James Cowling: an account of a visit to St.Agnes, Cornwall, in 1981, with some genealogical observations and sketches of the lives of one line of descendants of James Cowling born in 1802.* Hawthorn, Vic: the author, [1982?].

Cowmeadow
PERRY, DAVID. 'The history and genealogy of the Cowmeadow family', *J.G.F.H.S.* **36**, 1988, 26-8. 16-18th c.

Cox
C[OX]-W[ARBURTON], A.F. 'Cox families of the West of England', *D.C.N.Q.* **22**(18), 1942-6, 327-8. Of Devon, Dorset and Somerset
COX, A. 'Cox of Farway and Colyton', *D.C.N.Q.* **20**, 1938-9, 172-3. See also 31-2 & 77. Includes 17-19th c. pedigree.
COX, A.F. WARBURTON. 'Cox of the West of England', *N.Q.S.D.* **24**, 1946, 289-92.
COX, A.F.W. 'Further notes on Cox of South-East Devon', *D.C.N.Q.* **22**(17), 1946, 297-9.
NEVILL, EDMUND. 'Dorset freeholders: Cox of Beaminster', *N.Q.S.D.* **10**, 1907, 76-9. 16-19th c.

Coxe
WARBURTON-COX, A.F. 'Enquiry into the origin of the family of Coxe *alias* Coke(s) of the Hundred of Colyton', *D.C.N.Q.* **22**(7), 1943, 175-7. 16th c.

Crabtree
'John Crabtree, 1746-1812', *J.D.F.H.S.* **1**(2), 1988, 68-9. Lists his 6 marriages and 39 children!

Crane
See Cromwell

Craucombe
BATTEN, JOHN. 'Craucombe-Carew', *N.Q.S.D.* **6**, 1899, 49-56.

Crawley
See also Gibbs

Crawthorne
See also Arbalister

Creber
EDMONDSON, E.C., & TAYLOR,R. *The Creber connexion at Walkhampton.* Exmouth: [E.C.Edmondson], 1993. Medieval-20th c., includes pedigrees.

Cree
CREE, G.H. *The Cree family of Fife and Devon.* Oadby: Cree Family History Society, 1991. Includes pedigrees, 17-20th c.

Creemer
See Clarke

Cresswell
CAMPBELL, G. *The web of fortune: the narrative of an English family from the twelfth to the twentieth century.* Neville Spearman. 1965. Cresswell family of Wiltshire.

Crimp
CRIMP, STANLEY. 'The Crimp family: a beginning', *D.F.H.* **1**, 1977, 14-15. Pedigree, 18-20th c.

Croad
CROUCH, C.H. 'Croad and Meaden families', *Genealogical magazine* **6**, 1902-3, 307-8. Dorset and Devon.

Crocker
ALEXANDER, J.J. 'Crocker of Lyneham', *D.C.N.Q.* **14**, 1926-7, 30-2 & 74.
BRADY, EILEEN FRANCES. *My Crocker ancestors.* Bournemouth: the author, 1995. Of Huntshaw, Bishops Tawton and Fremington; includes pedigrees, 16-20th c., also pedigree of Chappell of Fremington, 17-19th c.
CROCKER, W.T. *The Crockers of Ashcombe Farm.* Canberra: Summit Press, 1979. Includes pedigree, 18-20th c.

HAYWARD, R.H.J. *The Crocker and Hayward family tree.* Wellington: the author, 1931.

Croker
See Churchill and Fox

Cromwell
BOUCHER, R. 'Oliver Cromwell's Wiltshire relations', *W.N.Q.* **7**. 1911-13, 25-32. Cromwell, Boucher and Crane families, 17th c.

SCHOMBERG, ARTHUR. 'Cromwell', *M.G.H.* 5th series **5**, 1923-5, 86-7. Extracts from Seend parish register, 17-18th c.

Crooke
See Hoode

Croom
See Gostlett

Crossman
HAINES, R.J. 'The Crossmans of Almondsbury', *J.B.A.* **32**, 1983, 11-13. Mainly 17th c.

Crudge
BAKER, JANE. *The Crudge family of Bristol and Devon: a family history.* [Bristol]: [the authors?], 1990. Includes pedigree, 18-20th c.

BAKER, JANE. *A Devon family: a general history of the Crudge family.* Bristol: the author, 1991. 16-20th c. Includes pedigrees.

Crupes
See Scrupes

Cruttwell
CRUTTWELL, HARRY ATHILL. *The chronicle of Crotall, Cruthal, Cruttall or Cruttwell and Bath.* [ ]: Camberley, Hickmott & Co., 1933. Of Wokingham, Berkshire, and Bath.

Cruwys
CRUWYS, M.C.S. *A Cruwys Morchard notebook, 1066-1874.* Exeter: J. Townsend & Sons, 1939.

CRUWYS, M.C.S. 'Records at Cruwys Morchard [presidential address]', *D.A.Tr.* **84**, 1952, 1-19. Includes pedigree.

PRIDEAUX, F.B. 'Cruwys of Morchard and East Anstey', *D.C.N.Q.* **13**, 1924-5, 134-7. Includes pedigree, 14-15th c.

Cudlipp
TAYLOR, ALAN. *Cudlipp of 17th century Tavistock.* Farnborough: A.J. C. Taylor, 1988. See also *Additional notes,* 1991.

Cullimore
HAYTER, ROY G. 'The Cullimores as carpenters and wheelwrights in the villages of Tytherington and Iron Acton', *J.F.G.F.H.S.* **61**, 1994, 16. Brief note, 19th c.
See also Merryweather

Culling
EVANS, H.R. 'The Cullings of Woodland', *D.C.N.Q.* **23**, 1947-9, 262-5, 293-5, 318-22 & 346-8. See also **24**, 1950-51, 98-9 & 102. 16-18th c.

Cunnington
CUNNINGTON, R.H. 'The Cunningtons of Wiltshire', *W.A.M.* **55**(200), 1954. 211-36. 18-19th c.

Curci
LYTE, HENRY C.MAXWELL, SIR. 'Curci', *S.A.N.H.S.* **66**(2), 1920, 98-126.

Curgenven
KENT, ALAN. 'Curgenven: ancient or modern', *C.F.H.S.J.* **47**, 1988, 24. 17-19th c.

P., J. 'Curgenven family', *D.C.N.Q.* **14**, 1926, 56-8. 17-19th c.

Curnow
CAVETT, DENISE. 'A typical 19th century Cornish family', *C.F.H.S.J.* **29**, 1983, 16-17. Curnow family.

CURNOW, E.A. *After the golden cockatoo: Cornwall & the story of the Thomas Curnow family & others.* [Salisbury Downs, South Australia]: E.A. Curnow, 1990.

CURNOW, NORMA. *Curnow cousins: a family history.* East Perth: the author, 1991. Supplement 1992. Of Cornwall and Australia, 19-20th c.

CURNOW, WILLIAM J. ed. *The Curnow family: a family history resource book.* Bedminster, New Jersey: Grand Curnow homecoming, 1990. 16-20th c., includes many pedigrees.

Cutcliffe
DRAKE, WILLIAM RICHARD, SIR. *Account of the family of Cutcliffe of Damage in Devonshire.* Privately printed, 1876.

Daccomb
COLBY, DR. 'Pedigrees from the visitation of Dorset, 1623', *M.G.H.* 2nd. series **2**, 1886, 238-9. Includes Daccomb and Foyle.

Dackombe
FRY, E.A. 'Templecombe register: Dackombe family', *N.Q.S.D.* **5**, 1897-8, 133.

'Sir John Dackombe, 1570-1618', *N.Q.S.D.*
33(341), 1995, 363-67; 33(342), 1995,
408-15. Includes pedigree shewing
relationships to Pitt and Mohun, 16-17th c.

Dabernon
BENSON, J. 'Dabernon', *D.C.N.Q.* 23(6), 1948,
182-4. Medieval.

Dadswell
BALCH, BARBARA. *A Dadswell family history
and genealogy, c.1560-1980.* London,
Ontario: the author, 1980. Gloucester
family.

Dalison
See Walker

Dallaway
'Dallaway family', *M.G.H.* 1, 1868, 285-7. Of
Warwickshire, Gloucestershire, *etc.,*
pedigree 17-19th c., with monumental
inscriptions.

Dallimore
MCGARVIE, MICHAEL. 'The Dallimores of
Nunney', *N.Q.S.D.* 30, 1974-9, 107-10.
16-19th c.

Damen
WIGG, LEN. 'The quest for Edith', *J.D.F.H.S.*
8(4), 1995, 140. Damen family; brief note,
18th c.

Damer
B., R.G. 'Damer *alias* Blandymore', *N.Q.S.D.* 17,
1923, 112-8. See also 20, 1930-32, 208-12. 16-
18th c.

Damerel
STREET, JOHN C. *Notes on a Damerel family of
Exeter.* Wisconsin: the author, 1994.
Includes pedigrees, 17-20th c.

Damery
DAMER, J.W. 'Damery family', *D.C.N.Q.* 10,
1918, 55. See also 94-6.

Dampier
W., W. 'Dampier of East Coker', *Notes &
queries* 154, 1928, 17. See also 195-6 & 227-
8.

Danby
BAKER, JANE. *Can you find me ? A Somerset
mystery: Francis Danby and his Somerset
connections.* Bristol: the author, 1991.
Includes pedigrees of Danby, 19th c., Poole,
19th c., and Fry 16-19th c.

Daneys
DENNY, H.L.L. SIR. 'The family of Le Daneys',
D.C.N.Q. 18(7), 1935, 316-8.
DENNY, HENRY L.L. 'Notes on the family of Le
Daneys', *N.Q.S.D.* 21, 1935, 39-42, 73-7 &
127-8

Daniel
BROAD, GWEN. 'Varied strands of inheritance:
the Daniel family', *C.F.H.S.J.* 66, 1992,
28.

Daniels
STANCLIFFE, CHRIS. 'The Daniels of Henbury,
Bristol', *J.B.A.* 70, 1992, 30-31. 19th c.

Danvers
MACNAMARA, F.N. *Memorials of the Danvers
family (of Dauntsey and Culworth), their
ancestors and descendants, from the
Conquest till the termination of the
eighteenth century ...* Hardy & Page, 1895.
Dauntsey, Wiltshire; Culworth,
Northamptonshire, Buckinghamshire and
Oxfordshire, etc., includes pedigrees. 14-
17th c.
USHFORTH, G. MCN. 'The story of Dauntsey',
B.G.A.S.T. 50, 1928, 325-1 5. Danvers
family; includes pedigree, 14-17th c.
LADE, J.J. 'The Yorkshire estate of the Danvers
of Dauntsey', *W.A.M.* 50(179), 1943, 214-8.
17th c.

Dark
DARK, ARTHUR. *A North Devon family: a
family history of some of the
descendants of the Darks of Parkham.* [ ],
1986. Includes loose folded pedigree, 16-
20th c.

Darracott
M., R.B. 'Darracott', *D.C.N.Q.* 16, 1930, 87-9.

Darrell
HALL, HUBERT. *William Darrell of Littlecote,
Wiltshire: a 16th century chronicle.* Dorrill-
Dorrell-Darrell Society, 1992. Includes
pedigree, medieval-16th c.
See also Calston

Dart
BATCHELOR, K.M. 'Notes on a Royalist family:
the Darts of Pentuan', *Old Cornwall* 5,
1951-61, 433-5. 17th c.

Daubeney/D'Aubeney
BURT, SAMUEL. 'The Daubeneys of Barrington',
Somerset year book 36, 1937, 99-100.
Medieval.

DAUBENEY, GILES. *The history of the Daubeney family.* Pontypool: Griffin Press, 1951. Medieval-19th c., of Somerset.

NEVILL, EDMUND. 'Dorset freeholders: Daubeny of Powerstock', *N.Q.S.D.* **90**, 1905, 255-8. 17-19th c.

GREENFIELD, B.W. 'On the Daubeney family and its connection with Gloucestershire', *B.G.A.S.T.* **10**, 1885-6, 175-85. 13-14th c.

HALL, I.V. 'The Daubeney's', *B.G.A.S.T.* **84**, 1965, 113-40; **85**, 1966, 175-201. Includes pedigree, 18-19th c.

ROUND, J. HORACE. 'A D'Aubeney cadet', *Ancestor* **12**, 1904, 149-51. 12-13th c., of Dorset.

See also Enga and Engayne

Daubrie

BUTTREY, PAM. 'The Daubrie family (four generations) recorded', *J.G.F.H.S.* **36**, 1988, 31-2. 17-18th c.

Daumarle

See Coode and Prowse

Daunt

DAUNT, JOHN. 'The Daunt family', *G.N.Q.* **2**, 1884, 286-8. 15-17th c.

DAUNT, JOHN. *Some account of the family of Daunt.* Newcastle-Upon-Tyne: J.M. Carr, 1881. Gloucester family.

Davie

See Dennis

Davies

'A Davies bible', *J.G.F.H.S.* **39**, 1988, 19-20. Birth, marriage and death registers in family bible.

Davy

TAPLEY-SOPER, H. 'The Davy family of Ottery St. Mary and Topsham, Devon', *D.C.N.Q.* **23**(5), 1948, 139-40.

Davys

FLETCHER, W.G. DIMOCK. 'Pedigree of Davys of Tisbury, Co. Wilts., of Rempstone, Co. Nottingham, and of Castle Donington and Loughborough, Co. Leicester', *Genealogist* **5**, 1881, 25-32. 16-19th c.

Dawe

COLBY, DR., & RYLANDS, J.P. 'Pedigrees from the visitation of Dorset, 1623: Dawe', *M.G.H.* 2nd series **2**, 1888, 255-6.

Dawson

See Massy-Dawson

Dean(e)

DEAN, COLIN. 'So many Deans in Dorset', *J.D.F.H.S.* **1**(3), 1988, 112-3. 18-19th c.

THRELFALL, JOHN B. 'Additions to the Deane ancestry in England', *N.E.H.G.R* **139**, 1985, 324-5. Of Chard, 15-17th c., includes probate record.

TURNER, D. 'An East Devon family, 1570-1646', *D.C.N.Q.* **29**(5), 1963, 147-9. Deane of Colyton.

See also Cooper Dean

Dearing

Abstracts of English records gathered principally in Devonshire and Essex, in a search for the ancestry of Roger Dearing, c.1624-1676, and Matthew Whimple c. 1560-1618. Boston: privately printed 1929. Dearing of Devon; Whimple of Essex. Numerous abstracts from a wide variety of sources.

De Berkeley

See De Cancia

De Boteville

BOTFIELD, BERIAH. *Stemmata Botevilliana: memorials of the families of de Boteville, Thynne and Botfield in the counties of Salop and Wilts.* J.B. Nichols and Sons, 1858. Also includes pedigrees of Leighton, Higgons, Haynes, Lake, Montgomery, Gresham, Baugh, Baker, Greve, and Hector families, with numerous extracts from original sources, medieval-19th c.

De Breuse

WATSON, G.W. 'Mary, Countess Marshall', *M.G.H.* 5th series **8**, 1932-4, 160. Of Gloucestershire; includes medieval pedigree of De Breuse.

De Cancia

PRIDEAUX, F.B. 'De Cancia and De Berkeley-De Canta families', *D.C.N.Q.* **15**, 1928-9, 27-30. Medieval.

De Chedder

GEORGE, W. 'The De Chedder family of Bristol and Cheddar', *S.A.N.H.S.* **34**(2), 1888, 114-6. 13-14th c.

De Chyrebury

H[EATHCOTE], T.G.J. 'De Chyrebury of Seend', *W.N.Q.* **4**, 1902-4, 414-6. See also **5**, 1905-7, 43-6 & 86-8. Medieval.

De Haviland

[DE HAVILAND, JOHN VON SONNTAG]. *Chronicle of the ancient and noble Norman family of De Haviland, originally of Haverland, in the Cotentin, Normandy, now of Guernsey, including the English branches of Havelland, now extinct, Haviland of Hawkesbury, Gloucestershire, also extinct, and Haviland of Somersetshire, with the documentary evidence.* [St. Louis]: Mekeel Press, 1895.

See also Daubeney

Deighton

DIGHTON, CONWAY. 'The Deightons of Gloucester', *G.N.Q.* **5**, 1894, 135-6. 17th c.

MORIARTY, G. ANDREWS. 'Some notes on Deighton, Gookin, Tervill, and Gifford of Brimpsfield', *B.G.A.S.T.* **66**, 1947, 246-54.

De La Mare

SMITH, S.N. 'The manor of Nunney-Delamere, Somerset', *M.G.H.* 5th series **10**, 1938, 35-42. Medieval descent of the manor in the De La Mare family.

De La Pole

See Botreaux

De La Zouch

See Botreaux

Delves

See Humphrey

De Miners

BADDELEY, ST. CLAIR. 'The De Miners family', *Notes and queries* **88**, 1919, 170-1. 12th c.

Denbow

ROBERTS, W.A. *The Denbow family book.* Kingsbridge: the author, 1985.

Dene

DEANE, MARY. *The book of Dene, Deane, Adeane: a genealogical history.* Elliot Stock, 1899. Includes pedigrees, 16-19th c.

SAYER, M.J. 'Pedigrees of county families, 2', *Genealogists' magazine* **19**(1), 1979, 359. Dene family.

Dening

WARREN, DERRICK. *Dening of Chard, agricultural engineers, 1828-1965.* S.I.A.S. survey 6. Taunton: Somerset Industrial Archaeological Society, 1989. Includes pedigree, 19-20th c.

Dennis

ROGERS, W.H. 'Orleigh: an ancient house', *D.A.Tr.* **58**, 1926, 185-92. Dennis and Davie families.

See also Kirkham

Dennys

BENSON, J. 'Robert Dennys of Manworthy', *D.C.N.Q.* **22**(19-20), 1946, 347-53. Dennys family history, 11-17th c.

DENNYS, R. 'Cheglinch, in the parish of West Down, Devon', *D.C.N.Q.* **23**(1), 1947, 24-6.

DENNYS, NICHOLAS. 'Nicholas Dennys, M.P. for Barnstaple, 1660-1678', *D.C.N.Q.* **23**, 1947-9, 116-8 & 145-51. Dennys family, 16-17th c.

DENNYS, RODNEY. 'Notes on the Dennys family,' *D.C.N.Q.* **24**, 1950-51, 212-3, & 222-5; **25**, 1952-3, 7-9, 38-41, 66-9, 96-101 & 110-11.

See also Donne

Densill

HUGHES, MICHAEL W. 'Corrections and additions to the pedigree of Densill', *Ancestor* **12**, 1905, 118-24. Medieval; of Cornwall.

Denys

BUSH, THOMAS S. 'The Denys family and their connections with the manors of Alveston, Siston and Dyrham', *Proceedings of the Bath Natural History and Antiquarian Field Club* **9**, 1901, 58-70. Includes wills, inquisitions post mortem and pedigree, 15-16th c.

Derby

MORIARTY, G. ANDREWS. 'Genealogical research in England: Derby', *N.E.H.G.R.* **79**(316), 1925, 410-49. See also **82**, 1928, 65-6. 17-18th c. Derby family of Sert Hill, Dorset: includes many will abstracts, deeds, Chancery proceedings, *etc.*

'Rev. Richard Derby, minister of Poole and vicar of Hilton, Dorset', *N.Q.S.D.* **12**, 1911, 212-4. See also 251-4. Pedigree, 17-18th c.

Detwiller

See Allin

Devenish

DEVENISH, BERTHA, ed. *Archives of the Devenish family collected by Henry Weston Devenish.* Weymouth: J.H.C. & B. Devenish, 1933. Of Hampshire, Sussex and Dorset.

DEVENISH, ROBERT J., & McLAUGHLIN, N. CHARLES. *Historical and genealogical records of the Devenish families of England and Ireland ...* Chicago: Lakeside Press, 1948. Of Dorset and Sussex.

Deverell

DEVERILL, PENELOPE. 'The medieval Deverells of Wilts and Bucks', *Origins: magazine of the Buckinghamshire Family History Society* 15(4), 1991, 95-6.

CHOPE, R. 'The Lord Dynham's lands', *D.A.Tr.* 43, 1911, 269-92. Notes on a survey taken in 1566.

CHOPE, R. 'The last of the Dynhams', *D.A.Tr.* 50, 1918, 431-92. Includes descent of Sir John Dynham, died 1501.

D'ewes

See Symonds

Dicke

See Dyer

Dickinson

BURDEN, JOY. *Winging Westward: from Eton dungeon to Millfield desk.* Bath: Robert Wall Books, 1974. Dickinson of King Weston; includes pedigree, 16-20th c.

Digby

See Churchill

Digges

See Harington

Dimock

FLETCHER, W.G.D. 'Dimock of Randwick and Stonehouse, Co. Gloucester', *Genealogist* 2, 1878, 181-3. See also 3, 1879, 326-7. 18-19th c.

FLETCHER, W.G.DIMOCK. 'The Dimocks of Gloucester', *G.N.Q.* 5, 1894, 269-71. 17-19th c.

FLETCHER, W.G.DIMOCK. 'The family of Dimock, of Randwick and Stonehouse', *G.N.Q.* 5, 1894, 240-9 and 269-71. Pedigree, 17-19th c.

FLETCHER, W.G.DIMOCK. 'Register extracts relating to the Dimock family', *Genealogist* 2, 1878, 213-4. 17-18th c.

Dinan

JONES, MICHAEL. *The family of Dinan in England in the later middle ages = La famille de Dinan en Angleterre au moyen age.* Dinan: Le Pays de Dinan Bibliotheque Municipale, 1987.

Dix

HORTON-SMITH, L.G.H. 'The Dix family of Cirencester and their Presbyterian and Unitarian connections', *Genealogical quarterly* 17(4), 1951, 147-55; 18(1), 1951, 3-8.

Dobell

'Detmore and the Dobell family', *C.K.L.H.S.B.* 5, 1981, 11-29; 6, 1981, 32-9. Includes pedigree, 18-20th c.

Doddridge

DODDERIDGE, SIDNEY E. 'Dudderidge *alias* Dodderidge of Devon, Somerset and Dorset', *N.Q.S.D.* 9, 1905, 157-65. See also 13, 1913, 328-30.

DODDERIDGE, SIDNEY E., & SHADDICK, H.G.HASTINGS. *The Dodderidges of Devon: with an account of the bibliotheca Doddrigiana ...* Exeter: William Pollard & Co., 1909.

DODDERIDGE, SYDNEY E. 'Dodderidge of Stogumber, Co. Somerset', *N.Q.S.D.* 14, 1915, 19-22. 16-18th c.

DODDERIDGE, SIDNEY E. 'Dudderidge *alias* Dodderidge of Devon, Somerset and Dorset', *N.Q.S.D.* 90, 1905, 157-65.

DODDERIDGE, SIDNEY E. 'Pedigree of Sir John Dodderidge, judge of the Kings Bench, and the Rev. Dr. Philip Dodderidge of Northampton', *M.G.H.* 5th series 1, 1916, 95-101. Of Devon and Pennsylvania, 16-19th c.

DODDERIDGE, S.E. 'Pedigrees of Dodderidge', *M.G.H.* 5th series 1, 1916, 68-72, 146-52, 195-8, 236-8, & 274-5. Addenda, 3, 1918-19, 127.

'Dodderidge of Doetheridge, Co. Devon, and Crowcombe, Co. Somerset', *M.G.H.* 4th series 5, 1914, 261-4.

'Pedigree of Dodderidge of Crowcombe, Co. Somerset, *M.G.H.* 4th series 5, 1913, 293-7.

Dodington

'Pedigree of Dodington, from visitations of Somerset, 1623', *Genealogist* 1, 1877, 23-8. See also 29 & 155-6.

COOPER, T. 'The families of Dodington and Collier', *Topographer & genealogist* 3, 1858, 568-75.

MARSHALL, GEORGE W. 'Genealogical notices of the family of Dodington, of Dodington, Co.Somerset', *Reliquary* 15, 1875-5, 86-90. Includes pedigree, 14-17th c., with will of George Dodington, 1618.

See also Marriott

Dolbeare

R., G.W. 'Dolbeare of Dolbeare', *D.N.Q.* **1**, 1900-1, 103.
'Pedigree of Dodderidge of Crowcombe, Co.Somerset', *M.G.H.* 4th series **5**, 1914, 293-7.
See also Cottell

Domett

NOBLE, ARTHUR H. 'Admiral Sir William Domett', *Genealogists' magazine* **15**, 1965-8, 26-30. Includes genealogical notes.

Donne

DENNYS, RODNEY. 'Gabriel Donne, Abbot of Buckfast', *D.C.N.Q.* **23**(2), 1947, 34-8. Notes on Donne-Dennys family connections, with pedigree, 15-16th c.

Doone

RAWLE, EDWIN JOHN. *The Doones of Exmoor.* Thomas Burleigh; Taunton: Barnicott & Pearce, 1903.
THORNYCROFT, L.B. *The story of the Doones in fact, fiction and photographs.* 4th ed. Taunton: Barnicotts, 1964.

Dorney

'Dorney family: extracts from the Uley registers', *G.N.Q.* **3**, **1887**, 440-1.

Dowdeswell

DOWDESWELL, E.R. 'Dowdeswell family', *G.N.Q.* **2**, 1884, 410-12. See also 530-2.

Dowling

GOULD, KENNETH J. 'The Dowlings of Somerset and Michigan', *G.T.* **5**(2), 1980, 12-13.

Down

AUTHERS, W. 'The Down family of Tiverton', *D.C.N.Q.* **31**, 1968, 62-3.
DOWNE, H. 'A booke of memoryall made by me Henry Downe of Barnestaple, merchant, the viii daye of June ... 1561', *M.G.H.* 3rd series **1**, 1896, 196-200. Primarily concerned with the history of the Downe and Hanmer families.
DRAKE, DAPHNE. 'Down family', *D.C.N.Q.* **20**, 1938-9, 233-4. See also 85, 188, 283-5, & 389.

Downton

SHRIMPTON, MARY. *Devon, Durham, and destiny: the story of two Englishmen and their families in Australia: the Simpsons from County Durham and the Downtons from Devonshire.* Camberwell, Victoria: M.F. Shrimpton, 1987.

Dowrich

TREASE, G.E. 'Dowrich and the Dowrich family of Sandford', *D.C.N.Q.* **33**, 1974, 37-8, 70-73, 113-7, 154-5, 208-11, 252-7, & 348-52.

Dowrish

ERSKINE-RISK, J. 'A forgotten episode in Devon history', *D.A.Tr.* **34**, 1902, 394-402.
Dowrish family, 17-18th c.
HUNT, JOHN G. 'The Dowrish pedigree', *D.C.N.Q.* **28**, 1959-61, 91-3.

Drake

ALEXANDER, J.J. 'Edmund Drake's flight from Tavistock', *D.C.N.Q.* **20**(8), 1939, 381-5.
DRAKE, D.S. 'Drakes of Ashe', *D.C.N.Q.* **20**(2), 1938, 92. Discusses whereabouts of the family muniments.
FULLER-ELLIOTT-DRAKE, ELIZABETH. *The family and heirs of Sir Francis Drake.* 2 vols. Smith, Elder & Co., 1911.
R. 'John Drake of Mount-Drake and Ash, Musbury, and Dorothy Button his wife', *N.G.D.C.* **4**, 1891, 19-20.
REICHEL, O. 'The family and heirs of Sir Francis Drake', *D.C.N.Q.* **9**, 1916, 32.
WERE, F. 'Drake and Skeffington', *D.C.N.Q.* **9**, 1917, 143-4.
WORTH, R.N. 'The Drakes in Tavistock', *N.G.D.C.* **1**, 1888, 86-7.
Buckland Abbey, Devon. National Trust, 1991. Home of the Drake family from the 16th c., includes Drake pedigree 16-20th c.
See also Strode

Drew

BAXTER, CAROL. *The Drews of Dromlohan: a preliminary history of the Drew family from Dromlohan townland, Kilcornan parish, County Limerick, Ireland.* St. Ives, N.S.W.: the author, 1996. Includes appendix, 'The Anglo-Irish Drew family and their ancestors', detailing the 16th c. Drew family of Devon.
KITE, E. 'Drew of Southbroom', *W.N.Q.* **7**, 1911-13, 303-8 & 441-8. 16-17th c., includes extracts from Devizes parish registers, etc.
MARTIN, EDWARD A. 'The evolution of a surname', *D.C.N.Q.* **32**, 1971-3, 113-9. Drew and Trewithan families of Gwennap and Stithians, Cornwall, 16th c.
MCKECHNIE, S. 'A Devonshire family of Georgian times', *D.C.N.Q.* **30**, 1965-7, 295-8.
'Genealogy of the family of Drew', *Topographer and genealogist* **2**, 1853, 209-13. Devon family.

Drockensford
See Botreaux

Drury
See Willis

Ducarel
TAYLOR, AILEEN. 'The Ducarel family of Newland', *F.F.* **16**, 1994, 33-6. 18th c.

Duck
COLBY, F.T. 'Family of Duck of Heavitree, Devon', *M.G.H.* N.S., **1**, 1874, 317-9. Pedigree, 16-19th c.

Duckworth
MCGARVIE, M. 'The Duckworths and the building of Orchardleigh House', *Ancient Monuments Society transactions* **27**, 1983, 119-45.

Dudbridge
DUDBRIDGE, BRYAN J. 'The descendants of Joseph Dudbridge the clothier', *J.G.F.H.S.* **39**, 1988, 17-18. 17-20th c.
DUDBRIDGE, B.J. 'The Dudbridge family in Bristol', *J.B.A.* **52**, 1988, 26-31. Mainly 18-19th c., includes pedigree.

Duder
PHILSON, MARIANNE. *The Duder family in New Zealand.* Auckland: Bush Press, 1990. Includes pedigree of the Duders of Devon, 16-19th c.

Dudderidge
See Doddridge

Duff
SIEDE, BETTY. 'Cornwall: a most unlikely source of Duff', *C.F.H.S.J.* **63**, 1992, 26-7. Duff family, 18-19th c.

Dugdale
S[CHOMBERG], A. 'Dugdale of Evercreech, Co. Somerset', *M.G.H.* 2nd Series **1**, 1886, 346. See also 368. Pedigree, 17-18th c.
SCHOMBERG, A. 'Dugdale of Seend, Co. Wilts', *M.G.H.* 2nd series **2**, 1888, 128. Pedigree, 16-17th c.
SCHOMBERG, ARTHUR. 'Dugdale of Wilts', *W.N.Q.* **1**, 1893-5, 174-5 & 194-200. See also **3**, 1899-1901, 87-90, 127-9, 179-81 & 517-8; **4**, 1902-4, 315-20; **5**, 1905-7, 473 & 474. Reprinted as *Dugdale of Seend.* Devizes: George Simpson & Co., 1924. Includes pedigree, 16-18th c., wills, monumental inscriptions, parish register extracts, deeds, etc.

Duke
ALEXANDER, J.J. 'Otterton notebook', *D.A.Tr.* **50**, 1918, 493-502. Notebook of Richard Duke of Otterton, early 18th c., containing much information on the Duke family.
DUKE, R.E.H. 'An account of the family of Duke of Lake', *W.N.Q.* **8**, 1914-16, 193-205, 241-51 & 289-300. See also 426. 15-19th c., includes folded pedigrees
DUKE, R.E.H. 'Pedigree of the Devonshire branch of the family of Duke, to illustrate the descent of Poerhayes and Otterton estate', *M.G.H.* 4th series **3**, 1910, 27-34. Includes monumental inscriptions from Otterton; 15-18th c.
SKINNER, A.J. 'John Duke's arms', *D.C.N.Q.* **14**, 1926-7, 361-2. Includes pedigrees of Passemer and Gill, 17-18th c., with Gill family monumental inscriptions at Honiton.
SKINNER, A.J. 'An Otterton note book', *D.C.N.Q.* **10**, 1918-19, 196-7. Marriage licence extracts relating to the Duke family.

Duket
DUCKETT, G.F., SIR. *Duchetiana: or history and genealogical memoirs of the family of Duket from the Norman conquest to the present time, in the counties of Lincoln, Westmorland, Wilts, Cambridge, and Buckingham* ... 2nd ed. J. Russell Smith, 1874. Includes pedigrees and many original sources.

Dummer
'Pedigree of Dummer of Penne Domer, Co. Somerset, and of Dummer, Co. Hants', *S.A.N.H.S.* **17**, 1871, 114-5. 12-17th c.

Duncan
DUNCAN, PAUL. *In service: the story of the Duncan family of Woodbury in Devon, with some distaff-sides and Australian off-shoots.* Western Australia: privately printed, 1995. Includes folded pedigree, 18-20th c.

Dunford
MECHAM, LILLIE DUNFORD. *Dunford genealogy.* Logan, Utah: the author, [198-?]. Trowbridge and U.S.A., 18-20th c.

Dunman
WILTSHIRE, ELAINE. 'The Dunman family', *G.T.* **9**(4), 1984, 112-4. Includes list of marriages, 1837-1911.

Dunning

DYMOND, ROBERT. 'Memoir of John Dunning, first Lord Ashburton', *D.A.Tr.* **8**, 1876, 82-112. Includes pedigree.

Dunsdon

GODDARD, J.R. *The Dunsdon family in Steeple Ashton, 1702-1885.* Newbury: [privately printed], c.1986. Includes pedigrees.

Dunstanville

BENSON, J. 'The De Dunstanvilles', *D.C.N.Q.* **20**, 1938-9, 194-204. Of Shropshire, Sussex, Wiltshire, Devon and Cornwall. Medieval; includes pedigrees.

Durnford

See Prowse

Dutilh

WAGNER, HENRY. 'Pedigree of Dutilh *alias* Rigaud', *M.G.H.* 3rd series **3**, 1900, 24. Of Frome and London; 18th c.

Dutton

Historical and genealogical memoirs of the Dutton family of Sherborne, in Gloucestershire, as represented in the peerage of England by the Right Hon. the Baron Sherborne. [ ]: privately printed, 1899. Includes pedigree. 16-18th c.

Memoirs of the Duttons of Dutton in Cheshire, with notes respecting the Sherborne branch of the family. Henry Sotheram & Co., Chester: Marshall & Meeson, 1901. Sherborne, Gloucestershire.

Dwelly

DWELLY, E. *Compendium of notes on the Dwelly family.* Fleet, Hants: the author, 1912. Medieval-19th c.

Dyer

DYER, A. O. 'Dyer of Wincanton and Roundhill', *N.Q.S.D.* **28**, 1968, 185-6.

MARTIN, E.H. 'Dyer family', *N.Q.S.D.* **10**, 1907, 97-107 & 145-57. See also **10**, 1907, 170; **11**, 1909, 177. 15-17th c.

'The origin of the Swinnerton Dyers, Baronets', *M.G.H.* 4th series **1**, 1906, 316-21. See also 4th series **2**, 1908, 45, 70 & 93-4. Somerset and Wiltshire; includes pedigree, 16-17th c., with wills of Rolfe, Dicke and Gerle.

See also Swinnerton

Dyke

PAINTER, G.C. 'Dyke family of West Somerset', *N.Q.S.D.* **7**, 1901, 192-6. See also 267-8 & 319-20.

Dymer

See Whitefield

Dynham

See Dinham

Earle

COLBY, DR., & RYLANDS, J.P. 'Pedigrees from the visitation of Dorset, 1623', *M.G.H.* 2nd. series **2**, 1888, 213-4. Includes Earle, and Ewens of Wincanton and Frampton, Dorset.

EARLE, ISAAC NEWTON. *History and genealogy of the Earles of Seacaucus with an account of other English and American branches.* Marquette, Michigan: Guelff Printing Co., 1924. Primarily of American interest, but also includes chapters on the Earles of Somerset, Wiltshire, Devon, Dorset, Essex, Norfolk, Lincolnshire and Lancashire.

EARLE, S.E. *A history of the Earle family from Wiltshire, England.* Brisbane: Uniting Church Print Shop, 1990. Includes pedigrees.

Easterbrooke

See Reynell

Easton

GENEALOGIST. 'The Easton family and the arms of the County of Devon', *W.A.* **9**(2), 1889, 24-8. See also 9(3-4), 1889, 50-6.

'The family of Easton, of Morchard Episcopi, Devon, and Bradford, Somerset', *W.A.* **6**(5), 1886, 125-9. See also 166-7, 169-70, 250, & 272-3. Medieval.

Ebbott

See Reed

Echyngham

'Echyngham of Echyngham, Sussex, and Brianston, Dorset', *N.Q.S.D.* **90**, 1905, 249-52 & 297-302. Medieval.

Eden

BARNARD, E.A.B. *The Edens of Honeybourne, Gloucestershire: an old time correspondence, 1785-1839.* Evesham: W & H. Smith, 1929.

Edgcumbe

EDGCOMBE, G. 'The surname Edg(e)combe/Edg(e)cumbe: origin of the form 'Edgcumbe' in the 16th century', *D.C.N.Q.* **36**(2), 1987, 65-8.

E[DGCOMBE], G. 'Edgcumbe', *D.F.H.* **48**, 1988, 5-8.

EDGCOMBE, GERALD. *My Edgcombe line, 1700 to 1995.* Edgcombe family history and genealogy supplement 1. Farnborough: A.J.C.Taylor, 1996. Includes pedigree.

GLANVILLE, G. 'Cotehele House and the Edgcumbe family', *Old Cornwall* **8**, 1973-9, 59-70. 13-16th c.

MARTIN, BINA ELIZABETH. *Edgcumbes of Edgcumbe: a supplement to parsons and prisons.* Fish Hoek: the author, 1976. Medieval-20th c.

MOUNT EDGCUMBE, EARL OF. 'The early history of the family of Mount Edgcumbe', *J.R.I.C.* **8**, 1883-5, 133-41. Medieval-16th c.

MOUNT EDGCUMBE, EARL OF. 'The early history of the family of Mount Edgcumbe', *Journal of the British Archaeological Association* **33**, 1877, 15-22. Medieval.

MOUNT EDGCUMBE, EARL OF. *Records of the Edgcumbe family.* Plymouth: W. Brendon & Son, 1888. Medieval-17th c., includes pedigree to 19th c.

TAYLOR, ALAN. 'Edgcombes at Tewkesbury', *Edgcombe family genealogy and history* **5**, 1989, 95-117. 17-19th c.

Cotehele, Cornwall. National Trust, 1991. Includes pedigree of Edgcumbe, 14-20th c.

Edgcumbe family genealogy and history. Farnborough: A.J.C. Taylor, 1988- . Includes many articles on the family in Cornwall and Devon, not otherwise listed here.

'Edward [Edgcombe] of Tewkesbury and Ellesmere.' *Edgcombe family genealogy and history* **8**, 1990, 183-7. 18-20th c. Descent.

Edgeworth

BUTLER, HARRIET JESSIE, & EDGEWORTH, HAROLD, eds. *The black book of Edgeworthstown and other Edgeworth memories, 1585-1817.* Faber & Gwyer, 1927

Edwards

BUTTREY, PAM. 'The Edwards of Hewelsfield and St. Briavels', *J.G.F.H.S.* **35**, 1987, 31-2. 18-19th c.

SKINNER, A.J.P. 'West Country families: Edwards', *N.Q.S.D.* **15**, 1917, 243-5. Of Dorset, Somerset, and Devon, 17-19th c.

See also Goddard, Martin and Pearce

Edye

See Oke

Eggardon

NEVILL, EDMUND. 'Dorset freeholders: Eggardon of Eggardon', *N.Q.S.D.* **10**, 1907, 3-8. 16-17th c.

Elford

ANTHONY, MARY. *The Red Funnel line: the story of the Elfords and the Oreston and Turnchapel Steamboat Company.* Plymouth: P.D.S., 1990. 19th c. family firm.

ELFORD, LAURA. *The Elfords: the story of an ancient English family.* [Camborne]: the author, c.1976.

ELFORD, LAURA. *Flesh on the bones.* Helston: Helston Printers, 1981. Elford family, mainly 17-20th c.

Eliot

ELIOT, CHARLES. 'Eliot: memoranda on fly-leaves of an old bible in the Port Eliot library', *M.G.H.* **2**, 1876, 39-43. Includes notes on baptisms, marriages, and deaths, from the family bible, and from St.Germans parish register, 16-19th c.

ELIOT, R. 'The pocket boroughs of the Eliot family at St.Germans, Liskeard and Grampound', *J.R.I.C.* N.S. **9**(4), 321-47. Mainly 16-17th c.

ELIOT, WILLIAM H. *Genealogy of the Eliot family.* New Haven: George B. Bassett & Co., 1854. Medieval-19th c., of Cornwall and the United States.

HORWOOD, ALFRED J. 'Port Eliot, Cornwall, the seat of the Earl of St.Germans', in HISTORICAL MANUSCRIPTS COMMISSION. *First report ...* C.55. H.M.S.O., 1.874, 41-4. Calendar of Eliot family letters and papers.

MORRIS, GEORGE J. 'The ravishment of Sir John Eliot's son', *Genealogist* N.S. **1**, 1884, 21-7. Early 17th c.

'The pedigree of the noble family of Eliot of Port Eliot in the county of Cornwall', *M.G.H.* **2**, 1876, 44-9. 15-19th c.

See also Pearce

Elkington

ELKINGTON, ARTHUR EDWARD HARDWICKE, & ELKINGTON, CHRISTINE MARY. *The Elkingtons of Bath, being the ancestry and descendants of George Elkington of Bath (1566-1640)*. Woodstock, Oxon: the author, 1959.

Ellacott/Ellicott

JOHNSON, DAVID J. *The Ellacott / Ellicott I.G.I. (U.K.) research assistant.* Warminster: David J. Johnson, 1996. Extracts from the *International genealogical index*, mainly from S.W. England.

LINDSAY, JOHN F. *The Ellicotts: a family history.* 2 vols. Canberra: J.Lindsay, 1991. Of Cornwall and Australia.

See also Churchill

Ellis

BAKER, THOMAS H. 'Ellis of Wilts', *W.N.Q.* **3**, 1899-1901, 45-6. See also **2**, 1896-8, 436 & 484. Extracts from Mere parish register, 17th c.

STABB, R. 'Ellis-Stabb connections?', *D.F.H.* **23**, 1982, 13-14. List of entries in family bible, 1820-1893.

STREET, JOHN C. *An Ellis family of Devon and Newfoundland.* Cross Plains, Wisconsin: the author, 1994. Of Woodbury; includes pedigrees, 18-20th c., including those of Tapscott, Ashford, Pinkham and Austin.

Ellison

See Smith

Elphinstone

HIRST, WILLIAM. 'A Three Towns fighting family', *Plymouth Institution ... transactions* **13**, 1898/9-1902/3, 122-33. Elphinstone family, 18-19th c.

Elton

ELTON, MARGARET. *Annals of the Elton family, Bristol merchants & Somerset landowners.* Stroud: Alan Sutton, 1994. Includes pedigrees, 17-20th c.

See also Mayo

Emery

See Turner

Endean

IVALL, D. ENDEAN. '- and downstairs', *C.F.H.S.J.* **34**, 1984, 18-19. Concerns the Endean family of Cornelly, mainly 19th c.

Endecott

LETHBRIDGE, ROPER, SIR. *The Devonshire ancestry and the early homes of the family of John Endecott, governor of Massachusetts Bay, 1629.* Exeter: W. J. Southwood, [1902?]

England

See Phillips

English

ENGLISH, JEAN. *History of the English family in Bath, 1770-1890.* Eastcote, Middlesex: Jean English, 1996. Includes pedigree.

Englefield

TRAPPES-LOMAX, T.B. 'The Englefields and their contribution to the survival of the faith in Berkshire, Wiltshire, Hampshire, and Leicestershire', *Biographical studies* **1**, 1951, 131-48. Roman Catholic family.

Ennor

See Ridington

Ensley

See Bater

Erasmus

See Rudman

Erisey

OATES, ALFRED STANLEY. 'Erisey and the Eriseys: an account of a Cornish manor and its ancient occupiers', *J.R.I.C.* N.S. 1(1), 1946, 61-70. Mainly 16-18th c.

Estcourt

LIGHT, MARY E. 'Estcourt of Swinley', *W.N.Q.* **2**, 1896-8, 351-7 & 399-408. 17-18th c.

SYMONDS, W. 'Estcourt of Salisbury, Rollestone and Long Newton', *W.N.Q.* **5**, 1905-7, 325-8. 17th c.

Estmond

SKINNER, A.J.P. 'Estmond of Lodge, Chardstock, Dorset', *N.Q.S.D.* **12**, 1911, 347-9. See also **13**, 1913, 210-12 for wills.

Ettrick

CURTIS, C.D. 'Monmouth rebellion: Anthony Ettrick', *N.Q.S.D.* **22**, 1938, 203-5. Includes 16-17th c. pedigree of a Dorset family.

Evans

EVANS, WILLIAM N. *Reminiscences of the Evans family formerly of Ottery St. Mary, Devon.* Manchester: R.G. Evans, 1894. 17-19th c.

MANLEY, F.H. 'The Evans family of North Wiltshire', *W.A.M.* **43**(143), 1925, 168-74. 17-18th c.

Evelegh

EVELEGH, ALDRIDGE. *Some notes on the Evelegh family.* Southsea: the author, 1965. Medieval-19th c.

Evelyn

EVELYN, HELEN. *The history of the Evelyn family.* Evelyn Nash, 1915. Of Surrey and Wiltshire, etc. 15-20th c.

FENTON, COLIN. 'The Evelyn family in Wiltshire', *W.A.M.* 58(209), 1961, 18-24. 16-18th c. Includes folded pedigree.

SCULL, G.D. 'Funeral of George Evelyn, West Dean, Wilts', *M.G.H.* 2nd series 1, 1886, 67-8. 1636; includes list of servants and gentlemen mourners.

'Genealogical memoranda relating to the family of Evelyn', *M.G.H.* 2nd series 1, 1886, 1-2, 82-3, 100, 152-6, 176-7, 210, 222-3, 229-34, 258-9, 296-7, 319-22, 332 & 352-6; 2, 1888, 8-11, 245, 38-9, 135-8, 184-6, 229, 245, 312 & 327-8; 3, 1890, 242-5, 267-8, 269-71 & 298-300. Surrey, Wiltshire and Hampshire. Includes pedigrees, 16-18th c., monumental inscriptions, parish register extracts, marriage licences, etc.

Everest

See Martin

Ewens

See Earle

Exelby

MOYLE, W.J.T. 'The Exelby family of St.Keverne', *C.F.H.S.J.* 5, 1977, 5-6; 16, 1980, 3-4. Medieval; also of Yorkshire.

Eyre

BAILEY, ROSALIE FELLOWS. *New England heritage of Rousmaniere, Ayer, Farwell, and Bourne families.* New York: [ ], 1960. Descended from the Eyre family of Wiltshire.

GANTZ, IDA. *Signpost to Eyrecourt: portrait of the Eyre family triumphant in the cause of liberty, Derbyshire, Wiltshire, Galway, c.1415-1856.* Bath: Kingsmead, 1975. Includes pedigree.

HARTIGAN, A.S. 'Eyre of Wilts', *W.N.Q.* 4, 1902-4, 506-8 & 562-6; 5, 1905-7, 27-31, 49-57, 97-104, 148-53, 218-22, 272-7, 309-13, 346-8, 416-21 & 468-72. See also 5, 1905-7, 426; 6, 1908-10, 189; 7, 1911-13, 421-2. 16-20th c.

RICHARDSON, MARY E.F. *A history of the Wiltshire family of Eyre.* Mitchell & Hughes. 1897. Includes pedigree, 12-19th c.

Falaise

BURSEY, PETER. 'William of Falaise', *N.Q.S.D.* 33(336), 1992 146-7. 11th c., includes pedigree showing link to Burci.

See also Burcie

Fane

CAREW, JOYCE. *Dusty pages: a story of two families and their homes.* Bridport: C. J. Creed, 1971. Fane and Fortescue families of Dorset, Devon, Somerset and Hampshire. Includes pedigree, 18-20th c.

See also Fortescue

Farmar

CHASEY, HAROLD. 'The diary of a young lady in Bath, 1842', *N.Q.S.D.* 33(336), 1992, 151-3. General discussion, with notes on the Farmar family.

Farren

'Pedigree of Farren of Tewkesbury, from deeds in the possession of the Rev. F.H. Hall', *M.G.H.* N.S., 1, 1874, 34. 17-18th c.

Farrington

See Morton

Farwell

See Eyre

Faull

FAULL, LILIAN M. *The Faulls of St.Ives.* Penzance: Headland Printing, 1972. 19-20th c.

Fawconer

BARTLETT, R.G. 'Fawconer of Salisbury', *W.N.Q.* 1, 1893-5, 571-2. See also 421.

MASKELYNE, ANTHONY S. 'Fawconer of Salisbury', *W.N.Q.* 2, 1896-8, 29-33 & 75-9. 17-18th c.

Fellowes

FELLOWES, EDMUND HORACE. *The family and descendants of William Fellowes of Eggesford.* Windsor: Oxley & Son, 1910. The family was also of Norfolk. 17-19th c.

Femell

See Symonds

Ferrers

ALEXANDER, J.J. 'The Ferrers', *D.C.N.Q.* 21, 1940-41, 57-62, 98-105, 157-62, & 195-9.

BENSON, J. 'The Ferrers', *D.C.N.Q.* 21, 1940-41, 57-62, 98-105, 157-62 & 195-9. Of Bere Ferrers, Devon, and Cornwall; medieval.

N., J.G. 'Devonshire charters, connected with the family of Ferrers', *Collectanea topographica et genealogica* 8, 1843, 33-5.

See also Chudderlegh

Ferris

RENDLE, R.S. 'The Ferris family of Exeter and other goldsmiths', *D.C.N.Q.* 34(7), 1981, 285-90.

Fettiplace

DUNLOP, J. RENTON. 'The family of Fettiplace,' *M.G.H.* 5th series 2, 1916-17, 93-100, 131-3, 183-92, 202-10, 242-56 & 282-92. Of Berkshire, Oxfordshire and Gloucestershire; pedigree, 13-20th c.

DUNLOP, J. RENTON. 'The Fettiplaces of Coln St. Aldwyn, Co. Gloucester', *M.G.H.* 5th series 3, 1918-19, 147-8. 17th c.

Fezzey

LEBUTT, MARIANNE. *The Fezzey family history.* Englewood, Ohio: the author, 1996. Of Devon and the United States, 18-20th c.

Ffooks

FFOOKS, EDWARD CAMBRIDGE. *The family of Ffooks of Sherborne in the county of Dorset, originally Ffooks of Marston Magna.* Welwyn Garden City: Alcuin Press, 1958.

Fiennes

See St. Barbe

Filmore

See Finnimore

Finnimore

PHILLIMORE, W.W. 'Finnimore and Filmore', *D.N.Q.* 2, 1902-3, 119-20. See also 138 & 215.

PHILLIMORE, W.P.W. 'On the origin of Finnimore and its allied surnames', *G.N.Q.* 2, 1884, 309-16.

Fisher

NEWTON, CECIL. 'The Fishers of Aldbourne', *W.F.H.S.* 54, 1994, 16-17. 18-19th c.

Fishley

LEARY, EMMELINE, & PEARSON, JEREMY. *By potters art and skill: pottery by the Fishleys of Fremington.* Exeter: Royal Albert Memorial Museum, 1984. Exhibition catalogue, including brief biographical notes, 18-20th c.

Fitz

RADFORD, G.H. 'Lady Howard of Fitzford', *D.A.Tr.* 22, 1890, 66-110. Includes pedigree showing descent from Fitz.

Fitzalan

BENSON, J. 'Fitz-Alan, Rohaut', *D.C.N.Q.* 25, 1952-3, 184-7. Medieval; of Dodbrook and Portlemouth.

Fitzjames

BROWN, FREDERICK. 'On the family of Fitzjames', *S.A.N.H.S.* 24(2), 1878, 32-42.

MAYO, C.H. 'The Fitzjames family of Somerset and later of Dorset', *N.Q.S.D.* 16, 1920, 54-68, 88-100, 128-38, 179-87, 218-27, & 247-55. 14-18th c.

HUMPHREYS, A.L., & WAINEWRIGHT, J.B. 'Fitzjames', *Notes & queries* 11th series 12, 1915, 202-4. See also 100.

Fitzmartin

'The Fitz-Martins', *D.C.N.Q.* 19(5), 1937, 211-5. See also 20(6), 1939, 287-8. Medieval.

Fitzroger

BENSON, J. 'Alice - Fitz-Roger, Bonville, Carminow, Rodney', *D.C.N.Q.* 24, 1950-51, 56-8. 14th c.

Fitzwalter

See Bonville

Fitz Waryn

See Botreaux

Fletcher

FLETCHER, N.K. 'Four Reverend Fletchers', *D.F.H.* 10, 1979, 8-10.

Flower

BARTLETT, R.G. 'Flower, North Wilts', *W.N.Q.* 1, 1893-5, 571-2. Brief extracts from 17th c. parish registers.

FLOWER, N.L. 'The Flower family of Somerset', *N.Q.S.D.* 29, 1974, 277-9. 16-20th c.

FLOWER, JEAN. 'The Flower family of Somerset', *N.Q.S.D.* 33(337), 1993. 203-6. 17th c.

S[TORY]-M[ASKELYNE], A.ST.J. 'Memoranda relating to the ancient Wiltshire family of Flower', *W.N.Q.* 8, 1914-16, 167-79 & 301-8. 16th c., includes brief pedigree.

Floyer

FLOYER, J. KESTELL. 'Pedigree of Floyer of India, etc.', *M.G.H.* 2nd series 4, 1892, 129-30. 17-18th c.

FLOYER, J.K., ed. *Pedigree of the family of Floyer, with evidences and notes.* [Esher]: [the editor], [1913]. Reprinted from *M.G.H.* 4th series 5, 1913, 303-7 & 346-51, and from *Visitation of England and Wales.*

FLOYER, J. KESTELL. 'Annals of the family of Floyer', *D.A.Tr.* **30,** 1898, 505-24.

Follett
HOLMAN, H. WILSON, *et al.* 'Follett pedigree', *D.C.N.Q.* **11,** 1920-21, 283. See also 306; **12,** 1922-23, 67-8; **13,** 1924-5, 15-16. 18th c., includes extracts from Topsham parish register.
WILSON, R.E. 'The Folletts', *D.C.N.Q.* **34,** 1979-81, 94-7 & 149-54. Includes 17-19th c. pedigrees.

Ford
REA, C.F. 'John Ford, vicar of Totnes, 1663', *D.C.N.Q.* **14,** 1926, 120-1 & 167.
FORD, K. ST. CLAIR. 'The Ford family miniature of Charles II with skull', *D.N.Q.* **1,** 1900-1, 157-8. See also 180.

Forrester
SKINNER, A.J.P. 'Forrester of Uplyme in Folke', **19,** 1929, 50-51. Includes monumental inscriptions, with extracts from parish registers.

Forsey
CAMPBELL-KEASE, JOHN. 'The medieval family of Forsey: an essay in local history, genealogy and heraldry', *D.N.* **109,** 1987, 21-4. Includes will of John Forsey of Bridport, 1457.

Forster
GOULSTONE, JOHN. 'The Forsters of Bristol and some descendants', *J.B.A.* **58,** 1989, 31-5. Includes pedigree, 12-18th c.

Fortescue
ALEXANDER, J.J. 'The early Fortescues', *D.C.N.Q.* **21**(6), 1941, 249-55.
FORTESCUE, EARL OF. 'Address by the president: some notes on the family of Fortescue', *D.A.Tr.* **88,** 1957, 1-20.
FORTESCUE, HUGH. *A chronicle of Castle Hill, 1454-1918.* W. H. Smith & Son, 1929.
FORTESCUE, THOMAS, LORD CLERMONT. *A history of the family of Fortescue.* 2nd ed. Ellis & White, 1880.
PERRY, F.A. 'The famous family of Fortescue', *Devon yearbook,* 1937, 49-52.
W., J. 'Arms of Fortescue', *W.A.* **1,** 1881, 22-3.
'The family of Fortescue', *London Devonian year book* **1910,** 36-8.
See also Fane and Fox

Forward
FORWARD, EDW. W. 'Forward family', *D.C.N.Q.* **13,** 1924-5, 295-6. See also **14,** 1926-7, 16-17 & 111-3. Includes parish register extracts, 16-18th c.

Foster
WARD, JOHN. 'Foster of Marlborough', *W.A.M.* **3**(8), 1857, 244-5. Includes folded pedigree, 17-19th c.
See also Hawkes

Fourdrinier
See Withy

Fowell
PAISLEY, T.B. 'The Fowells of St.Ives, engineers and traction engine makers', *Newcomen Society transactions* **36,** 1966, 25-46. Includes pedigree of Fowell, 19-20th c., and notes on Box family, 19th c.
SMITH, M.G. 'The Fowells of Fowlescombe', *D.C.N.Q.* **36**(1), 1987, 29-32.

Fowler
FOWLER, JEAN E. *A short account of the Fowler family from 1550 to 1891.* [Corsham]: [privately printed], 1899. Of Warwickshire and Wiltshire; includes pedigrees, 18-19th c.
FOWLER, W.G., 'The Fowlers of Kings Stanley and Stonehouse', *J.B.A.* **10,** 1977, 14-17; **12,** 1978, 23-7; **14,** 1978, 6-10.
'Fowlers of Gloucestershire', *G.N.Q.* **1,** 1881, 223-5, 282-4 & 450-1; **2,** 1884, 55-7, 172-5, 324-6 & 405-9. Includes wills, *inquisitions post mortem, etc.,* not completed.

Fox
CLAY, CHRISTOPHER. *Public finance and private wealth: the career of Sir Stephen Fox, 1627-1716.* Oxford: Clarendon Press, 1978. Includes pedigrees, 17-18th c.
FOSTER, JOSEPH. *A revised genealogical account of the various families descended from Frances Fox of St. Germans, Cornwall, to which is appended a pedigree of the Crokers of Lineham and many other families connected with them.* Head, Hole & Co., 1872. Includes folded pedigree, 17-19th c.

FOX, CHARLES HENRY. *A short genealogical account of some of the various families of Fox in the West of England, to which is appended a pedigree of the Crokers of Lineham, and also sketches of the families of Churchill, Yeo, Pollard, Coplestone, Strode, Fortescue and Bonvile*. Bristol: T. Kerslake & Co., 1864. With folded pedigrees, 17-19th c., including one of the Hingston family. Lineham in Yealmpton, Devon.

FOX, CHARLES H. *Chronicles of Tonedale: two centuries of family history*. Taunton: Barnicott & Son, 1879. Fox family, 18-19th c.

FOX, CHARLES HENRY. 'Genealogical memoranda relating to the family of Fox of Brislington, Clifton *etc., etc.*', *M.G.H.* N.S. **1**, 1874, 114-8. See also 283-5. Pedigree, 18-19th c.

FOX, GEORGE. 'Find the great grandparents', *J.D.F.H.S.* **2**(2), 1989, 54-5. Fox pedigree, 19-20th c.

FOX, HUBERT. *Quaker broadcloth: the story of Joseph and Mariana Fox and the cousinry at Wellington*. Buckfastleigh: the author, 1981.

GANDELL, H.L. 'The Holland baronies', *Coat of arms* **10**, 1969, 276. Fox family of Wiltshire, 18th c.

NORGATE, MARTIN. 'Edward and James Fox, pipemakers of Trowbridge', *W.A.M.* **78**, 1983, 128-9. 17th c.

'Genealogical memoranda relating to the family of Fox, of Brislington, etc.', *M.G.H.* N.S., **1**, 1894, 114-8 & 283-5. Includes pedigree.

See also Churchill and Were

Francome

'The Francome family', *W.N.Q.* **4**, 1902-4, 29-34. 16-18th c.

Freeman

LEGA-WEEKES, ETHEL. 'The Freemans of Ashburton, Buckfastleigh, Bovey Tracey, etc', *D.A.Tr.* **45**, 1913, 450-54.

DOWDESWELL, E.R. 'Notes on the Freeman family of Bushley, 1620-1700', *G.N.Q.* **3**, 1887, 168-70.

See also Marshall

Freke

FREKE, RALPH, & FREKE, JOHN. 'A pedigree or genealogy of the family of ye Frekes for nearly 200 years ...', *Ancestor* **10**, 1904, 179-212; **11**, 1904, 33-54. Of Dorset and Somerset; pedigrees, 16-18th c.

French

Go ... Be fruitfull and multiply: a history of the Francis French, John Badcock and Edward French families and their descendants from the late eighteenth century to 1989. Hobart: The French and Badcock Family Book Committee, 1989. Of Cornwall and Tasmania.

Friend

SEARLE, MURIEL V. 'The Friend family of Kelston', *J.B.A.* **46**, 1986, 30-32. 19th c.

Frome

PRIDEAUX, F.B. 'Fordington manor', *N.Q.S.D.* **19**, 1929, 110-12. Includes pedigree of Frome family, 14-15th c.

Froude

HOOPPELL, R.E. 'The Froudes or Frowdes of Devon', *D.A.Tr.* **24**, 1892, 441-57.

Fry

FRY, EDWARD ALEXANDER. 'Fry of Yarty', *S.A.N.H.S.* **49**(2), 1903, 65-70.

FRY, GEORGE S. 'Fry of Glastonbury', *N.Q.S.D.* **19**, 1929, 69-71. Includes 15th c. pedigree.

FRY, GEORGE SAMUEL. *The Saxon origin of the Fry families*. C. Rogers & Co; Dorset Printing Works, 1928. Dorset family.

Fuge

THOMAS, J.D. 'Fuge family', *D.C.N.Q.* **31**, 1968-70, 192-3. 18-19th c.

Fuidge

SCHOMBERG, ARTHUR. 'Bible entries', *M.G.H.* 3rd series **2**, 1898, 194. Relating to the Fuidge and Gardiner families of Marlborough and Bath, Somerset, 18-19th c.

Fulford

BROWN, F. 'Pedigrees from the visitation of Dorset, 1623: Fulford', *M.G.H.* 2nd series **2**, 1888, 76-8. Includes brief will extracts.

ALEXANDER, J.J. 'Early owners of Fulford manor', *D.A.Tr.* **70**, 1939, 199-211. 13-15th c.

POPE, F.J. 'The Dorset descendants of Sir Francis Fulford', *N.Q.S.D.* **11**, 1909, 12-14. See also 69-70. 17-18th c.

Fuller

FULLER, J.F. 'Fuller of Bath', *M.G.H.* 5th series **1**, 1916, 137-43. See also **4**, 1922, 62. Pedigree, 18-19th c.

FULLER, J.F. 'Fuller of Bristol', *M.G.H.* 5th series **4**, 1920-22, 60-62. 18-19th c.

Furneaux

FURNEAUX, H. 'Furneaux family: genealogical notes', *M.G.H.* N.S., **2**, 1877, 193-7. Of Paignton and Churston Ferrers Devon; also of Landrake, Cornwall. Extracts from parish registers, deeds, monumental inscriptions, etc., 16-18th c.

FURNEAUX, H. 'Furneaux family genealogical notes: extracts from a pocket-book ... ', *M.G.H.* N.S., **2**, 1877, 218-22. 18th c., includes marriage licences, etc.

FURNEAUX, H. 'Notices of the family of Furneaux from the eleventh to the fifteenth century', *M.G.H.* 3rd series **3**, 1900, 272-6; **4**, 1902, 7-11.

FURNEAUX, H. 'Pedigree of the family of Furneaux of Paignton and Buckfastleigh, Devon, afterwards of Swilly, near Plymouth', *M.G.H.* N.S., **2**, 1877, 171-5. 16-19th c.

HAMLYN, WILLIAM. *The Furneaux family.* Taunton: Hammett & Co., [1920]. Of Fenottery, Devon, Ashington, Somerset, *etc.,* medieval-19th c.

LYTE, H. MAXWELL. 'The co-heirs of Furneaux', *N.Q.S.D.* **16**, 1920, 281-5.

'Descendants of Matthew Furneaux', *Collectanea topographica et genealogica* **1**, 1834, 243-8. Medieval.

See also Rowe

Fursdon

FURSDON, DAVID. *Fursdon: home of the Fursdon family.* Tiverton: Marlands, 1984. Includes pedigree, 14-20th c.

Furse

CARPENTER, H.J. 'Furse of Morsehead: a family record of the sixteenth century', *D.A.Tr.* **26**, 1894, 168-84.

WALTON, HUGH. 'Oxford: Jericho and the Furse family of Devonshire', *Oxfordshire local history* **3**(8), 1992, 338-44. 16-19th c.

Fussell

ATTHILL, R. 'A dynasty of ironmasters', *Country life* **131**, 1962, 1254-9. Fussell and Horner families of Somerset.

FRY, GEORGE S. 'John Fussell: a forgotten Blandford worthy, 1622-59', *N.Q.S.D.* **21**, 1935, 15-18. See also 70. Includes pedigree, 17-18th c.

Fust

FUST, JENNIFER H. 'Fust family: extracts from Hill registers', *G.N.Q.* **3**, 1887, 587-94.

FUST, JENNIFER H. 'The Fust family portraits', *G.N.Q.* **4**, 1890, 102-27. See also 201. List of portraits, including much genealogical information, with notes on arms.

Galabin

WAGNER, H. 'Pedigree of the Huguenot family of Galabin', *M.G.H.* 4th series **2**, 1908, 252-4.

Gale

GALE, FRED R. 'Gale of Bolehyde, Co. Wilts', *Notes & queries* **170**, 1936, 292-4, 312-4 & 331-2. 13-18th c.

Galpin

GALPIN, GEORGE LUCK. *The family of Galpin of Staffordshire and Dorset.* Chiswick Press, 1926. Includes Grey, Hannam, Nuntley and James.

Gandy

GANDY, CLIFFORD N. *Branches of the Gandy family: genealogy & historical notes.* 2nd ed. Crondall: the author, 1994. Originally of Devon, but with branches in many counties. Primarily pedigrees, 16-20th c.

Garde

MORIARTY, G. ANDREWS. 'Genealogical research in England; Garde: parentage of Roger Garde, the first New England mayor', *N.E.H.G.R.* **82**, 1928, 69-70. See also 185. Includes extracts from Alvington, Devon, parish registers, 16-17th c.

Gardiner

See Chivers, Fuidge and Hastings

Garland

Garlandhayes: report. Ilford: N.G. Furlong, 1981.
See Whitfield

Garlick

HALL, I.V. 'The Garlicks, two generations of a Bristol family (1692-1781)', *B.G.A.S.T.* **80**, 1961, 132-59. Includes pedigree, 18th c.

Garne

GARNE, RICHARD O. *Cotswold yeomen and sheep: the Garnes of Gloucestershire.* Regency, 1984. Includes pedigrees, 16-20th c.

Garrard

S., J. 'Crawlboys', *W.N.Q.* **7**, 1911-13, 32-4. Garrard family, 18th c.

Gater

KELLAND, WILLIAM HENRY. 'The Gater family', *W.A.* **4**, 1885, 103-4. Includes pedigree, 17-19th c., with parish register extracts. *See also* Clarke

Gauntlett

See Heal

Gay

'The Gay Bicentennial', *W.A.* **5**, 1885, 123-8. Includes notes on the pedigree of John Gay, the Barnstaple poet. *See also* Harington

Gayer

COLE, C.F. 'Memoranda relating to the Gayer family', *M.G.H.* 2nd series **4**, 1892, 126. 17-18th c. *See also* Pearce

Gayner

GAYNER, MARGARET. *From Smithy to computer: a history of one Gayner family, 1582-1983.* [ ]: [the author?], 1985. Gloucestershire family, includes pedigrees.

Gayre

GAYRE, G.R., & GAIR, R.L. *Gayre's booke: being a history of the family of Gayre.* 4 vols. Phillimore, et al, 1948-59. Of Scotland, Cornwall, etc., includes pedigrees, medieval-19th c.

Geddes

SMITH, RICHARD J. 'Geddes family of Alderbury', *W.F.H.S.* **50**, 1993, 9-11. 18-19th c.

Gee

GEE, HENRY. *Gee of Freshford and London: an attempt to trace the history of the family and of other holders of the name.* Chiswick Press, 1916. Also of Lincolnshire. Includes folded pedigree, 16-20th c.

Geen

GEEN, M.S. *An ordinary Devon family: Geen of Okehampton.* Crediton: Phillips & Co., 1975. Includes pedigree, 18-20th c.

Geere

GEARE, R. HOLWELL. 'Geere of Heavitree and Kenn, and Geer of U.S.A', *D.C.N.Q.* **28**, 1959-61, 261-3 & 291-5. See also **29**, 1962-4, 9; **31**, 1968-70, 250.

Gennys

ROBBINS, ALFRED F. 'Gennys of Launceston and Ireland', *Notes & queries* 12th series **1**, 1916, 249-51. See also 126, 193, 299 & 489-90; 12th series **2**, 1916, 114. 16-17th c.

Gerard

See Bulley

Gerle

See Dyer

Gernon

See Gresley

Gibb(e)s

ALDENHAM, LORD. *Pedigree of the family of Gibbs, of Clyst St. George, Co. Devon, Aldenham, Co. Hertford, Tyntesfield, Charlton, and Barrow Court, Co. Somerset.* Privately printed, 1904.

ALDENHAM, HENRY H., LORD. *Pedigree of the family of Gibbs, of Pytte in the parish of Clyst St. George.* 3rd ed. Mitchell, Hughes and Clarke, 1932. 16-19th c.

GIBBS, HENRY HUCKS. 'Pedigree of Gibbes of Bedminster and Bristol, allied to Harington of Kelston, Somerset', *M.G.H.* 2nd series **1**, 1886, 3-6.

GIBBS, JOHN ARTHUR. *The history of Antony and Dorothea Gibbs and of their contemporary relatives, including the history of the origin & early years of the house of Antony Gibbs and Sons.* Saint Catherine Press, 1922. Of Exeter and London, 18-19th c., includes folded pedigrees of Gibbs, Hucks of Hertfordshire, and Crawley.

GIBBS, RACHEL. *Pedigree of the family of Gibbs of Pytte in the parish of Clyst St. George.* 4th ed. Richmond: Kingprint, 1981. Includes folded pedigree, 16-20th c.

HUNSDON, LORD. *The history of Gibbs of Fenton in Dartington, County Devon.* St. Catherine Press, 1925. 14-20th c., includes extracts from wills, deeds, *etc.*, with pedigrees of Wadham, 15-17th c., and Gibbs, 14-19th c.

Giddy

GEDYE, NICK. 'Davies Gilbert and his ancestors', *C.F.H.S.J.* **78**, 1995, 10-11. Giddy family; includes pedigree, 17-19th c.

GIDDY, JOYCE. 'Early emigrants to New Zealand', *C.F.H.S.J.* **37**, 1985, 17-18. Of Boyton; 17-19th c.

GIDDY, JOYCE. *Giddy: the yeoman pioneer: the story of George and Sally Giddy and their family*. Morrinsville, N.Z.: the author, c.1986. Of Cornwall and New Zealand, etc., includes pedigrees 17-20th c.

Gidley
See also Ridington

Giffard
BAZELEY, WILLIAM. 'Brimpsfield Castle and its owners', *B.G.A.S.T.* **20**, 1895-7, 233-40. Giffard family, medieval.

BENSON, J. 'The Giffards', *D.C.N.Q.* **23**(2), 1947, 38-41.

BENSON, J. 'Walter Giffard and "De La Hull"', Hulham, *D.C.N.Q.* **22**(5), 1943, 146. 13th c.

DYMOND, R. 'Gifford or Giffard of Yeo, Devon', *M.G.H.* N.S., **2**, 1877, 312-3. Pedigree, 14-17th c.

FANE, ARTHUR. 'Brief notice of the family of Giffard of Boyton', *W.A.M.* **3**(4), 1855, 100-108. Medieval.

GIFFARD, HARDINGE F. 'Giffards jump', *D.A.Tr.* **34**, 1902, 648-703. Includes pedigree.

LANGSTON, J.N. 'The Giffards of Brimpsfield', *B.G.A.S.T.* **65**, 1944, 105-28. Includes pedigrees, 11-14th c.

PESKETT, H.M. 'The inheritance of Giffard of Weare', *D.C.N.Q.* **32**(9), 1973, 266-71. Medieval.

RICHARDSON, DOUGLAS. 'Boyton: the church, the Giffards, and their successors', *Hatcher review* **1**(9), 1980, 26-33. Medieval Giffard family.

ROUND, J. HORACE. 'Giffard of Fonthill Giffard,' *Ancestor* **6**, 1903, 137-47. Wiltshire; medieval.

WROTTESLEY, GEORGE. *The Giffards*. [ ], 1902. Reprinted from the *Proceedings of the Wm. Salt Society*. Study of 32 branches of the family, mainly in the South-West.

'The family of Giffard', *Devonian year book* **1912**, 29-31.

'The Giffard ring', *W.A.* **9**(12), 1890, 220-1. Includes pedigree, 17-18th c.

See also Redvers and Stowford.

Gifford
See Deighton

Gilbert
EDWARDS, J.M. 'Spotlight: Portland. A heritage of stone: the Gilberts', *G.T.* **13**(2), 1988, 65-6.

PINK, W.D. 'The Gilberts of Devonshire', *W.A.* **6**(10), 1887, 237-8.

ROBINSON, E.B. 'Names occurring in deeds and documents at Exeter City Library (SCS) re Gilbert family of Sandridge in Stoke Gabriel', *D.F.H.* **45**, 1988, 6-7.

THORNTON, J. WINGATE. 'The Gilbert family', *N.E.H.G.R.* **4**, 1850, 223-32. Includes pedigree, medieval-17th c.

Compton Castle, Devon. National Trust, 1979. Includes pedigrees of Gilbert and Raleigh, 14-20th c.

'Gilbert family of Compton and Greenway, Devonshire.' *Essex Institute historical collections* **17**, 1880, 40-41. Folded pedigree, 15-17th c.

Gill
GILL, H.D. *Random notes on the Tavistock Gills*. Lamerton: the author, 1954.

GILL, H.D. *Further notes on the Tavistock Gill family and some of their connections*. Lamerton: the author, 1957.

LITSCHI, F. 'Two Preston families', *Dorset year book* 1982, 39-42. Gill and Guppy families.

See also Duke

Gillard
GILLARD, JEFFREY J. *Thick on the ground*. Melbourne: the author, 1978. Of Somerset and Australia.

Gilling
G., A.H. 'A Somerset yeoman family', *N.Q.S.D.* **10**, 1907, 72-6. Gilling of South Brent, 14-20th c.

Gillingham
'Gillingham family of Dorset', *N.Q.S.D.* **8**, 1903, 77-8, 131-6, & 153-6. See also **8**, 1903, 354-5; **9**, 1905, 37-8.

Gillman
GILLMAN, ALEXANDER WILLIAM. *Searches into the history of the Gillman or Gilman family, including the various branches of England, Ireland, America and Belgium*. Elliot Stock, 1895. Includes chapters on the family in Wales, London, Surrey, Ireland, Hertfordshire and Essex, Gloucestershire, Kent, Norfolk, *etc., etc.*, with folded pedigrees, medieval-19th c.

Glanville

GLANVILLE-RICHARDS, WM. URMSTON S. *Records of the Anglo-Norman house of Glanville from A.D.1050 to 1880.* Mitchell & Hughes, 1882. Of Devon, Cornwall, and many other counties; includes pedigrees. 10-19th c.

KING, E. 'Glanville of Launceston: from the registers of St.Mary Magdalene, Launceston', *M.G.H.* N.S. **4**, 1884, 7-9. 16-17th c.

'Glanville of Ashburton, Devon', *M.G.H.* N.S., **4**, 1884, 16-17. Parish register extracts.

'Glanville of Halwell: extracts from the registers of Whitchurch, Co. Devon', *M.G.H.* N.S., **3**, 1880, 418-9 & 431-2.

Glynn

BEAZLEY, F.C. 'The pedigree of Glynn of Glynn in the county of Cornwall, and of Liverpool in the County Palatine of Lancaster', *Genealogist* N.S. **24**, 1908, 145-63. 15-19th c., includes wills.

BEAZLEY, F.C. 'Further notes on the family of Glynn', *Genealogist* N.S. **25**, 1909, 266. Extracts from the Cardinham bishops' transcripts, 17th c.

Goddard

BAREFOOT, MICHAEL. *My Great Grandmother was Cornish: an insight into some inter-related families from Derbyshire, Staffordshire, Devon, and in particular, Cornwall: the Goddards, Narramores, Loverings, Brewers and Edwards.* [ ]: J. Barefoot Ltd., 1989. Includes pedigrees, 18-20th c.

GODDARD, R.W.K. 'Goddard of Englesham: a New England branch', *W.N.Q.* **3**, 1899-1901, 481-96. 17-19th c.

HARMS, JOHN W., & HARMS, PEAR GODDARD. *The Goddard book.* 2 vols. Baltimore: Gateway Press, 1984-90. Goddard family of North Wiltshire and the U.S.A., etc., 16-20th c. Includes pedigrees.

JEFFERIES, RICHARD. *A memoir of the Goddards of North Wilts, compiled from ancient records, registers and family papers.* Swindon: Goddard Association, 1987. Originally published 1873. Medieval-19th c.

KNAPP, KENNETH NORTHCOT. 'Goddard of Swindon', *Swindon review* **2**, 1946, 7-9.

See also Perne and Harington

Godolphin

DIMONT, ELISABETH. *Godolphin family portraits, 1610-1781.* Salisbury: Godolphin School Benevolent Fund, 1987. Includes pedigree, 17-18th c.

HADOW, G.E. 'House of Godolphin', *J.R.I.C.* N.S. **13**(4), 1898, 407-22. 16-18th c.

MARSH, F.G. *The Godolphins.* New Milton: Smith & Son, 1930. Of Godolphin, Cornwall, Coulston, Wiltshire, *etc.* Includes folded pedigree, 15-20th c.

MURRIN, T.H. 'Under the badge of a white eagle: the Godolphins', *Old Cornwall* **8**, 1973-9, 221-6, 276-8, 316-20, 380-7, 445-50 & 487-91. Medieval-18th c.

Golde

ROGERS, W.H.H. 'Golde-Strechleigh of Seaborough, Somerset, and Ermington, South Devon', *N.Q.S.D.* **7**, 1901, 91-8. 13-16th c.

ROGERS, W.H. HAMILTON. 'Golde-Strechleigh of Seaborough, Somerset, and Ermington, South Devon', *N.Q.S.D.* **7**, 1901, 91-8. Reprinted in his *Archaeological papers relating to the counties of Somerset, Wilts., Hants., and Devon.* [ ]: reprinted for the author, 1902.

Goldsborough

BENETT-STANFORD, J.M.F. 'Families of East Knoyle', *W.A.M.* **51**(185), 1946, 386-404. Notes on Goldesborough, Still, Mervyn, Hunton, Brethers, and Toope families, mostly with pedigrees.

GOLDSBROUGH, A. *Memorials of the Goldesborough family.* Cheltenham: E.J. Burrow & Co., 1930. Originally of Yorkshire, but of Wiltshire, Somerset, Dorset, and various other counties from the 15th c.

Goldstone

H[AMMOND], J.J. 'Goldstone of Alderbury', *W.N.Q.* **7**, 1911-13, 322-5. 17th c.

See also Goulstone

Goldwyer

BAYLEY, A.R. 'Goldwyer of Somerford Grange and Salisbury Close', *Genealogists' magazine* **7**(9), 1937, 455-9. Somerford Grange, Hampshire. 16-19th c.

Gollop

FOX, MARGARET M.O. 'The Gollops of Bowood and Strode, Dorset', *N.Q.S.D.* **30**, 1974-9, 65-7. See also 111. 17-19th c.

LITSCHI, F., & GOLLOP, K.S. 'The Gollops of
Bowood and Strode of Netherbury in
Dorset', *Dorset year book* 1987, 12-14.

Goodden
NOTLEY, JOHN E.B. 'Compton House, Dorset',
N.Q.S.D. **30**, 1974-9, 405-18. Goodden and
Abington families.

Goodenough
LIGHT, MARY. 'The Goodenoughs of Sherston',
W.N.Q. **3**, 1899-1901, 385-403. 17-18th c.
Sherston Magna.

Goodhinds
GOULSTONE, J. *The Goodhinds of Saltford:
notes, wills and pedigrees.* [2nd ed.]
Alsager: G. Pratten, 1989.

Gookin
HUDLESTON, C. ROY. 'Sir Vincent Gookin of
Highfield, Gloucestershire', *B.G.A.S.T.* **64**,
1943, 113-7. Includes pedigree, 16-17th c.,
and will, 1638.
See also Deighton.

Gordon
See Pitman

Gorges
BROWN, FREDERICK. 'Pedigree of Sir Ferdinando
Gorges', *N.E.H.G.R.* , **29**, 1875, 7-11. Of
Wraxall, 16-18th c.
BROWN, FREDERICK. 'The Gorges family',
N.E.H.G.R. **29**, 1875, 40-47. 16-17th c., of
Somerset.
GORGES, RAYMOND. *The story of a family
through eleven centuries, illustrated by
portraits and pedigrees, being a history of
the family of Gorges.* Boston,
Massachusetts: Merrymount Press, 1944.
Dorset and Somerset family.
WHITMARSH, J. 'The Gorges of Wraxall etc.',
W.A. 1882, 189-90. 14-17th c.
'Funeral certificate: Dame Ann Gorges, 1620',
M.G.H. N.S., **4**, 1884, 55.
See also Maynard, Knight and Prowse

Goslett
POYNTON, F J. 'Gostlett of Marshfield, allied to
Harington of Kelston', *M.G.H.* N.S., **4**,
1884, 2-4. Includes extracts from Kelston
parish register and monumental
inscriptions for Croom family, and a
pedigree of Harington of Bitton,
Gloucestershire.
See also Harington and Hooke.

Goss
MOYLE, A.N, & MOYLE, I.N. *History of Goss
family: Devonshire to Midlands, Tasmania,
1804-1993.* Launceston, Tasmania: L.B. &
J.A. Moyle, 1993.

Gostlett
'Gostlett of Marshfield allied to Harington of
Kelston', *M.G.H.* N.S., **3**, 1880, 454-5; N.S.,
4, 1884, 2-5. Of Marshfield, Gloucestershire, and Kelston, Somerset; includes
parish register entries relating to Gostlett
and Croom families with pedigree of
Haringtona of Bitton, Gloucestershire, 17-
18th c.

Gough
MULLIN, DAVID. 'The Gough family of the New
Inn, Bream', *New regard* **4**, 1988, 24-34.
Includes pedigree. 16-17th c.

Gould
See Baring-Gould

Goulstone
GOULSTONE, J. *Goulstone, Gouldstone and
Goldstone: genealogical records for Bristol,
Somerset, etc.* Bexleyheath: J. Goulstone,
1986.

Gournay
See Gurney

Grace
PARKER, GRAHAME. 'The Grace trail', *J.B.A.* **53**,
1988, 26-9. Includes pedigree. 18-20th c.

Granger
See Bater

Granville
See Grenville

Gray
WHITTON, DONALD C. *The Grays of Salisbury:
an artist family of nineteenth century
England.* San Francisco: East Wind
Printers, 1976.

Green
BUTTREY, P.M. 'Gloucestershire Greens',
J.G.F.H.S. **39**, 1988, 13-14. 18-19th c.
See Mortimer

Greene
HOPWE, C. 'The Greenes of Bowridge Hill,
Gillingham, Dorset', *Dorset year book*
1984, 73-6. 16-18th c.
MORIARTY, G. ANDREWS. 'Gleanings from
English records: Greene', *N.E.H.G.R.* **103**,
1949, 185-8. Of Gillingham, Dorset, 16-17th c.

Greenslade

ELLEN, JO. *The hammer and the anvil: a history of the Greenslade/Moore family from South Molton, Devon to Maldon, Victoria, with a section on the Greenslade/Norton family of Lopen, Somerset.* Nunawading: [the author?], 1992. 18-20th c.

Gregor

NORTH, CHRISTINE. 'The Gregors of Trewarthenick', *C.F.H.S.J.* **58**, 1990, 34-8. 17-19th c.

PASCOE, W.H. 'The Gregors of Cornwall - upstairs', *C.F.H.S.J.* **34**, 1984, 17-18. 13-18th c.

Grene

See Bisse

Grenfell

HOOPER, J.E. 'The Grenfell family', *Old Cornwall* 3(10), 1941, 433-5.

Grenville

BENSON, J. 'Grenville', *D.C.N.Q.* **26**, 1954-5, 15-18. Medieval.

FITCH-NORTHEN, CHARLES. 'A revision of the Grenville pedigree', *D.C.N.Q.* **34**, 1978-81, 154-61. See also 254. Medieval-16th c.

GRANVILLE, ROGER. 'An account of Sir Thomas Grenvile's tomb in Bideford church, and also of the Long Bridge of Bideford', *E.D.A.A.S.Tr.* 3rd series 1, 1892, 11-16. 1513.

FITCH-NORTHEN, CHARLES. 'A revision of the Grenville pedigree', *D.C.N.Q.* **34**, 1978-81, 154-61. See also 254. Medieval-16th c.

GRANVILLE, ROGER. 'The Grenvilles: a race of fighters', in SNELL, F.J. *Memorials of old Devonshire.* Bemrose & Sons, 1904, 34-62.

GRANVILLE, ROGER. *The history of the Granville family, traced back to Rollo, first Duke of Normandy, with pedigrees, etc.* W. Pollard & Co., 1895.

TAYLOR, THOMAS. 'The genesis of a myth', *Ancestor* 3, October 1902, 98-104. Grenville family, 18-19th c.

REICHEL, OSWALD J. 'History of the Granville family', *D.C.N.Q.* 5, 1908-9, 145-7. See also 218-9, & 6, 1910-11, 22-5. Includes pedigree, 12-15th c.

ROUND, J.H. 'The Granvilles and the monks', in his *Family origins and other studies.* Tabard Press, 1970. Originally published: Constable, 1930.

WORTHY, CHARLES. 'Notes, genealogical and historical, being a second essay towards a history of Bideford', *D.A.Tr.* **16**, 1884, 670-702. Primarily concerned with the Grenville family.

The Grenvilles. Journeys into Cornwall's past. [ ]: Bethany Books, [198-?].

Gresham

See De Boteville

Gresley

CARTER, WILLIAM F. 'Gresley and Gernon', *Genealogist* N.S. **35**, 1919, 176-7. 15th c.

Greve

See De Boteville

Greville

G., I.E. 'The Greville-Jame marriage', *B.G.A.S.Tr.* **76**, 1957, 171-2. c.1501.

PAGET, M. 'The Grevill pedigree', *C.K.L.H.S.B.* **8**, 1982, 7-18. 17-18th c

Grey

See Galpin

Gribble

GRIBBLE, DOROTHY ROSE J. *Gribble annals IV: kinships. Gribbles of Barnstaple, from church records and the researches of Henry Edward Gribble and his cousins.* Highclere: Plantagenet Productions, 1994. 19th c., includes pedigree.

Gribble annals 3: family letters. Highclere: Plantagenet Productions, 1992. c.1870-1940.

Grigg

GRIGG, S.C. 'The Grigg family of Kilkhampton in Cornwall', *C.F.H.S.J.* 3, 1977, 9-13. Includes pedigree, 18-19th c.

KENT, ALAN. 'Early Griggs of St.Dennis', *C.F.H.S.J.* **62**, 1991, 28. 17th c.

WALTERS, B. 'Grigg twigs', *G.T.* 13(2), 1988, 45.

Grove

HAWKINS, DESMOND. 'Grove of Fern House, Wilts', *N.Q.S.D.* 31. 1980-85. 120-22. 15-16th c.

HAWKINS, DESMOND, ed. *The Grove diaries: the rise and fall of an English family 1809-1925.* Wimborne: Dovecot Press, 1995. Of Ferne House, Donhead St. Mary, Wiltshire. Includes biographical dictionary of people mentioned.

See also Hanham

52

Guise

DAVIES, G., ed. 'Memoirs of the family of Guise', *Camden third series* **28**, 1917, 83-177. See also index, 178-84. Includes pedigrees, 15-18th c., of Elmore, Glos.

MACLEAN, JOHN, SIR. 'Elmore and the Guise family', *B.G.A.S.T.* **3**, 1878-9, 49-78. Includes pedigree of Guise, 13-18th c.

Gumb

ALEXANDER, J.J. '[Genealogical notes on Daniel Gumb, stone-cutter, 1703-1776]', *D.C.N.Q.* **14**, 1926, 79-82.

Gundry

MEAD, C.J.H. 'The Gundry family of Cornwall', *D.C.N.Q.* **25**, 1952-3, 125-8. 18-19th c.

'Nathaniel Gundry, Justice of Common Pleas', *N.Q.S.D.* **12**, 1911, 129-31. Warren of Musbury, Devon, and Gundry of Lyme Regis, Dorset; pedigree, 17-18th c.; also concerned with Warren of Musbury, Devon.

Gunning

GOULSTONE, J. *The Gunnings of Cold Ashton in Gloucestershire*. Bexleyheath: the author, 1991.

GUNNING, CHARLES JOHN HOPE, & WARDER, ALFRED. *Genealogy of the Gunning family, 1400-1907*. A. Prickett: [ ], 1907.

Guppy

See Gill

Gurney

GURNEY, DANIEL. *The record of the house of Gourney*. 4 pts in 3 vols and supplement. John Bowyer Nichols and John Gough Nichols, 1848-58. Pt.1. The Gourneys in Normandy. Pt.2. The Gourneys or Gurneys of Swathings and West Barsham, in Norfolk. Pt.3. The Gurneys of Keswick, in Norfolk. Pt.4 The Gourneys of Somerset, from the survey to the reign of Henry IV.

Gye

HUNT, JOHN G. 'The ancestry of Mary Gye, wife of the Rev. John Maverick', *N.E.H.G.R.* **115**, 1961, 248-53. See also **122**, 1968, 282-3. Prowse and Gye families of Sandford, *etc.* 15-16th c.

Gyverney

HARBIN, E.H. BATES. 'Walter Fichet's grant of lands to Simon Michel, circa 1300', *S.A.N.H.S.* **64**(2), 1918, 46-60. Includes pedigrees of Gyverney, 12-14th c., and Michel, 13-17th c.

Haccombe

SHEARLEY, A.W. 'Haccombe', *D.A.Tr.* **50**, 1918, 323-52. Includes pedigree of Haccombe, 11-14th c.

Hache

See also Arbalister

Hadrill

MUNROE, MAVIS. 'Hadriel? Hatherell? Hadrell? Hadrill?', *W.F.H.S.* **6**, 1982, 23-5. 19th c.

Haimes

HAIME, JOHN W. *The Haimes: a Dorset family*. Colehill: the author, 1970.

Haines

See King

Hale

HALE, WILLIAM MATTHEW. *The family of Hale*. [Rake]: privately printed, 1936. Gloucestershire family.

LINDLEY, E.S. 'Hale of Alderley', *B.G.A.S.T.* **74**, 1955, 199-202. Includes pedigree of Hale, 16-20th c., and Blagden, 17-19th c.

Halfyard

HALFYARD, ROBERT R. *The Halfyard family register: the ancestors and descendants of Richard Halfyard (1744-1815) and Elizabeth Churchill (1752-1828)*. St. Catherine's, Ontario: Halfyard Heritage, 1994. Originally of Farrington, Devon, but primarily concerned with the United States. Includes wills of Stephen Puddicombe of Bovey Tracey, 1716, James Puddicombe, 1678 and Richard Halfyard of Bovey Tracey, 1798.

Hallewell

SANDERS, GEOFFREY. 'The Hallewell family', *B.G.A.S.T.* **92**, 1973, 190-97. 19th c.

Halse

CHUBB, L.J. 'John Halse', *D.C.N.Q.* **31**, 1968-70, 153-4. See also 191. Includes 17-18th c. pedigree

Halwell

GEARE, RALPH HOLWELL. 'Admiral of the Fleet Sir John Halwell', *D.C.N.Q.* **25**, 1952-3, 195-201. Medieval; includes genealogical notes.

GEARE, R. HOLWELL. 'Richard Halwell, armiger, of South Pool near Exon', *D.C.N.Q.* **26**, 1954-5, 110-11. Halwell family, 15-16th c.

Hamblyn

SHAW, M.N. *Hamblyn family history, 1841, 1855, 1976: Plymouth to New Plymouth.* [Wyndham, New Zealand]: the author, 1971. Of Devon and New Zealand; 19-20th c.

Hamlett

LANE, G.B. 'The Hamlett family', *C.K.L.H.S.B.* **9**, 1989, 38-46. Includes pedigree, 18-20th c.

Hamley

BENSON, J. 'The Hamleys, Talbot and Champernowne', *D.C.N.Q.* **19**, 1936-7, 265-70. Medieval; includes pedigrees of Hamley and Talbot.

HAMLEY, DOUGLAS W. *The Hamley, Hambly, Hamlyn group of families: historical and genealogical notes.* Norwich: D.W. & J.C. Hamley, 1977. Of Cornwall and various other counties, medieval-19th c. Includes many parish register extracts.

HAMBLY, EDMUND H. *The family of Hamley, Hambly, Hamlyn and Hambling.* Gloucester: John Bellows, [192-?]. Medieval-20th c., includes many parish register extracts.

HAMBLY, ERIC H. 'The origin of Hamley and Hambly', *C.F.H.S.J.* **49**, 1988, 27. Medieval. *A family for ever?* Hamley, Hambley and Hamlyn Family History Society, forthcoming.

See also Talbot

Hamlyn

The Hamlyn family. Truman Press, 1933. 14-20th c.

WORTHY, CHARLES. *The history of the suburbs of Exeter, with general particulars of the landowners, lay and clerical, from the Conquest to the present time, and a special notice of the Hamlyn family, together with a digression on the noble houses of Redvers and of Courtenay, Earls of Devon.* Henry Gray, *et al,* 1892.

Hamm

See Allin

Hammill

HIGGANS, JOHN. 'The French connection', *C.F.H.S.J.* **12**, 1979, 9-11. See also **14**, 1979, 10-11. 17-20th c. Perhaps a Huguenot family.

Hancock

HANCOCK, F. *Hancock of Somerset: some notes on a yeoman family.* Taunton: Barnicott & Pearce, 1919.

Hand

DEACON, LOIS. *Hardy's grandmother, Betsy, and her family.* Monographs on the life, times and works of Thomas Hardy **34**. St. Peter Port: Toucan Press, 1968. Hand family, 18-19th c.

See also Hardy

Hanham

HAWKINS, DESMOND. 'Hanham and Grove families', *N.Q.S.D.* **31**, 1980-85, 243-4.

Hanmer

WILLIAMS, H. FULFORD. 'The Hanmer family of North Devon', *D.C.N.Q.* **27**, 1956-8, 16-17. See also 212-5 & 247-8.

See also Down

Hannam

HANNAM, D.C. 'The Hannams of Purse Caundle', *N.Q.S.D.* **28**, 1968, 119-23, 165-9, 209-11, 316-8, & 330-3.

HANNAM, D. C. 'The Hannams of Wimborne Minster', *N.Q.S.D.* **31**, 1980-5, 27-31, 68-71, 117-9 & 161-4.

See also Galpin

Harbin

RAWLINS, SOPHIA W. 'Joseph and Alexander Harbin: two Barbadian merchants, their families and descendants', *Journal of the Barbados Museum and Historical Society* **11**(1), 1951, 28-33. Somerset family; 17th c.

Harcourt

CLOWES, R.L. 'Harcourt of Bradninch, near Exeter', *D.C.N.Q.* **16**, 1930-31, 12-13.

HARCOURT-BATH, W. 'Harcourts of Bridgetown, Totnes', *D.C.N.Q.* **15**, 1929, 349-51.

Harding

HARDING, ROSS. *From the Axe and the Brue: a Harding family history.* Canberra: Ross Harding, 1992. Migrants to Australia.

REID, R.D. *Some account of the family of Harding of Cranmore, Co. Somerset, together with notes on the Yeoman family of Wanstrow.* Bristol: J. W. Arrowsmith, 1917. 18-19th c.

ROYAL, NICHOLAS JOHN. *Harding family: a short history and narrative pedigree from 1480 to the present day.* [ ]: privately printed, 1970.

Hardwick

STUCKEY, KEN. 'My Gran Hardwick', *Yatton yesterdays* **6**, 1989, 17-18. Includes list of Hardwicks in the 1851 census for Yatton and Kenn.

Hardy

DODDERIDGE, SIDNEY E. 'Stinsford and the Hardy family', *N.Q.S.D.* **19**, 1929, 106-9. Includes pedigree, 16-20th c.

TUNKS, BRENDA. 'An author in the family', *J.D.F.H.S.* **1**(1), 1987, 21-3. Hardy; includes pedigree, 18-20th c.

TUNKS, B.M. 'A re-examination of R.G. Bartelot's version of Thomas Hardy's ancestry', *N.Q.S.D.* **33**(336), 1992, 154-6. 17-19th c.

TUNKS, BRENDA. 'The John Hardys of Puddletown, Owermoigne and Tolpuddle', *N.Q.S.D.* **33**(337), 1993, 181-94. Includes pedigree, 17-19th c.

TUNKS, BRENDA. *Whatever happened to the other Hardys?* Poole: Brenda Tunks, 1990. Of Bockhampton, Puddletown, *etc.* 18-20th c.

SQUIBB, G.D. 'Thomas Hardy's maternal grandparents', *N.Q.S.D.* **31**, 1980-5, 315-6. Hardy and Hand families of Dorset.

See also Hand and Honeybun

Harington

GRIMBLE, IAN. *The Harington family.* Jonathan Cape, 1957.

MORE, J.H. 'Family portraits: only a name', *Listener* 6.9.1956, 336-8.

POYNTON, F.J. 'The last days of Harington at Kelston', *M.G.H.* 2nd series **1**, 1886, 316-8 & 338-40.

POYNTON, F.J. 'Pedigrees showing the connection of Harington of Kelston, Somerset, with the Wiltshire families of Digges, Thorner, Goddard, and White', *M.G.H.* 2nd series **1**, 1886, 37-40.

POYNTON, FRANCIS J. 'Who was Margaret, wife of William, V Lord Harington, 1418?', *Genealogist* N.S., **9**, 1893, 78. Includes will of Robert Hylle of Spaxton, Somerset.

'A brief account of the complaint made by Sir John Harington of Kelston, Kt., to the Star Chamber, against his brother-in-law Edward Rogers of Cannington, Somerset', *M.G.H.* N.S., **4**, 1884, 261. c. 1602.

'A brief memoir and some other notes of John Harington of Kelston, M.P. for Bath, 1646-54-56', *M.G.H.* N.S., **3**, 1880, 398-401.

'A memoir of Captain John Harington of Corston and Kelston, Somerset, M.P. for Somerset, 1654, M.P. for Bath city, 1658', *M.G.H.* N.S., **4**, 1884, 22-4 & 33-6.

'Extracts from the registers of the parishes of Kelston and Corston, Somerset, and from Bitton in Gloucestershire', *M.G.H.* N.S., **3**, 1880, 194-7. Relating to the Harington family.

'Genealogical table shewing the descent of Harington of Somerset from the reign of Henry VIII to A. D. 1700 ... ', *M.G.H.* N.S., **4**, 1884, 190-6.

'George and Roger Harington, alderman of Bristol: were they members of the Kelston family?' *M.G.H.* N.S., **3**, 1880, 119-20. 17th c., includes wills.

'Harington of Corston in the county of Somerset', *M.G.H.* N.S., **4**, 1884, 274-7, 291-6 & 378-83. 18-19th c.

'Harington of Somerset, and Chetwynd of Ingestre, Staffordshire', *M.G.H.* N.S. **3**, 1880, 316-8 & 388-401. 16-18th c., includes pedigree of Chetwynd of Bristol.

'Notes upon the pedigree of John Harington of Stepney', *M.G.H.* N.S. **4**, 1884, 206-8. Notes on the estates of his wives, Etheldreda née Malte, and Isabella née Markham, in Somerset, Berkshire and Hertfordshire, 16th c.

'Pedigree of Harington, Co.Cornwall, and of Worden in Shebbear, Co.Devon', *M.G.H.* N.S. **3**, 1880, 333-6. 17-18th c. Includes notes on Rous of Landrake.

'Some notes on Devonshire families allied to Harington of Worden in Shebbear, viz, Yeo of Heanton and Shebbear, Gay (probably the poet's kindred), Somers of North Tawton, Brent of Newton St. Petrock and Shebbear', *M.G.H.* N.S., **3**, 1880, 364-8. Includes 17-19th c. extracts from parish registers.

'The genealogy of Harington', *M.G.H.* N.S. **3**, 1880, 436-8. Includes pedigree of Gostlett of Marshfield, Gloucestershire, 16-17th c.

'The genealogy of Harington of Kelston, Co. Somerset, resumed from A. D. 1700', *M.G.H.* N.S., **4**, 1884, 366-7.

'The Haringtons of North Devon, descending from those of Somerset', *M.G.H.* N.S., **3**, 1880, 333 & 346-8. 16-17th c., includes pedigree, entries from parish register of Shebbear, monumental inscriptions and parish register extracts relating to the family of Rous of Landrake, Cornwall.
The pedigree of the Harrington family (reprinted from an ancient book). Mitre Press, [195-?]. Extracts from parish registers.
'The political jeopardy of John Harington, esq., in 1660, and by what friends he was rescued from it', *M.G.H.* N.S., **4**, 1884, 33-6.
See also Bave, Gibbes, Gostlett, Horner and Rogers

Harnden
VIVIAN, A. 'The Harnden family', *D.F.H.* **9**, 1979, 14-16.

Harris
HARRIS, EDWARD M. 'Ottery St. Mary origin of Thomas Harris', *N.E.H.G.R.* **27**, 1973, 27-8. 17th c.
HARRIS, SUE. 'The Harris family', *Search: journal of the Banwell Society of Archaeology* **18**, 1982, 24-33. 19-20th c., of Banwell, Somerset.
MALMESBURY, EARL OF. 'Some anecdotes of the Harris family', *Ancestor* **1**, 1902, 1-27. 17-18th c. of Wiltshire.
POOL, ANNE. 'Harris of Kenegie', *Old Cornwall* **4**(7), 1948, 224-7. 17-19th c.

Harrison
'Extracts from the parish register of West Quantoxhead, Co. Somerset, relating to the family of Harrison', *Genealogist* **2**, 1878, 24-6.
See also Pitman

Hart
FAIRBROTHER, E.H. 'Hart family of West Dorset', *N.Q.S.D.* **12**, 1911, 167-9.

Hartland
PAGET, M. 'The Hartland pedigree', *C.K.L.H.S.B.* **7**, 1982, 13-15. 16-19th c.

Harvey
GORE, DAVID. *A Cornish inheritance: the Harveys of Chacewater.* Lower Basildon, Berks; David Gore, 1997. Not seen
HARVEY, G.H. *The Harvey families of Inishowen, Co.Donegal, and Maen, Co.Cornwall.* Folkestone: F. Weatherhead, 1927. Medieval-19th c., includes folded pedigrees.

HARVEY, C. 'Pedigree of Harvey of Maen in Cornwall', *M.G.H.* 3rd series **4**, 1902, 229-32; 4th series **4**, 1912, 167-70. 15-19th c.
VALE, EDMUND. *The Harveys of Hayle: engine builders, shipwrights, and merchants of Cornwall.* Truro: Bradford Barton for Harvey & Co., 1966. Includes pedigree, 17-19th c.
See also Martin and Mead

Harward
BRAGGE, N.W. 'Hayne House and the Harward family', *D.C.N.Q.* **30**, 1967, 270-4.

Haskell
HASKELL, WINTHROP ALLISON. 'English origins of the Haskell family', *N.E.H.G.R.* **138**, 1984, 223-7. Haskell of Charlton Musgrove, 16-17th c.
'Haskell', *G.T.* **13**(2), 1987, 57. Entries from a family bible relating to a Dorset family.

Haskett
MORIARTY, G. ANDREWS. 'Haskett: genealogical information concerning the Hasketts of Marnhull and elsewhere', *N.E.H.G.R.* **77**, 1923, 71-77 & 110-33; **78**, 1924, 54-63; **84**, 1931, 229-31, 273-86 & 433-5. Of Henstridge, 16-17th c., includes wills, parish register extracts, Chancery proceedings, lay subsidies, deeds, *etc.*, with wills of William Seavier, 1604, Mariane Sevier, 1607, John Hillier, 1619, and Katherine Sampson, 1627.

Hastings
LARKEN, GEOFFREY. 'The unknown cousin: Warren Hastings and Barbara Gardiner', *W.A.M.* **72/3**, 1980, 107-118. Includes pedigree showing relationship of Hastings and Gardiner, 17-18th c.

Hatch
'Memorials of the families of Hatch in Devonshire', *Genealogist* **1**, 1877, 313-20 & 368-75.
See also Audley

Hathaway
BLAKE-MIZEN, LINDSEY. 'Dwellers on the heathway', *F.F.* **23**, 1996, 21-5. Hathaway family of St. Briavels, medieval.

Haviland
See Daubeney and De Havilland

Hawker
OGGINS, VIRGINIA D., & OGGINS S. 'Some Hawkers of Somerset', *S.A.N.H.S.* **124**, 1979/80, 51-60. 11-13th c.

Hawkes
'Hawkes-Foster', *Genealogical quarterly* **41**, 1974-5, 107. Wiltshire families; pedigree, 18th c.

Hawkins
HAWKINS, MARY W.S. *Plymouth armada heroes: the Hawkins family, with original portraits, coats of arms and other illustrations,* Plymouth: William Brendon and Son, 1888. Includes folded pedigree, 16-19th c.

LEWIS, MICHAEL. *The Hawkins dynasty: three generations of a Tudor family.* Allen & Unwin, 1969. Includes some details of descendants.

JOHNSTONE, E. 'The Hawkins family of Trewithen', *C.F.H.S.J.* **37**, 1985, 14-16.

WILLOUGHBY, RUPERT. 'Hawkins of Abbotsbury, Portesham and Martinstown', *N.Q.S.D.* **33**(334), 1991, 58-77. Includes pedigree, 16-20th c.

Hawley
S. 'Does an heir to the barony of Hawley exist?', *Genealogist* **1**, 1877, 161-3. 17-18th c.

Hawthorne
'The Hawthorne family', *C.K.L.H.S.B.* **18**, 1987, 5. Includes pedigree, 16-18th c.

Hayden
HAYDEN, W.B. *The Haydens in England and America: a fragment of family history.* James Speirs, 1877. Of Norfolk, Watford, Devon, and the U.S.A; 13-19th c.

Haydon
HAYDON, N.W.J. 'Haydon family', *D.N.Q.* **2**, 1902-3, 96.

ROGERS, W.H.H. 'Haydon of Woodbury and Ottery St. Mary', *D.N.Q.* **1**, 1900-1, 225-40. Reprinted in his *Archaeological papers relating to the counties of Somerset, Wilts, Hants and Devon.* [ ]: The Author, 1902.

Hayman
W., E. 'Hayman family', *D.C.N.Q.* **9**(4), 1916, 119-20. Extracts from Totnes parish register, 16th c.

Hayne
'Hayne genealogical memoranda: Sherborne registers, Dorset', *M.G.H.* N.S., **4**, 1884, 290.

Haynes
POYNTON, F.J. 'The family of Haynes of Westbury-on-Trym, Wick and Abson, and other places in Gloucestershire', *B.G.A.S.T.* **9**, 1884-5, 277-97. See also **10**, 1885-6, 226-9. Includes pedigree, 15-18th c., wills, and monumental inscriptions.
See also De Boteville

Hayward
'Pedigree of Hayward', *M.G.H.* 3rd series **4**, 1902, 207. Gloucestershire, 18-19th c.
See also Crocker and Hopton

Heal
HEAL, AMBROSE, & HEAL, EDITH. *The records of the Heal family.* [ ]: privately printed, 1932. Primarily of Somerset and Dorset, includes folded pedigrees (in pocket) of Heal, 16-20th c., Standerwick of Gillingham, Dorset, and Gauntlett of Market Lavington; also monumental inscriptions, parish register extracts, wills, etc.

Hearle
HEARLE, DUNCAN. 'The Hearles of West Looe', *Old Cornwall* **8**, 1973-9, 23-5. 17-19th c.

Heath
DRAKE, WILLIAM RICHARD, SIR. *Heathiana: notes genealogical and biographical of the family of Heath, especially of the descendants of Benjamin Heath, D.C.L., of Exeter.* Privately printed, 1882.

Heathfield
See Elliott

Heane
HEANE, WILLIAM C. *Genealogical notes relating to the family of Heane.* Mitchell & Hughes 1887. Originally published *M.G.H.* 2nd series **2**, 167-8, 180-2 & 209-12. Gloucester family. Includes extracts from registers, monumental inscriptions, wills and pedigree, 17-19th c.

HEANE, WILLIAM C. 'The Heane family', *G.N.Q.* **3**, 1887, 232-3. Parish register extracts.

Heard
FULLER, JOHN FRANKLIN. 'Pedigree of Heard, formerly of Wilts, now of Co. Cork', *M.G.H.* 2nd series **4**, 1892, 209-14. 17-19th c.

Hearne
See Martyn

Heaven

LANGHAM, M. 'The Heaven family of Lundy, 1836-1916', *D.A.Tr.* **118**, 1986, 93-121.

LANGHAM, MYRTLE. *A Lundy album.* Reigate: the author, 1980. Heaven family; 19th c.

Heberden

WILKIN, W.H. 'Rev. Canon Thomas Heberden', *D.C.N.Q.* **16**, 1930-31, 272-4. Includes monumental inscriptions, 1843, and genealogical notes.

'Heberden pedigree', *Cricklade Historical Society bulletin* **10**, 1975, 5. 19-20th c.

Hector

See De Boteville

Hedges

See Lacy

Hellier

BROADLEY, A.M. 'Thomas Hellier of Whitchurch Canonicorum', *N.Q.S.D.* **13**, 1913, 108-10. Includes pedigree, 16-18th c.

Helyard

See Perne

Henbury

C., G.E.L. 'Henbury and Smith families', *D.C.N.Q.* **15**, 1928-9, 91-2. 18-19th c. entries from a family bible.

Hender

DAUBER, GAYLE & TIMSBURY, CHERYL. *The story of the Hender family.* Grovedale, Victoria: G. Dauber, 1992. Cover title: *The hammer and the anvil.* Of Cornwall and Australia.

Hendra

HENDRA, PETER. 'Eighteenth century connections: the Hendras of Gwinear', *C.F.H.S.J.* **16**, 1980, 10-11. Includes pedigree.

Henley

See Maynard

Henning

O., V.L. 'Henning family', *N.Q.S.D.* **21**, 1935, 10-12. 18th c.

SAYER, M.J. 'Pedigrees of county families, 4 & 5', *Genealogists magazine* **20**, 135 & 157-60.

Henville

DAVIS, F.N. 'The Henville family', *N.Q.S.D.* **15**, 1917, 287-9. Dorset family, 18-19th c.

Herbert

LEVER, TRESHAM. *The Herberts of Wilton.* John Murray, 1967. Includes pedigree, 16-20th c.

OLIVER, F.L. 'Heraldic glass of Wolfeton House, Dorset', *D.N.* 66, 1944, 76-83. Includes pedigrees of Herbert and Trenchard.

WORKMAN, TONY. 'The butcher, the baker and the milkman: a cautionary tale', *J.G.F.H.S.* **54**, 1992, 12-13. Herbert family, 19th c.

Hereford

HERFORD, A.F. 'The Hereford family of Plymouth', *Ancestor* **7**, 1903, 71-4.

'Hereford, Herford or Hurford family of Devonshire', *M.G.H.* N.S., **3**, 1880, 268. 15-18th c.

Herring

GENEALOGIST. 'John Herring', *W.A.* **4**, 1885, 263-4. Pedigree of Herring, 17-18th c.

Hervey

HARVEY, C. 'A pedigree showing that Francis Hervey, son of Anthony Hervey of Swarland, was rector of St.Breage in Cornwall', *M.G.H.* 4th series **4**, 1912, 165-70. Swarland, Northumberland; pedigree 16-17th c.

Heyron

KRAUSS, RUSSELL. 'John Heyron of Newton Plecy, Somerset', *Speculum* **10**(2), 1935, 187-9. 14th c.

Heyward

HEYWARD, RICHARD. *The Heyward family of Devon: a genealogy of descendants of the Heywards of Langstone in the parish of Manaton, Devon, England, and other Heyward families, 1580-1936, together with an account of the origin of the name.* Pasadena: Star-News, 1936.

Hicks

HICKS, JOHN. 'Researching the Hicks family', *C.F.H.S.J.* **9**, 1978, 13-17. Includes pedigree, 18-19th c.

HICKS BEACH, WILLIAM, MRS. *A Cotswold family: Hicks and Hicks Beach.* William Heinemann, 1909. 16-19th c.

HICKS, NORMAN. '"Budley" Hicks of Bodmin', *C.F.H.S.J.* **49**, 1988, 11-13. Includes pedigree, 18-19th c.

KILFOY, HELEN HICKS. *Hicks-Thurber family history: Robert and Zoe.* [United States]: [privately printed], 1982. Cornish-American family, 17-20th c.

POYNTON, FRANCIS J. 'A doubtful point in the genealogy of Hicks of Beverston as it appears in *Burkes peerage and baronage*', *B.G.A.S.T.* **11**, 1886-7, 260-5. Includes pedigree, 17-19th c.

RUVIGNY AND RAINEVAL, MARQUIS DE. 'The family of Hicks', *Genealogical magazine* **5**, 1901-2, 449-452, 501-7, & 538-45; **6**, 1902-3, 24-9.
'Some account of the later Hicks's of Stinchcombe', *G.N.Q.* **10**(87), 1913, 1-9.

Higgins
See Grenville

Higgons
See De Boteville

Highmore
HIGHMORE, N.J. 'Highmore family of Dorset', *N.Q.S.D.* **3**, 1893, 218-20.

Hill
ALEXANDER, J.J. 'The Hill pedigrees', *D.C.N.Q.* **15**, 1928-9, 220-1. See also 254-7 & 367-9.
BLACKMUN, SIDNEY T. 'The Hills of Eastington', *J.G.F.H.S.* **56**, 1993, 29. Brief note, 18-19th c.
HILL, T.S. 'Pedigree of the family of Hill', *M.G.H.* 2nd series **4**, 1892, 266-70. 17-19th c.

Hillersdon
HUMPHERY-SMITH, CECIL R. 'The Hillersdon roll', *D.C.N.Q.* **24**, 1950-51, 79-83.

Hillier
HORTON-SMITH, L.G.H. 'The Hillier family of Cirencester from 1635, together with the family of Parry, and supplement', *B.G.A.S.T.* **64**, 1943, 211-39. 17-20th c.
See also Haskett

Hinder
HODSDON, JAMES. *The Hinders of Minety and their descendants, 1840-1979.* Cheltenham: the author, 1979.

Hine
See Lane

Hingston
PRIDEAUX, W.F. 'Hingeston or Hingston family', *D.C.N.Q.* **6**, 1910-11, 164-7.
See also Fox

Hippisley
JONES, I. FITZROY. 'Hippisley, Northleigh, Sparkes, Toller and Tothill families', *D.C.N.Q.* **20**, 1938-9, 134-5. 17th c. extracts from a family bible.
JONES, I. FITZROY. 'Sir John Cox Hipisley', *Genealogists' magazine* **6**(11), 1934, 505-6.

Hippisley-Seaman
JEBOULT, EDWARD. *The Hippisley-Seaman family of Shiplette Manor, Bleadon, Somerset.* [Taunton?]: [the author?]. 1891.
See also Seaman

Hiscock
NOBLE, LEN. *Village folk: the Hiscocks: a Ramsbury family: experiments in oral history.* Locale series **4**. Trowbridge: Wiltshire County Council Library & Museum Service, 1990. 19-20th c.

Hoar
HOARD, LYON J. 'The English ancestry of Hezekiah Hoar of Taunton, Massachusetts', *N.E.H.G.R.* **141**, 1987, 222-33. Of Axminster, Sidmouth, *etc.*, 15-17th c.

Hoare
WOODBRIDGE, KENNETH. *Landscape and antiquity: aspects of English culture at Stourhead, 1718 to 1838.* Oxford: Clarendon Press, 1970. In part, a history of the Hoare family.
See also Hore

Hobbs
HOBBS, GRAHAM. 'Will the next ancestor sign in please ?' *J.G.F.H.S.* **59**, 1993, 16-17. Signatures of Hobbs family, originally of Kingsclere, Gloucestershire.

Hobhouse
HOBHOUSE, CHARLES PERCY. *Some account of the family of Hobhouse and reminiscences.* Leicester: Johnson Wykes & Co., 1909. Somerset family. Includes pedigree, 18-20th c.
HOBHOUSE, HENRY. *Hobhouse memoirs.* Taunton: Barnicott & Pearce, 1927. 14-20th c.

Hoblyn
'Armorial bookplates: Robert Hoblyn and Edward Hoblyn', *M.G.H.* N.S. **3**, 1880, 353. 18-19th c.

Hodges
'The Hodges family of Shipton Mayne', *G.N.Q.* **1**, 1881, 360-3. See also 455-7; **2**, 1884, 27, for wills, monumental inscriptions, *etc.*, 17th c.

Hodkins

BRADENEY, JOSEPH ALFRED. *Genealogical memoranda relating to the families of Hopkins of Llanfihangel Ystern Llewern, Co. Monmouth, and Probyn of Newland, Co. Gloucester.* Mitchell & Hughes, 1889. Includes pedigree, 17-18th c., parish register extracts, etc.

Hody

DILKS, T. BRUCE. 'The Hody family', *N.Q.S.D.* **24**, 1946, 22-5. 15th c.

'Notices of the family of Hody', *Collectanea topographica et genealogica* **6**, 1840, 22-31. Includes wills of John Hody of Pillesdon, Dorset, 1441, and of John Jewe, 1416.

Holberton

DAVY, J. 'The family of Holberton or Holbeton, Devon', *D.N.Q.* **2**, 1902-3, 89-97.

Holbrow

PHILLIMORE, W.P.W. *Some account of the family of Holbrow, of Kingscote, Uley and Leonard Stanley in Gloucestershire.* Phillimore & Co., 1901.

Holder

See Berkeley

Holdsworth

FREEMAN, RAY. *The contributions of the Holdsworth and Newman families to Dartmouth.* Dartmouth: Dartmouth History Research Group. [1992]. Originally published by Devon History Society, 1985. 18-19th c.

Holeway

'Holeway family', *D.C.N.Q.* **22**(5), 1943, 155-6. Extracts from 15th c. court roll.

Holland

LEGA-WEEKES, ETHEL. 'The Hollands of Bow Hill in St. Thomas's, Exeter', *D.C.N.Q.* **18**(7), 1935, 300-5.

Holman

HOLMAN, ALFRED LYMAN. 'John Holman and his descendents', *N.E.H.G.R.* **72**(287), 1918, 185-203; **72**(288), 1918, 286-311.

Holwell

DYMOND, R. 'Holwell family', *M.G.H.* N.S., **2**, 1877, 416-7. 18th-19th c.

GEARE, RALPH HOLWELL. 'Holwells of Bampton, Tiverton, Sampford Peverell and Bradninch', *D.C.N.Q.* **26**, 1954-5, 8-10.

GEARE, RALPH HOLWELL. 'Holwells of Woodbury', *D.C.N.Q.* **26**, 1954-5, 72-5. 16-18th c.

Honeybun

NEWNHAM, ZENA M. 'Did Thomas Hardy attend Gr. Gr. Grandfather's wedding', *J.D.F.H.S.* **5**(1), 1991, 31-2. Honeybun family; includes pedigree, 19th c.

Honeycombe

STEEL, DON. *Discovering your family history*, ed. Bryn Brooks. British Broadcasting Company, 1980. A basic textbook designed to complement a television service. Largely based on records relating to the Cornish Honeycombe family; includes pedigrees.

Hood

BARTELOT, R.G. 'The naval Hoods of Dorset and Somerset', *N.Q.S.D.* **17**, 1923, 23-39.

Hoode

HUDD, KEN. 'Was your Hoode ancestor a Crooke ? Or, what's in a name ?', *W.F.H.S.* **56**, 1995, 30-32. Hoode *alias* Crooke family, 16-18th c.

Hooke

TODD, FREDERICK W. *Humphrey Hooke of Bristol and his family and descendants in England and America during the seventeenth century.* New Haven: Tuttle, Morehouse & Taylor, 1938. Includes pedigree of Hooke, 15-17th c., also of Young 15-17th c., Gostlett, 16-17th c., and Scrope of Oxfordshire, 16-17th c., with Hooke wills, etc

Hooker

ALEXANDER, J.J. 'Ancestors of John Hooker', *D.C.N.Q.* **15**, 1928, 113-6. 14-16th c.

Hooper

H., R.P. 'Extracts from the registers of Salisbury Cathedral relating to the family of Hooper, of New Sarum and Boveridge', *Genealogist* N.S. **2**, 1885, 42. 16-17th c.

HOOPER, HILDA J. 'Hoper: origin of the name', *D.C.N.Q.* 18-20. See also 64, 92, & 118-9.

HOOPER, H.J. 'Hoper: a surname or an occupation?', *D.C.N.Q.* **21**(5), 1941, 212-3.

HOOPER, H.J. 'Hooper of Modbury', *D.C.N.Q.* **21**(7), 1941, 326-9.

See also Rawlins

Hopkins

HOPKINS, H. HANFORD. *Captain John Hopkins, mariner of Philadelphia and Bideford in Devon, and his alleged forebears and descendants: a narrative.* Baltimore: the author, 1977.

Hopton

HAINES, ROBERT J. 'The Hopton and Hayward families of Berkeley and Frocester', *J.G.F.H.S.* **57**, 1993, 12-15. 18th c.

RUTTON, W.L. 'Pedigree of Hopton of Suffolk and Somerset', *M.G.H.* 3rd series **3**, 1900, 9-12, 49-53, & 81-6.

Hore

HOARE, EDWARD. *Some account of the early history and genealogy, with pedigrees from 1330, unbroken to the present time, of the families of Hore and Hoare with all their branches ...* Alfred Russell Smith, 1883. Devon, London, and various other counties; includes pedigree, 17-19th c.

HOARE, RICHARD COLT, SIR. *Pedigrees and memoirs of the families of Hore of Rishford, Com. Devon; Hoare of Walton, Com. Bucks; Hoare of London, Com. Middlesex; Hoare of Stourton, Com. Wilts; Hoare of Barn-Elms, Com. Surrey, Hoare of Boreham, Com. Essex.* Bath: Richard Cruttwell, 1819. Includes pedigrees, medieval-19th c.

Hornblower

JENKINS, RHYS. 'Cornish engineers: the Hornblowers', *D.C.N.Q.* **11**, 1920, 10-17. 18-19th c.

Hornbrook

BUSH, THOMAS LLOYD, & BUSH, LOUISE HORNBROOK. *The times of the Hornbrooks: tracing a family tradition.* Cincinnati: General Printing Co., 1977. 15-20th c., of Devon and the United States.

Horneck

CLUER, B.R. 'The Horneck family of Plymouth, 1666-67', *D.C.N.Q.* **33**, 1974-7, 79-80.

Horner

'Family of Horner, Co. Somerset', *M.G.H.* N.S., **4**, 1884, 160-66. Includes pedigree, 16-19th c., wills, *etc.*
See also Fussell

Horsey

BROWN, F. 'Pedigrees from the visitation of Dorset, 1623: Horsey', *M.G.H.* 2nd. series **2**, 1888, 43-8. Includes wills.

BATTEN, JOHN. 'The Horsey family', *S.A.N.H.S.* **43**(2), 1897, 84-93.

WEBB, PETER. 'John Horsey of Martin and his kinsmen at the time of the dissolution of the monasteries: the triumphs and tribulations of a West Country family in the 1530s and 1540s', *Hatcher review* **3**(21), 1986, 10-22. Includes 15-16th c. pedigrees.

Hosford

HOSFORD, NORMAN F., & HOSFORD, DAVID H. *The Hosford genealogy: a history of the descendants of William Hosford, sometime resident of Beaminster, Dorsetshire, Dorchester, Massachusetts, Windsor, Connecticut and Calverleigh, Devonshire.* West Kennebunk: Phoenix Publications, 1993. Primarily of American interest, but includes useful West Country information, 16-17th c.

Hoskins

HOSKINS, WILLIAM. 'The early history of the Hoskyns of Beaminster', *N.Q.S.D.* **24**, 1946, 48-55. Includes 14-16th c. pedigree.
See also Parsons

Houlton

BOUCHER, R. 'Genealogical notes on the Houlton family', *W.N.Q.* **6**, 83-5, 110-13, 167-70, 211-13 & 270-72. 16-19th c., wills, etc., with pedigree, 17-18th c.

How

See Phillipps

Howard

MILLER, A.C. 'Lady Howard and her children', *D.A.Tr.* **102**, 1970, 87-104.
See also Fitz, Rowe and Stafford

Howell

NORGATE, MARTIN. 'George Howell, pipemaker, of Warminster', *W.A.M.* **79**, 1984, 243. 17-18th c.

Huchyns

See Tyndale

Hucks

See Gibbs

Huddesfield

See Rogers

Hugo

HUGO, FRANCIS.H.M. *A pedigree of the family of Hugo of St.Feock, Co.Cornwall.* Guernsey: Frederick Clarke, 1932. 16-19th c.

HUGO, FRANCIS H.M. 'Clan Hugo papers, I: a preliminary note on the surname Hugo in Devon and Cornwall', *D.C.N.Q.* 23(7), 1948, 205-12. Medieval.

HUGO, FRANCIS H.M. 'Clan Hugo papers, II: notes on minor Hugo branches', *D.C.N.Q.* 23, 1947-9, 391-5. Mainly 18-19th c.

HUGO, FRANCIS H.M. 'Clan Hugo papers, III: more minor Hugo branches', *D.C.N.Q.* 24, 1950-51, 49-52. See also 99-100. 16-19th c.

HUGO, FRANCIS H.M. 'Clan Hugo papers, IV: further minor Hugo branches', *D.C.N.Q.* 24, 1950-51, 186-90 & 209-11. See also 25, 1952-3, 203-4. 16-19th c.

HUGO, FRANCIS H.M. 'Hugos no Huguenots', *Notes & queries* 156, 1929, 4-7, 25-7 & 44-5. See also 68-9. Medieval-19th c.

Hull

HULL, ROBERT E. *The ancestors and descendants of George Hull (ca. 1590-1659) and Thamzen Michell, of Crewkerne, Somerset, Dorchester, Massachusetts, Windsor and Fairfield, Connecticut.* Baltimore: Gateway Press, 1994.

Humphrey

FITCHETT, PAULINE. *My dear brother: a family history: Humphrey, Delves, Cleaver.* Wellington, N.Z., P. E. Fitchett 1990. Families of Sussex, Devon and New Zealand, 19-20th c.

S[KINNER], A.J. 'Humphry family, Honiton', *D.C.N.Q.* 10, 1918, 56.

SKINNER, A.J. 'Ozias Humphry, A.R.A., F.S.A', *D.C.N.Q.* 11, 1920-21, 116-20. Humphrey pedigree, 16-18th c., with wills of George Humphry, 1759, and his widow Elizabeth, 1790.

Hungerford

DAVIS, E.L. *Is your name Hungerford? A short history of the famous Hungerford family, with references to the town of Hungerford in Berkshire and the township of Hungerford in Queensland, Australia.* Hungerford: the author, 1984. Berkshire, Wiltshire and Australia. 15-20th c.

FLETCHER, J.M.J. *The Hungerfords and their memorials, past and present: two lectures* ... Salisbury: Bennett Bros., [1936]. Medieval.

HOARE, RICHARD COLT, SIR. *Hungerfordiana, or, memoirs of the family of Hungerford.* [ ]: J. & R. Hungerford, 1981. Originally published Shaftesbury: Typis Rutterianis, 1823. Medieval-18thc.

JACKSON, J.E. 'On the Hungerford chapels in Salisbury Cathedral', *W.A.M.* 2(4), 1855, 83-99. Includes notes on medieval family.

KIRBY, J.L., ed. *The Hungerford cartulary: a calendar of the Earl of Radnor's cartulary of the Hungerford family.* Wiltshire Record Society 49. 1994. 15th c.

MILWARD-OLIVER, FREDERICK FRANCIS, MRS. *Memoirs of the Hungerford, Milward and Oliver families.* Privately published, 1930. Wiltshire families, medieval - 19th c.

W., J. 'Extracts from the registers of Welford, Berks., and Hungerford, and Bedwyn Parva, Wilts., chiefly relating to the family of Hungerford', *Collectanea topographica et genealogica* 5, 1838, 359-62.

WILMOT, E.A. EARDLEY. 'The Hungerford family of Windrush', *G.N.Q.* 1, 1881, 272-3. 16-18th c.

See also Botreaux and Molyns

Hunt

ATKINSON, D.R. 'Jeffry Hunt pipes', *W.A.M.* 66, 1971, 156-61. Hunt family of pipemakers, 17th c.

LEGA-WEEKES, E. 'Hunt family in Devonshire', *D.C.N.Q.* 9, 1916-17, 158.

Huntley

HUNTLEY, GORDON. 'The Huntley and Penny families of Wiltshire and Monmouthshire', *W.F.H.S.* 5, 1982, 22-3.

Hunton

See Goldesborough

Hurford

See Hereford

Hurll

WORDSWORTH, CHR. 'The conversion of Mary Hurll, lace-maker's apprentice at Marlborough, 1675, with her indentures, 21 June, 1671', *W.A.M.* 35(107), 1907, 103-13. Includes apprenticeship indentures.

Hussey

MAYO, C.H. 'The Hussey family of Marnhull, Dorset', *N.Q.S.D.* 15, 1917, 220-4.

SCANTLEBURY, R.E. 'The Husseys of Marnhull, Dorset', *Biographical studies* 2(1), 1953, 55-65. 17-18th c.

SMITH, CHRISTOPHER. 'The Husseys of Marnhull', *South Western catholic history* 2, 1984, 32-43. 17-19th c.

Hutchins

BOWER, H.B. 'Giles Hutchins, gent., M.P. for Salisbury', *M.G.H.* 5th series 7, 1929-31, 284. 16-17th c.

HUTCHINGS, JACK RANDOLPH. & HUTCHINGS, RICHARD JASPER. *Hugh Hutchins of old England: the history of the Hutchins families of the old and new worlds.* Baltimore: Gateway Press, 1984. Includes pedigrees, 16-20th c.

Hutchinson
JENNINGS, HELEN. 'A family named Hutchinson,' *Family history* 19(153), N.S., 129, 1997, 11-28; 19(154); N.S., 130, 1998, 56-67. To be continued. Of Lincolnshire, Devon and the United States, 16-20th c.

Huthnance
See Ridington

Huxtable
WHYBROW, C. 'Huxtable of Swincombe', *D.C.N.Q.* 30, 1965-7, 105-14.

Huyshe
ROGERS, W.H. HAMILTON. 'Huyshe of Somerset and Devon: a pedigree', in his *Archaeological papers relating to the counties of Somerset, Wilts, Hants and Devon.* [ ]: The Author, 1902. Reprinted from *S.A.N.H.S.* 43, 1897, 1-44. 12-19th c.

Hyde
HAMMOND, J.J. 'Notes on the Hydes of Wilts and Cheshire', *W.N.Q.* 6, 1908-10, 337-44, 385-90, 433-7 & 498-503; 7, 1911-13, 116-7 & 377-80. See also 7, 1911-13, 41-2, 96 & 160-61. Includes folded pedigree, 15-18th c.

JONES, W.H. 'Lord Clarendon and his Trowbridge ancestry', *W.A.M.* 9(27), 1862, 282-90. Includes pedigree of Hyde and Langford, 16-17th c.

'The Hyde family and Trowbridge', *W.N.Q.* 1, 1893-5, 156-9. See also 234. 17-18th c.

See also Mohun

Hylle
See Harington and Loryng

I'Ans
HARTMAN, LOIS I. *Remembered in this land.* Pasadena: House of Printing, 1978. Includes pedigrees, 17-20th c.

Inch
INCH, ARTHUR. 'The Inch clan: a history and analysis of the Inch clan in England and Wales from circa 1375-1981', *C.F.H.S.J.* 33, 1984, 10-11.

INCH, A.R. 'In search of the Inch clan', *C.F.H.S.J.* 2, 1976, 5-8. 19-20th c.

Ingoldsthorpe
See Botreaux

Ireland
See Clayfield-Ireland

Isaac
'Pedigree of Isaac of Westdown, etc., Co. Devon', *Genealogist* 4, 1880, 118-9. See also 120-1.

Isham
LONGDEN, H. I. 'Isham family of Somerset', *N.Q.S.D.* 1, 1890, 110-11. See also 139-40. 17th c.

LONGDEN, H.I. 'Isham family of Somerset', *N.Q.S.D.* 2, 1891, 317-8.

LONGDEN, H. I. 'Isham family of Somerset', *N.Q.S.D.* 3, 1893, 126-30. Includes wills of William Isham of Bodrugan, Cornwall, 1572, Thomas Isham, 1588, and Roger Isham, 1653, both of Bradon, Isle Brewers, John Isham of Langport-Eastover, 1675, and parish register entries from Edmonton, Middlesex.

LONGDEN, H. I. 'Isham family of Somerset', *N.Q.S.D.* 3, 1893, 221-3.

Ivie
'Ivie family', *W.N.Q.* 8, 1914-16, 286. Extracts from Malmesbury parish registers, 17th c.

Jackson
PLUMMER, JOHN. 'Two John Jacksons from Dartmouth, Devon', *N.E.H.G.R.* 144, 1990, 29-38. 16-17th c.

See also Raymond

Jacob
JACOB, HENRY W. *A history of the families of Jacob of Bridgwater, Tiverton and Southern Ireland.* Taunton: Wessex Press, 1929.

Jacobs
JOSEPH, Z. 'The Jacobs of Bristol, glassmakers to King George III', *B.G.A.S.T.* 95, 1977, 98-101. 18-19th c.

Jago
BRYANT, E.D.K.H. 'Jago of Gerrans, Gorran, and Mevagissey', *D.C.N.Q.* 15, 1929, 301-3. 17-18th c.

James
See Galpin

Janns
See Martin

Jaques
'[Jaques family]', *W.N.Q.* 1, 1893-5. 323-4. See also 130 & 529. 17-19th c.

Jason

MANLEY, F.H. 'Notes of the family of Jason of Broad Somerford', *W.N.Q.* **7**, 1911-13, 181-4, 241-5, 291-8, 361-5, 396-403 & 457-60. 16-18th c. Includes wills and pedigree, etc.

Jay

TAYLOR, J.C. 'Jay of Whitecliffe Park, Berkeley, Glos.', *M.G.H.* 5th series **6**, 1926-8, 212-3. Pedigree, 16-18th c.

Jelf(s)

JELF, LEONARD A. 'Research into Jelf/Jelfs', *J.G.F.H.S.* **61**, 1994, 15. Brief note on one-name research.

JELF, LEONARD A. 'More Jelf/Jelfs', *J.G.F.H.S.* **69**, 1996, 11-12. Brief note, 18th c.

'James Jelf, 1763-1842', *J.G.F.H.S.* **55**, 1992, 12-14; **56**, 1993, 15-17; **57**, 1993, 17-19.

Jellard

See Bulley

Jenkin

JENKYN, A.W. *Jenkyn - exclusively Cornish.* Amesbury: the author, 1987. Medieval-18th c., includes many wills, etc.

PHILLIPS, RUTH M. 'Jenking family', *D.C.N.Q.* **31**, 1968-70, 251. 19th c.

Jenkinson

DENNY, HENRY LYTTLETON LYSTER. *The manor of Hawkesbury and its owners.* Gloucester: J. Bellows, 1920. Jenkinson family, 16-20th c., includes pedigree.

Jenner

FYNMORE, R.J. 'Jenner, of Gloucestershire and Wiltshire,' *G.N.Q.* **10**, 1914, 49-59. Includes pedigree, 18-19th c.

Jennings

JENNINGS, H.R. 'The Jennings family in Cornwall', *Old Cornwall* **4**, 1943-50, 284-7 & 316-9. Mainly 17-19th c.

See also Knight

Jerningham

BERGIN, MICHAEL. 'The Jerninghams and Painswick,' *Gloucestershire and North Avon Catholic History Society journal* **15**, 1990, 2-7. 16-19th c.

LANGSTON, J.N. 'The Jerninghams of Painswick,' *B.G.A.S.T.* **83**, 1964, 99-118. 16-18th c.

Jerrard

JERRARD, FREDERICK BARTHOLOMEW JOSEPH. *The Jerrard family and its Chideock branch.* Lymington: King, 1912.

See also Bulley

Jessop

COLBY, DR., & RYLANDS, J.P. 'Pedigrees from the visitation of Dorset, 1623', *M.G.H.* 2nd. series **2**, 1888, 312-3. Includes Jessop and Martin.

Jesty

WALLACE, E. MARJORIE. *The first vaccinator: Benjamin Jesty of Yetminster and Worth Matravers and his family.* Wareham: Anglebury-Bartlett, 1981. 18-19th c.

Jewe

See Hody

Job

JOB, ROBERT BROWN. *John Job's family: a story of his ancestors and successors and their business connections with Newfoundland and Liverpool, 1730-1953.* 2nd. ed. St. Johns, Newfoundland: Telegram Printing, 1954. Also of Devon.

Johnson

MONEY, WALTER. 'The family of James Johnson, successively Bishop of Gloucester and Worcester,' *B.G.A.S.T.* **8**, 1883-4, 324-41. Includes pedigree, 17-19th c., with monumental inscriptions.

MONEY, WALTER. 'The family of James Johnson, successively Bishop of Gloucester and Worcester', *B.G.A.S.Tr.* **9**, 1884-5, 356-7. Pedigrees of American branch of the family, 18th c.

See also Colby

Jolliffe

JOLLIFFE, JEAN SAXE. *Richard Jolliffe and his descendents, 1800-1980: from Tremaine Parish, Cornwall, England to Palmyra, Wisconsin.* Brookfield, Wisconsin: [ ], 1980.

Jones

MORIARTY, G. ANDREWS. 'Genealogical research in England: Jones', *N.E.H.G.R.* **81**, 1927, 488-92; **82**, 1928, 55-63. Of Bridgwater. 16th c., includes wills, parish register extracts, deeds, etc.

See also Matthews

Jordan

SALE, J. 'The Jordan family of Withy Holt', *C.K.L.H.S.B.* **20**, 1988, 37-9. 19-20th c.

SOUTHALL, J.P.C. 'Miss Cicely Jordon of Dorsetshire in England', *Virginia magazine of history & biography*, **54**(4), 1946, 340-1. Notes on the family of Samuel Jordan, early 17th c.

See also Mortimer

Julian

MALCOLM, MADGE. *The Julian jigsaw.* Taranaki, New Zealand: Julian Re-Union Committee, 1987. Of Cornwall and New Zealand; includes pedigrees, 17-20th c.; also pedigrees of related families.

See also Ridington

Karslake

WILKIN, W.H. 'A clerical family', *D.C.N.Q.* **16**, 1930-31, 316-9. See also **17**, 1932-3, 128. 17-19th c.

Keats

See Pitman

Keene

LOXTON, N.. & PARKER, R. 'The Bennett-Keene papers', *Search: journal of the Banwell Society of Archaeology* **14**, 1978, 4-23. Includes pedigree of Keene, 17-20th c.

See also Bennett

Kekewich

CARTER, WILLIAM FOWLER. 'The name and family of Kekewich', *Genealogist* **6**, 1882, 8-11. 14-15th c.

CARTER, WILLIAM FOWLER. 'The Kekewich family', *Genealogist* N.S. **26**, 1910, 8-15 & 72-82. 15-16th c., includes extracts from Chancery proceedings.

Kelland

GENEALOGIST. 'Kelland of Kelland', *W.A.* **4**, 1885, 264-5. Extracts from Totnes parish register, 16-17th c.

O'REILLY, DAVE. 'Kellands of Somerset', *Kelland family* **6**, 1991, 162-5. Mainly extracts from 19th c. census returns.

STANLEY, MICHAEL. *Kelland/Kellond family charts: South Devon.* Walsall: Kelland/Kellond Family Circle, 1997.

STANLEY, MICHAEL. *Mid-Devon Kelland family charts.* Kelland/Kellond Family Circle, 1996.

Kelland family. London: June Bennett, 1988- . Includes many useful articles not otherwise mentioned here. There is a separate index for vols. 1-5, 1988-90.

Kelland & Kellond families: register of members interests. London: June Bennett, 1991.

See also Clarke

Kelly

O'DONNELL, JENNY. 'The Kelly family', *C.F.H.S.J.* **40**, 1986, 24-5. 18-19th c.

Kemp/Kempe

HITCHIN-KEMP, FRED. *A general history of the Kemp and Kempe families of Great Britain and her colonies ...* Leadenhall Press, 1902. Of Kent, Hampshire, Norfolk, Suffolk, Essex, Middlesex, Cornwall, Staffordshire, Sussex, *etc.* Includes pedigrees, medieval-19th c.

KEMP, GEORGE EDWARD. *Kemps of Ollantigh and Kemps of Poole: being a brief outline of the ancient Kemp family of Olantigh manor, Wye, Kent County, and a brief history of the Kemp family of Poole, Dorset, England, and some of the descendants in the United States.* Seattle: McKay Printing Co., 1939.

KEMPE, JOHN. *A family history of the Kempes.* Stanford: Peter Spiegl & Co., 1991. Of Cornwall, London, Australia, etc., medieval-20th c.

Kempthorne

See Ley

Kenrick

KENRICK, W. BYNG, ed. *Chronicles of a nonconformist family: the Kenricks of Wynne Hall, Exeter, and Birmingham.* Birmingham: Cornish Bros., 1932.

Kent

KENT, GEORGE. *The Kents on the hop, 1381-1989: a family story.* Cambridge: the author, 1989. Gloucestershire family.

'Kent of Boscombe', *W.N.Q.* **6**, 1908-10, 431; **7**, 1911-13, 228-35. See also **6**, 1908-10, 238 & 431-2. 17th c., includes wills.

Kerr

KERR, RUSSELL J. *A history of the family of Kerr, of the House, Newnham, Gloucestershire, which is descended from the houses of Ferniehurst and of Ancrum.* Gloucester: John Bellows, 1923.

Kerslake

BAYLEY, A.R. 'Sidbury, Devon', *D.N.Q.* **1**, 1900-1, 132. Murder of Richard Kerslake, 1664.

Kestell

CORNISH, VAUGHAN. *Kestell, Clapp & Cornish: records of homelife and travel.* Sifton Praed, 1947. Of Salcombe Regis, 17-20th c.

Keynes

GIBBON, R. G. 'The Keynes family in Somerset and Dorset', *N.Q.S.D.* **30**, 1974-79, 104-5.

Kidman

KIDMAN, T.H.F. *Kidman family history.* Cirencester: the author, 1984. Of Whitminster, Gloucestershire, *etc.* Includes many pedigrees.

Killigrew

WORTH, R.N. 'The family of Killigrew', *J.R.I.C.* **3**(12), 1871, 269-82. 17th c.

WORTH, R.N. 'The Killigrew Bible', *M.G.H.* N.S. **1**, 1874, 370-1. 17th c.

King

KING, CAMERON H. 'English records of the King family of Suffield, Conn.', *N.E.H.G.R.* **58**, 1904, 347-8. Extracts from Ivybridge parish registers, 16-17th c.

KING, EDWIN JAMES. *Records of the family of King, formerly of Leigh-upon-Mendip, Somerset.* Privately printed, 1937.

KING, RUFUS. 'Extracts from English parish registers relating to King and Haines families', *N.E.H.G.R.* **43**, 1889, 256-7. Somerset and Oxfordshire, 16-17th c.

LAMBOURNE, MURIEL. 'There's a good time coming: the King family from Bristol to Melbourne, 1854/7', *J.B.A.* **82**, 1995, 18-20.

M[AYO], C.H. 'King entries in the Sherborne register', *N.Q.S.D.* **3**, 1893, 144-6.

M[AYO], C.H. 'King of West Hall, Dorset', *N.Q.S.D.* **3**, 1893, 137-43. See also 260.

POOLE, H.J. 'King entries in the Stowell register', *N.Q.S.D.* **3**, 1893, 260-1.

'Memoranda relating to the family of King: Sherborne registers (Dorset)', *M.G.H.* N.S., **4**, 1884, 264-6. Extracts from the parish register.

'Memoranda relating to the family of King, Castle Cary registers (Somerset)', *M.G.H.* N.S., **4**, 1884, 346-50.

Kingdon

KINGDON, F.B. *The Kingdon family.* Stanley Press, 1932. Of Devon, medieval-20th c., includes pedigrees.

KINGDON, A.S. *The Kingdon family: a second look.* 2nd ed. Privately published, 1974. Also supplements, 1975 and 1977. Includes pedigrees.

Kingscote

POTTER, ARTHUR KINGSCOTE. 'The Kingscote of Kingscote', *Local history bulletin* **49**, 1984, 3-6. Brief note, 12-19th c.

See also Berkeley.

Kingsley

HUXLEY, ELSPETH. *The Kingsleys: a biographical anthology.* George Allen & Unwin, 1973. Mainly their writings, but includes biographical notes.

See Martin

Kingston

See Lisle

Kipling

JACKSON, RALPH. 'The Lockwood Kiplings at Tisbury, Wiltshire', *Hatcher review* **2**(16), 1983, 278-84. 19th c.

Kirch

See Rudman

Kirkham

ALEXANDER, J.J. 'Blagdon and the Kirkhams', *D.C.N.Q.* **17**, 1932-3, 106-11. 13-17th c., also Dennis, 13th c.

Kirton

REID, R.D. 'A local fragment', *Somerset year book* **37**, 1938, 98-102. Kirton family; includes pedigree, 18-19th c.

Kitson

COZENS, D.H. 'The Kitson diaries', *D.C.N.Q.* **33**, 1974, 3-9, 73-7, 120-24 & 159-65. Includes pedigree, 17-19th c.

KITSON, J.L. 'Kitson family', *N.Q.S.D.* **17**, 1923, 194-7. See also 225.

Knapp

MOODY, ROBERT. *An account of the Knapp family of Gloucestershire and their descendants.* [ ]: the author, 1964. Includes pedigree, 16-20th c.

Knatchbull

See Brydges

Knevett

L., C.E. 'Funeral certificate of Sir Henry Knevett and his lady', *Topographer and genealogist* **1**, 1846, 469-73. 1598.

Knight

CIMA, B.M. 'The Knights of Cannington and Axminster', *E.C.A. [English catholic ancestor] journal* **2**(2), 1986, 35-7. Includes pedigree, 17-20th c.

HALL, I.V. 'The connexions between John Knight, Junior, and the Jennings, Latch and Gorges families, 1641-1653', *B.G.A.S.T.* **74**, 1955, 188-99.

HALL, I.V. 'The connexions between John Knight, Jnr., and the Parsons and Jennings families, 1641-79', *B.G.A.S.T.* **70**, 1951, 119-25.

HALL, I.V. 'John Knight Junior, sugar refiner at the Great House on St. Augustine's Back (1654-1679): Bristol's second sugar house', *B.G.A.S.T.* **68**, 1949, 110-64. Includes pedigrees of Challoner, Knight and Cary, 16-17th c.

See also Nicholas

Knipe

WILLIAMS, J. ANTHONY. 'The decline of a recusant family: the Knipes of Semley', *W.A.M.* **59**, 1964, 170-80. See also *E.C.A. [English Catholic Ancestor] journal* **2**(4), 1987, 79-86. 17-19th c.

Knolles

See Lower

Knott

SCHURMAN, GLORIA KNOTT. *William Knott of Ashburton, Devon England: the history of the Knott family and related families.* Ferndale, Michigan: the author, 1995. 18-20th c., also of the United States.

Lacy

CRAIG, ALGERNON TUDOR. 'Pedigree of Lacy *alias* Hedges of Alderton, Wilts', *M.G.H.* 5th series **2**, 1916-17, 84-9. 16-19th c.

Laity

RUSCH, FRANCES DENEEN. *The ancestors and descendents of Ralph Laity of Bostrase Farm, St. Hilary, Cornwall.* Wauwatosa, Wisconsin: [ ], 1992.

Lake

W., J. 'Family and arms of Lake', *W.A.* **3**, 1884, 45-6.

See also De Boteville

Land

MOZLEY, A. 'The Land family of Woodbeare Court, Plymtree', *D.A.Tr.* **23**, 1891, 215-24.

Landrey

GREGORY-SMITH, T.G. 'The Landreys & the Carew Arms, Sheviock', *C.F.H.S.J.* **60**, 1991, 21-22. 18-19th c.

Lane

HALL, I.V. 'Temple St. Sugar House under the first partnership of Richard Lane and John Hine (1662-78)', *B.G.A.S.T.* **76**, 1957, 118-40. Includes pedigrees of Lane, 16-18th c., and Hine, 17-18th c.

JONES, I. FITZROY. 'Note: John Lane, Chancellor of Lichfield', *S.A.N.H.S.* **93**, 1947, 135-6. Notes on several 15th c. Somerset clergymen of this name.

Laney

POWELL, DAVID, & BRYDON, MARY. 'The Laney family of Banwell', *Search: journal of the Banwell Society of Archaeology* **21**, 1985/6, 27-37; **22**, 1987, 39-57. Includes pedigrees, 18-20th c., of Banwell, Somerset.

Lang

'Lang family of Devon', *Notes & queries* **170**, 1936, 429. Extracts from parish registers.

Langdon

LANGDON, A.T. 'A Cornish royalist family in the seventeenth century', *D.C.N.Q.* **25**, 1952-3, 89-93 and 116-20. Langdon family.

Langford

FERRIS, J.P. 'The Langford inheritance', *N.Q.S.D.* **29**, 1974, 2-4, 25-7, 52-4, 86-7, & 106-7.

OLIVER, V.L. 'Langford of Trowbridge, Co. Wilts', *W.N.Q.* **3**. 1899-1901, 426-7. Extracts from parish register, 16-17th c.

'Langford family', *W.N.Q.* **1**, 1893-5, 166. Brief note, 14-18th c.

See also Hyde

Langley

COSS, PETER R. *The Langley family and its cartulary: a study in late medieval 'gentry'.* Dugdale Society occasional papers, **2**. Stratford-Upon-Avon: the Society, 1974. Includes pedigree, 13-15th c., of Warwickshire and Gloucestershire.

Langmead

See Cock

Langton

DAVIS, GRAHAM P. *The Langtons at Newton Park.* Bath: Fyson & Co., 1976. Includes pedigree, 17-19th c.

Langworthy

LANGWORTHY, JOHN U. 'The Langworthy family of the South Hams and Rhode Island', *Kingsbridge History Society recorder* **3**, 1990, 7-10. 17-18th c.

Lanyon
'The Lanyons of Lanyon, Madron: an incident in the family history', *Old Cornwall* **6**, 1961-7, 319-20. See also **8**, 1973-9, 562-6. Medieval.

Larpent
WOODS, IVY M. 'What's in a name?', *Devon historian* **31**, 1985, 14-15.

Latch
See Knight

Laurence
'Laurence pedigree', *M.G.H.* **1**, 1868, 199-211. Of Lancashire, Dorset, Cambridgeshire, Somerset, Gloucestershire, London and Buckinghamshire; medieval-17th c.

Lavor
PITMAN, H. A. 'Henry Pitman, chirurgeon to the Duke of Monmouth', *N.Q.S.D.* **21**, 1935, 104-6. Includes pedigree of Lavor, 17th c.

Law
See Turner

Lawdy
LODEY, JOY. 'Lawdy! Lodey!' *Family tree magazine* **9**(3), 1993, 15-16. 16-20th c.

Lawrence
DURNING-LAWRENCE, EDITH J. *Family history of the Lawrences of Cornwall.* Truslove and Bray, 1915. 18-19th c.
LAWRENCE, RICHARD GWYNNE. 'The Lawrence family, of Bourton-on-the-Water', *G.N.Q.* **2**, 1884, 15-17. 17-18th c.
'Lawrence genealogy', *M.G.H.* **1**, 1868, 232-7. Gloucestershire; 16-19th c.
'Lawrence pedigree, from the visitation of Dorsetshire, 1565-1623', *M.G.H.* **1**, 1868, 201.
'Lawrence pedigree, from the visitation of the county of Somerset, 1623', *M.G.H* **1**, 1868, 203.
See also Paulet and Poulett

Lea
LEA, JAMES HENRY, & LEA, GEORGE HENRY. *The ancestry and posterity of John Lea, of Christian Malford, Wiltshire, and of Pennsylvania in America, 1503-1906.* Philadelphia: Lea Bros., 1906.

Leach
STEPHENS, WILLIAM. 'Leach family', *D.C.N.Q.* **6**, 1910-11, 42-3. 17th c., of St.Eval.

Leachland
MORIARTY, G. ANDREWS. 'Genealogical research in England: Leachland', *N.E.H.G.R.* **81**, 1977, 320-23 & 486-7; **82**, 1928, 63-5. Of Taunton and Colyton, *etc.,* 16-17th c., includes wills and parish register extracts, lay subsidies, Chancery proceedings, etc.

Leaker
RENDELL, S.D., & RENDELL, J.N. 'A name on the war memorial', *Search: journal of the Banwell Society of Archaeology* **17**, 1983, 48-51. Leaker family of Banwell, Somerset, 19-20th c., includes pedigree.

Leaman
PEARCE, MAUREEN & PEARCE, MALCOM. *Routes from Devon: a Leaman trail.* Chesterfield: M & M Pearce, 1992. Includes pedigrees, 18-20th c.

Lean
KENT, ALAN. 'Sir John Maclean, K.B., F.S.A., 1811-1895', *C.F.H.S.J.* **67**, 1993, 28-9. Discussion of Lean and Maclean genealogy, medieval-19th c.

Legg
MONK, MURIEL. 'The Leggs of Sandford Orcas', *G.T.* **15**(3), 1990, 89. Pedigree, 18-20th c.

Leigh
DENNISON, SHEILA. 'Nympsfield and the Leigh family', *Gloucestershire & North Avon Catholic History Society journal* **13**, 1990, 4-13. 19-20th c
'The visitation of the county of Cornwall ... 1620', *M.G.H.* **1**, 1868, 12-13. Pedigree of Leigh.
See Parker 1868.

Leighton
See De Boteville

Leir
'The Priory, Ditcheat, Somerset: a family and architectural history', *Transactions of the Ancient Monuments Society* N.S., **24**, 1980, 75-125. Home of the Leir family, 18-20th c.

Lethaby
WEST, W.R. 'The indomitable Lethabys', *Wesley Historical Society (Plymouth and Exeter District branch) proceedings* **1**(9), 1966, 145-62. 18-19th c.

Lethbridge
B[RUSHFIELD], T.N. 'Regnar Lothbrog the Dane and his Devonshire descendants', *D.N.Q.* **1**, 1900-1, 214-8. See also 255.

LETHBRIDGE, ROPER, SIR. *The Lethbridges: A Devonshire clan.* Exeter: Southwood & Co., 1900. Includes a 'calendar of Lethbridge papers preserved at Exbourne Manor'.
WEST, W.R. 'The indomitable Lethabys', *Wesley Historical Society (Plymouth and Exeter District Branch): Proceedings*, 1(9), 1966, 145-62. 18-19th c.
Royal descents of Sir John Hesketh Lethbridge, of Sandhill Park, Co. Somerset. John Camden Hotten, 1871.

Leversage
See Bampfylde

Levet
COLBY, DR., & RYLANDS, J.P. 'Pedigrees from the visitation of Dorset, 1623', *M.G.H.* 2nd series **2**, 1888, 354-5. Levet and Lovell families.

Leweston
BARTELOT, R. GROSVENOR. '[Leweston pedigree]', *N.Q.S.D.* **25**, 1950, 60. 15-16th c.

Lewis
WILKIN, W.H. 'Lewis of Honiton: a scholastic family', *D.C.N.Q.* **19**, 1936-7, 29-30. See also 322-3.

Ley
BOASE, C.W. 'The Leys of Beerferris and old Plymouth', *W.A.* **3**, 1884, 76 & 83-4.
MARTYN, W.W. 'Notes on the family of Ley in Beer Ferrers', *W.A.* **4**, 1885, 112-4. Pedigree, 17-19th c., of Ley alias Kempthorne of Kempthorne in Devon, and Tonacombe, Morwenstow, Cornwall, 15-19th c.
SKINNER, RAYMOND J. 'The declaracion of Ley: his pedigree', *D.C.N.Q.* **37**(2), 1992, 58-64; **37**(3), 1993, 101-6. Ley family; 17th c. account of the medieval family history.

Lidstone
LIDSTONE, HUGH R.G. *Lidstone of the South Hams of Devon.* Plymouth: Lidstone Family History Society, 1989. Medieval-20th c.
The Lidstorian. Plymouth: Lidstone Family History Society, 1978-

Linley
BLACK, CLEMENTINA. *The Linleys of Bath.* New ed. M. Secker, 1926. Reprinted Frederick Muller, 1971. 18-19th c.

Lisle
NORRIS, H. 'George Lisle of Compton D'Urville', *N.Q.S.D.* **3**, 1893, 84-8. Includes genealogical information.

ROGERS, W.H. HAMILTON. 'Lisle-Kingston-Lisle, of Wodeton, Isle of Wight, Thruxton, Hants and of Wilts and Dorset', in his *Archaeological papers relating to the counties of Somerset, Wilts, Hants and Devon.* [ ]: the author, 1902.

Litelcote
MORRIS, G.F.W. 'Litelcote, Coplestone and Morris families', *D.N.Q.* **1**, 1900-1, 188-9.

Little
LITTLE, E. CARUTHERS. *Our family history.* Gloucester: John Bellows, 1892. Little family: includes notes on Palling, Carruthers, Butler and White families.

Littleton
'Armorial bookplates: Littleton of Cornwall', *M.G.H.* N.S. **4**, 1884, 166. 15-17th c.

Livingstone
See Pearce

Lloyd
SLEE, JOHN. 'Seven generations of the Lloyd family of masons', *Commmorative art* **34**, 1967, 147-9. Of Great Bedwyn.

Lobb
ELAND, G.E. *The Lobb family from the sixteenth century.* Oxford University Press, 1953.
LOBB, DOUGLAS. *Lobbery: 20,000 Lobbs around the world.* 2 vols to date. Truro: Lobb Genealogical Records, 1992-5. Originally of Cornwall. Extensive.

Lochhead
LOCHHEAD, J. *A reach of the river: a family chronicle, 1880-1954.* Gillingham: Blackmore Press, 1955. Dorset family

Lockett
LOCKETT, R. CYRIL. 'Family of Lockett', *N.Q.S.D.* **90**, 1905, 61-5. See also 114. Of Somerset, Dorset, Devon, and Cornwall.

Loders
EAGERS, K. 'The Loders', *G.T.* **13**(2), 1988, 47.

Lodey
See Lawdy

Long
CHITTY, WALTER. *Historical account of the family of Long of Wiltshire.* Gilbert and Rivington, 1889. Includes pedigree, 17-19th c.

LONG, L.H. 'Long family of Exeter', *D.C.N.Q.* 23(5), 1948, 155.
LONG, WILLIAM. 'Long of Wraxall, Draycote, &c., Co. Wilts.', *M.G.H.* 2nd series 3, 1880, 58(f). Folded pedigree, 15-19th c.
'Long of Semington, Trowbridge, Whaddon, Monkton, &c., Co. Wilts; Beckington, Stratton and Downside, Co. Somerset', *M.G.H.* N.S., 3, 1880, 396 (insert). 16-18th c.
'Pedigree of the Longs of Semington: Rood Ashton and Preshaw branches', *M.G.H.* N.S. 2, 1880, 46(f). Preshaw, Hampshire. 16-19th c.

Longden
LONGDEN, H. ISHAM. 'Longden family of Gloucester', *G.N.Q.* 3, 1887, 36-7, 214-6, and 244-6.
LONGDEN, HENRY ISHAM. 'Pedigree of Longden', *M.G.H.* 3rd series 3, 1900, 101-8. Of Gloucestershire, London, *etc.*, 17-19th c.
LONGDEN, H. ISHAM. 'The family of Longden', *G.N.Q.* 5, 1894, 230-33. 17-18th c.

Longe
DIGHTON, CONWAY. 'Longe of Ashelworth', *G.N.Q.* 10, 1904, 22-6. Extracts from the parish register, 1566-1674.

Longuespee
QUIRQ, ROGER. The Longuespee family', *Friends of Salisbury Cathedral* 17, 1947, 11. Medieval.

Lory
SHEPHERD, LETTA LORY. *The Lorys of Cornwall.* Ann Arbor: Edwards Brothers, 1962. Medieval-20th c.

Loryng
GREENFIELD, B.W. *Pedigree of Sir Nigel Loryng, K.G., and Hylle of Spaxton, with references, wills, etc.* Mitchell and Hughes, 1883. 14-15th c.

Lovel
BAIN, J. 'The Lovels of Castle Cary and Hawick', *Genealogist* N.S., 4, 1887, 214-5.
LANDON, L. 'The Lovels of Castle Cary', *N.Q.S.D.* 18, 1926, 173-6. 12th c.

Lovering
See Goddard

Lower
'The visitation of the countie of Cornwall, 1620', *M.G.H.* 2, 1876, 18. Pedigrees of Lower, 17th c., and Knolles, 15-17th c.
'Lower of Trelask', *M.G.H.* 1, 1868, 266. Pedigree, medieval-17th c.
See also Leigh

Ludlow
BAYNE, WILLIAM WILFRID. 'The Ludlows of Hill Deverill', *Virginia magazine of history and biography* 54(3), 1946, 255-7.
'Certified pedigree of Ludlow, of Hill Deverill, Co. Wilts', *W.A.M.* 26(77), 1892, 173. Folded pedigree, 15-19th c.
Pedigree of Ludlow of Hill Deverill, Co. Wilts. Privately printed, [1897].
MAYO, C.H. 'Ludlow of Chipping Sodbury', *G.N.Q.* 5, 1894, 443-5. Includes extracts from parish registers etc.

Lupus
TAYLOR, THO. 'Lupus', *Ancestor* 5, April 1903, 224-5. Medieval.

Lush
HULL, ROBERT E. *The Lush family history: the descendents of Edmund Lush of East Knoyle, Wiltshire, England; married March 1717/18, Elizabeth Eliot. Descendants now living in Australia, Canada, and the United States of America.* Baltimore: Gateway Press, 1987.
LUSH, GORDON J. *Lush of Hazelbury Bryan.* Ferndown: the author, 1995. 18th-20th c.

Luttrell
Mohun

Luxmoore
LUXMOORE, CHAS. F.C. *The family of Luxmoore.* Exeter: William Pollard & Co., 1909. Includes wills, deeds, pedigrees, etc., mainly 17-19th c.

Luxton
CORNWELL, JOHN. *Earth to earth: a true story of the lives and violent deaths of a Devon farming family.* Harmondsworth: Penguin, 1982. Luxton family; includes pedigree, 18-20th c.

Lyddon
HOBBS, K.M., et al. *The Lyddons of Twitchen.* [ ]: [the author], 1990. 19-20th c.

Lyde
CAUNTER, F. LYDE. *Lyde records.* Solicitors' Law Stationery Society, 1933.

Lyne
LYNE, ROBT. EDWIN. 'The Lyne family, of Little Compton', *G.N.Q.* 2, 1884, 34-7.

Lyne-Glubb

MCCORMACK, E.E. 'History of the Lyne-Glubb family', *Old Cornwall* **7**, 1973, 491-8.

Lyons

PAUL, ROLAND W. 'The arms of Lyons of Long Ashton, Somerset', *Proceedings of the Clifton Antiquarian Club* **6**, 1908, 208-15.

Lysons

GLOCESTRIENSIS. 'The Lysons Family', *G.N.Q.* **2**, 1884, 533-5.

GRAY, IRVINE. 'The Lysons family', *B.G.A.S.T.* **81**, 1962, 212-3. Includes pedigrees, 16-20th c.

MESSAM, W. 'The Lysons family connection with Rodmorton', *Local History bulletin* **39**(actually **41**), 1980, 5-8. 18-19th c.

Lyte

GEORGE, WILLIAM. *Lytes Cary manor house, Somerset, and its literary associations, with notices of authors of the Lyte family, from Queen Elizabeth to the present time.* Bristol: William George, [188-?]

LYTE, H.C. MAXWELL. *The Lytes of Lytescary.* Taunton: Barnicott & Pearce, 1895. Reprinted from *S.A.N.H.S.* **38**(2), 1892, 1-100. For Supplement, see **77**(2), 1931, 115-35. Includes pedigree.

Mabbutt

See Merryweather

Mace

MACE, CHARLES A. 'Mace family', *Notes and queries* 12th series **11**, 1922, 156-7. See also **150**, 1926, 410. Parish register extracts.

Maddeford

PERROTT, TERRY. *Notes on the Maddeford family of South Devon and South Australia.* Canberra: T. Perrott, 1982.

Machen

MACHEN, H.A. 'The Machen family, Gloucestershire', *B.G.A.S.T.* **64**, 1943, 96-112. Includes pedigree, 16-20th c.

Maffey

DAVIS, F.N. 'Maffey family', *N.Q.S.D.* **18**, 1926, 233-5. 18-19th c. Of Dorset and Wiltshire.

Main

See Bond

Mainwaring

BUCK, H.M. 'Oliver Mainwaring', *D.C.N.Q.* **5**, 1908-9, 50-62, & **9**, 1916, 3-4. Includes pedigree.

MORGAN, H.G. 'What's in a name?', *Devon historian* **12**, 1976, 22-5. Manwaring of Dawlish, 18th c.

Makeig

BAYLISS, W.J. 'The Makeigs of Cardigan: Bristol fashion', *J.B.A.* **5**, 1976, 23-6; **6**, 1977, 22-4; **7**, 1977, 12-14. Of Cardigan and Bristol; 18-19th c.

Mal(l)et

BATTEN, J. 'Malet of Enmore, Somerset', *N.Q.S.D.* **3**, 1893, 255-8. Primarily medieval deeds.

MALET, ARTHUR. 'Notes on the Malet family', *S.A.N.H.S.* **30**(2), 1884, 74-5. 12th c.

MALET, ARTHUR. *Notices of an English branch of the Malet family, compiled from family papers and other authentic sources.* Harrison & Sons, 1885. Medieval-19th c., includes pedigrees.

MALET, G.E.G. 'The origin of the Malets of Enmore', *Genealogists' magazine* **8**(6), 1939, 316-24.

MALLET, MATILDE. 'Origin of the name of Mallet and various ways of writing it', *N.Q.S.D.* **21**, 1935, 51-4. See also 83.

MARSHALL, G. W. 'The Malets of St. Audries', *S.A.N.H.S.* **16**(2), 1870, 35-40. Includes pedigree, 14-17th c., and parish register extracts.

'The Mallets of Ash', *N.Q.S.D.* **20**, 1930-32, 255-7 & 265-8; **21**, 1935, 8-10.

Malte

See Harington

Maltravers

S[TEINMAN], G.S. 'Pedigree of Maltravers, Baron Maltravers', *Collectanea topographica et genealogica* **3**, 1836, 77-9. Dorset family.

S[TEINMAN], G.S. 'Pedigree of Mautravers of Litchet, and of Crowell and Hook', *Collectanea topographica et genealogica,* **6**, 1840, 334-61.

Manley

See Pitman

Manwaring

See Mainwaring

March

See Burt

Marisall

MARSHALL, GEORGE W. 'The Marisall family', *G.N.Q.* **1**, 1881, 74-80.

Marisco

BROOKS, ERIC JOHN. 'The family of Marisco', *Journal of the Royal Society of Antiquaries of Ireland* **61**, 1931, 22-38 & 89-112. Of Lundy Island, Somerset and Ireland; medieval.

POWICKE, F.M. 'The murder of Henry Clement and the pirates of Lundy Island', *History* **25**, 1941, 285-310. Marisco family; medieval.

Markham

See Harington

Marriott-Dodington

MARSHALL, G.W. 'Pedigree of Marriott-Dodington of Horsington', *Reliquary* **13**, 1872-3, 244-5. 17-19th c.

'Pedigree of Marriott-Dodington of Horsington', *Genealogist* **1**, 1877, 81-4.

Marsh

C[OCKAYNE], G.E. *Some notice of various families of the name of Marsh.* Exeter: William Pollard and Co., 1900. Includes notice of Marsh of Hannington, Wiltshire, 17-19th c., with wills; also notices of Marsh families from various other counties.

PARKER, ALEC MORGAN. *A Marsh family from Wiltshire.* Melbourne: Universal Multiowners, 1979. 16-20th c., primarily a biographical dictionary of Marsh and related families.

'Marsh connections', *G.T.* **13**(2), 60. Lists families linked by marriage in Wareham area.

Marshall

M., G.W. 'The Marshalls of Exeter', *Genealogist* **4**, 1880, 11-17.

MARSHALL, GEORGE. 'Marshall of Selaby, Co. Durham and Freeman of Batsford, Co. Gloucester', *G.N.Q.* **1**, 1881, 131-5. 17-18th c.

See also De Breuse and Trowbridge

Martin

BENSON, J. 'Pons Martinorum', *D.C.N.Q.* **21**(4), 1940, 168-9. 13-14th c.

HUDLESTON, C. ROY. 'The Martins of Redland Court, Bristol', *B.G.A.S.T.* **56**, 1934, 83-93. Includes pedigree, 17-18th c.

I'ANSON, BRYAN. *The history of the Martyn or Martin family.* Janson & Co., 1935. Puddletown family.

MARTIN, BINA ELIZABETH. *Parsons and prisons: Temple Chevalier Martin (1842-1933): his ancestors and his descendants.* Fish Hoek, South Africa: the author, 1972. 18-20th c., includes pedigrees of Janns, Kingsley, Edgcumbe, Parkyn, Everest, Chevallier and Courtenay.

MARTIN, EDWARD A. *The Martin family of Stithians in Cornwall.* 4th ed. Ipswich: the author, 1991. 16-20th c., includes many pedigrees.

MARTYN, MICHAEL. 'From Davidstow (Dewstow), North Cornwall: a Martyn, Martin, Marten family and its descent', *C.F.H.S.J.* **64**, 1992, 26-30. 16-20th c.

WATSON, W.G. WILLIS. *The house of Martin: being chapters in the history of the West of England branch of that family.* Exeter: William Pollard & Co., 1906. Devon and Dorset.

WILLIAMS, M. 'Genealogical memoranda relating to the Martyn family', *M.G.H.* N.S., **1**, 1874, 385-96. Includes pedigrees, wills, parish register extracts, etc.

See also Burcie and Pollard

Martyn

WHITAKER, J. 'The Martyns and the Hearnes: recollections of a grandson', *C.K.L.H.S.B.* **22**, 1989, 16-26.

Marwood

FORTESCUE-FOULKES, R. 'The Marwoods of Honiton and Colyton', *D.C.N.Q.* **32**, 1971, 48-51, 71-3 & 110-13.

SKINNER, A.J. 'Marwood and Blackaller families', *N.Q.S.D.* **11**, 1909, 321-5. Of Colyton; includes monumental inscription of Bridget Marwood, 1622, and will of Thomas Blackaller, 1659.

VIGORS, PHILIP D. 'Marwood family', *W.A.* **9**(8-9), 1890, 153-4.

Masling

GREENFIELD, BENJ. W. 'Extracts from the parish register of Wootton Bassett, taken October 1842', *M.G.H.* N.S. **1**, 1874, 119-20. Mainly concerns Masling or Masklin family, 16-18th c

Mason

'Funeral certificate: Edmond Mason, D.D., Dean of Salisbury', *M.G.H.* 2nd series **1**, 1886, 310.

Massinger

GRAY, IRVINE E. 'Philip Massinger: an archive problem', *Journal of the Society of Archivists* 2(7), 1963, 319-21. Includes brief pedigree of Massinger of Gloucester, 16-17th c.

Massy-Dawson

Massy-Dawson and Poore pedigrees. Frome: Selwood Printing Works, 1937. 18-20th c., pedigrees, with biographical notes on many associated families.

Mate

SIRR, HUBERT H.F. 'An enquiry into the antecedents of the families of Mate and Sirr', *Huguenot Society proceedings* 19(5), 1958, 226-37. Mate of Dorset and Kent; Sirr of London.

Matravers

MATTRAVERS, PHILIP. 'The Matravers families', *Family history journal of the South-East Hampshire Genealogical Society* 1(5), 1975, 100-102. Includes pedigree, 19-20th c.

Matthews

GRAY, IRVINE. 'Records of four Tewkesbury vicars, c. 1685-1769', *B.G.A.S.T.* **102**, 1984, 155-72. Matthews and Jones families, 18th c.

MATTHEWS, GRAHAM. *The Matthews and Knapp families of West Wiltshire.* Coventry: the author, 1987. 18-19th c. 'Line of descendants, 1585-1928', *J.D.F.H.S.* 2(1), 1989, 15-17. Matthews pedigree, 1669-1923.

See Ridington

Maunsell

STATHAM, EDWARD PHILIPS. *History of the family of Maunsell (Mansell, Mansel).* 2 vols in 3. Kegan Paul, Trench & Co., 1917-20. Of Glamorganshire, Somerset, Carmarthenshire, Northamptonshire, Yorkshire, etc.

Maurice

MAURICE, DICK. 'Six generations in Wiltshire', *W.F.H.S.* **8**, 1982. 14-18. Maurice family, 18-20th c., includes pedigree.

Mautravers

See Maltravers

Maverick

CRESSWELL, BEATRIX F. *The Mavericks of Devonshire and Massachusetts.* Exeter: J. G. Commin, 1929.

FRENCH, ELIZABETH. 'Genealogical research in England: Maverick', *N.E.H.G.R.* **69**, 1915, 146-59. 16-17th c., includes wills, extracts from Awliscombe parish register, *etc.*

May

MOLYNEAU, EDNA MAY. *May: a Cornish family - roots and branches.* Vineland, N.J.: the author, 1982. 17-20th c.

Mayell

MAYELL, F.L. *In search of ancestors.* Research Publishing, 1975. Account of the author's experience researching the Mayell family.

Maynard

DEMAIN-SAUNDERS, C. 'The early Maynards of Devon and St. Albans', *Genealogists' magazine* 6(12), 1934, 591-641.

LANDON, M. 'Serjeant Maynard's children', *D.C.N.Q.* 33(6), 1976, 200-203.

LANDON, M. 'Serjeant Maynard's wives', *D.N.Q.* 33(5), 1975, 156-8. i.e. Elizabeth Henley, Jane Selhurst, Margaret Gorges, and Mary Barmondin; 17th c.

Mayo

MAYO, C.H. *A genealogical account of the Mayo and Elton families of Wilts and Herefordshire, and some other adjoining counties, together with numerous biographical sketches, to which are added many genealogies ... of families allied by marriage to the family of Mayo, and a history of the manors of Andrewes and Le Mote, in Cheshunt, Hertfordshire.* 2nd ed. 1908. Mayo of Wiltshire, Dorset, Gloucestershire and Herefordshire; Elton of Herefordshire.

Mayow

MCKIE, DOUGLAS. 'John Mayow (1641-79)', *Old Cornwall* **4**, 1943-50, 89-93. Includes genealogical notes.

Mcadam

HALL, R. de Z. 'John Loudon McAdam and his descendents in Somerset', *N.Q.S.D.* **27**, 1961, 258-61.

Mead

MEAD, CECIL JOHN HAARLEM. *A record of the Mead and West families in county of Cornwall, from 1751-1941.* Falmouth: Cornish Echo (194-?]. Also includes notes on Harvey family.

MEAD, C.J.H. 'The Mead family of St.Gluvias', *D.C.N.Q.* **22**, 1942-6, 277-9, 292-5 & 305-8. 16-19th c.

Meaden

See Croad

Meardon

MEARDON, MAURICE. *The family of Meardon.* Didcot: the author, 1992. Of Devon and the United States, *etc.,* pedigrees, 19-20th c.

Meggs

COLBY, DR., & RYLANDS, J. P. 'Pedigrees from the visitation of Dorset, 1623', *M.G.H.* 2nd. series **2**, 1888, 378-9. Includes Meggs and Peverell. For Peverell, see also **3**, 1890, 11.

Melford

See Clarke

Menhinick

SHAW, THOMAS. *The Menhinick family, Meneghy Nyot: the history and genealogy of a Cornish family.* Rotherham: the author, 1950. 16-20th c., includes many pedigrees.
SHAW, THOMAS. 'The Menhinick family', *Old Cornwall* **4**, 1943-50, 398-404.

Mercer

SKINNER, A.J. 'Mercer of Ottery St. Mary', *D.C.N.Q.* **9**, 1917, 164-72.

Merewether

See Townsend

Meriet

GREENFIELD, B. W. *Genealogy of the Somersetshire family of Meriet traced in an unbroken line from the reign of the Confessor to its extinction in the reign of King Henry V.* Taunton: J. F. Hammond, 1883. Reprinted from *S.A.N.H.S.* **28**(2), 1882, 99-215. Includes folded pedigree, 11-15th c.

Merivale

MERIVALE, ANNA W. *Family memorials.* Exeter: Thomas Upward, 1884. Merivale family, of Northamptonshire and Devon.

Merrick

MERRICK, D. 'Merrick: my roots were built in Somerset', *G.T.* **13**(4), 1988, 134.

Merryweather

MERRYWEATHER, ALAN. *Merryweather of Mere and Sedgehill, Wiltshire: a family history, with notes on the families of Amiel, Chandler, Cullimore, Mabbett, Sanderson, Welsh and others.* 2nd ed. Bussage: the author, 1989.

MERRYWEATHER, ALAN. 'Some Merryweathers of Mere and Sedgehill', *W.F.H.S.* **47**, 1992, 27-30. 18-19th c.

Mervyn

DRAKE, SIR WILLIAM RICHARD. *Fasciculus Mervinensis: being notes historical, genealogical and heraldic of the family of Mervyn.* Metchin & Son., 1873. Includes pedigrees, 16-19th c. Of Wiltshire, Sussex and Devon, etc.
VAVASOUR, HENRY MERVYN, SIR. 'Mervyn', *M.G.H.* **1**, 1868, 289-91. Funeral certificate of Sir John Mervyn, 1566.
'Tabular pedigree of the Fountel-Gifford branch of the Mervyn family', *M.G.H.* N.S. **1**, 1874, 358-65. Fonthill Gifford. 16th c., includes *inquisition post mortem* and wills.
'Tabular pedigree of the Pertwood branch of the Mervyn family', *M.G.H.* N.S. **2**, 1877, 3-11. 15-19th c.
See also Goldesborough

Methuen

See Rowe

Meurdrae

See Bocland

Michell

MICHELL, DONOVAN HENRY. *The Michells: a short history of a Cornish family.* Gorran: the author, 1986.
MICHELL, F. BICE. *Michell: a family of Cornish engineers, 1740-1910.* Penzance: Trevithick Society, 1984. Includes pedigree.
MICHELL, GEORGE B. 'Michell of Cannington', *S.A.N.H.S.* **73**, 1927, 80-5. 15-17th c.
See also Gyverney and Hull

Midelney

ROSS, D. MELVILLE. 'Sir Ralph de Midelney', *S.A.N.H.S.* **61**, 1916, 143-56.

Milborne

MILBOURN, THOMAS. 'The family of Milborne of Somerset and Monmouthshire', *M.G.H.* 5th series **3**, 1918-19, 130-40, 197-203, 235-44; **4**, 1920-22, 22-5, 45-51, 63-9, 91-4, 113-6, 137-8, 165-78, 192-6 & 220-28. 15-19th c.

Mildmay

LANKESTER, R.P.A. *A history of Hazlegrove House, in the parish of Queen Camel, Somerset.* Sparkford: Kings School Bruton Junior School, 1958. Largely Mildmay family history, includes pedigree, 16-18th c.

SAGE, EDWARD J. 'Mildmay of Marks, Shawford and Hazel Grove', *M.G.H.* **2**, 1876, 263-7. Marks, Essex, Shawford, Hampshire, and Hazle Grove, Somerset; pedigree, 17-18th c.

Mildren
TWINING, SANDRA. *Mildren family history: a history of the Mildren and associated families in Cornwall and Australia.* Seacombe Gardens, South Australia: the author, 1991. Includes pedigrees, 17-20th c.

Milford
MILFORD, J.R. 'Milford Family', *D.C.N.Q.* **31**, 1968-9, 121.

Mill
GRAHAM, ELSIE. 'The Mill family of Sailors' Gully, Eaglehawk and Redruth', *C.F.H.S.J.* **30**, 1983, 19. 19-20th c.

Milledge
MILLEDGE, DEREK. 'The Milledge sherrifs of Poole', *J.D.F.H.S.* **8**(1), 1994, 18-19. 17th c.

Miller
See Wills

Millett
M[ILLETT], V.V. 'A Hampshire sailor in Devonport', *D.C.N.Q.* **29**, 1962-4, 227-30. See also 113-5. Discusses the marriage of John Smith and Thomasine Millett, 1748, and the Cornish ancestry of Thomasine.
See also Vivian

Milsom
MILSOM, PHILIP. 'Was my ancestor a bigamist?' *W.F.H.S.* **53**, 1994, 12-14. Milsom family, 18-19th c.

Milward
See Hungerford

Mimms
MIMMS, PETER. *Only for life: a labouring family from Civil War to Second World War.* Bournemouth: the author, 1995. Of the East Midlands, Southwark and Bermondsey, and Devon, 17-20th c.

Mitchell
See Clarke

Moase
MOASE, CLIFFORD REAGH. *Moase of Devon: an account of the descendants of one of Devon's immigrants to Prince Edward Island, Henry Moase, and some of his ancestors.* Fredericton, New Brunswick: The Author, 1982.

Modesley
HUDSON, HAZEL, & NEALE, FRANCIS. 'A busy day in Wedmore church, 1350', *N.Q.S.D.* **33**(336), 1992, 171-3. Concerns the proof of age of William Modesley or Mudgley.

Moel
SHEPPARD, W.L. 'Two comments on complete peerage articles', *Genealogists' magazine* **16**, 1971, 550-3.
See also Prowse

Moeles
ROGERS, W.H.H. 'Lady Alice de Moels of North Cadbury', *N.Q.S.D.* **7**, 1901, 49-55. For pedigree, see also p.126-7
ROGERS, W.H.H. 'Moeles-Botreaux of North Cadbury, Somerset', *N.Q.S.D.* **6**, 1899, 289-95. See also 359, & **7**, 1901, 21-2, 63-4, 127, & 142-3. Medieval.
Both the foregoing papers are reprinted in Rogers's *Archaeological papers relating to the counties of Somerset, Wilts., Hants., and Devon. [ ]: the author, 1902.*
See also Coode

Mohun
LYTE, H. C. MAXWELL. *Dunster and its lords, 1066-1881.* Exeter: W. Pollard, 1882.
LYTE, H. C., SIR. *A history of Dunster and the families of Mohun and Luttrell.* 2 vols. St. Catherine's Press, 1909.
MORIARTY, G. ANDREWS. 'Genealogical research in England: Mohun (or Moone) - Hyde', *N.E.H.G.R.* **81**, 1927, 91-4, 178-86 & 314-20. See also **82**, 1928, 66-9. Of Dorset, 16-17th c., includes wills, *inquisitions post mortem,* Chancery proceedings, *etc.*
MORIARTY, G. ANDREWS. 'The origin of the Mohuns of Fleet', *N.E.H.G.R.* **103**, 1949, 21-4. Includes folded pedigree, 14-16th c.
TRINICK, MICHAEL. 'The manor of Polrode and the Mohun family', *D.C.N.Q.* **36**(2), 1987, 61-2. 17th c.
Dunster Castle, Somerset. National Trust, 1991. Includes notes on the Mohun and Luttrell families with pedigree of Luttrell, 13-20th c.
See also Dackombe

Molford
See Cottell

Molesworth
'Pedigree of Molesworth', *M.G.H.* N.S. **2**, 1877, 280-3. 13-17th c.

ALLEN, ROBERT JOSEPH. 'Steele and the Molesworth family', *Review of English studies* **12**, 1936, 449-54. 17-18th c.

Molyns

ROGERS, W.H.H. 'Molyns-Hungerford, of Farleigh Hungerford, Somerset', *N.Q.S.D.* **6**, 1899, 337-43. See also **7**, 1901, 22-3. Reprinted in Rogers's *Archaeological papers relating to the counties of Somerset, Wilts., Hants., and Devon.* [ ]: reprinted for the author, 1902. Medieval.

Monoux

BOSWORTH, GEORGE F., & SAUNDERS, CONSTANCE DERRAIN, eds. *Original documents relating to the Monoux family.* Walthamstow Antiquarian Society official publications **19**. Walthamstow: the Society, 1928. Of Walthamstow, Essex, London, Gloucestershire and Worcestershire. Includes deeds, *inquisitions post mortem*, wills *etc.*

Monk

See Carkeet and Grenville

Montacute

KITE, ed. 'Some notes on the Montacutes, Earls of Salisbury', *W.N.Q.* **4**, 1902-4, 481-93 & 529-43. Medieval; includes pedigree, *etc.*

Montagu

CUNNINGTON, WILLLAM. 'Memoir of George Montagu', *W.A.M.* **3**(7), 1857, 87-94. Includes folded pedigree of Montagu of Lackham, 17-19th c.

DORLING, E.E. 'A Montagu shield at Hazelbury Bryan', *Ancestor* **8**, 1904, 215-7.

WOOLLEY, T. G. *From Bryan to Percy: some notes on the genealogical tree hanging in Hazelbury Bryan church.* Dorchester: Longmans, 1952. Cover title: *Church of St. Mary and St. James, Hazelbury Bryan.* Includes pedigree of Montague, 14-15th c.

'Montagu of Sutton Montagu, Bevyn of Lufton, Muttlebury of Ashill in Ilminster, Smith of Thornecombe, Devon', *N.Q.S.D.* **20**, 1930-2, 18-19, 40-42, & 75-8.

Montgomery

See De Boteville

Moon

See Mohun

Moore

MOORE, CECIL. *Genealogical memoranda of the family of De La Moor, or Moore, de Moorehayes, in the parish of Cullompton, in the County of Devon, from A.D.1120 (circa) to A.D.1844.* Mitchell & Hughes, 1884. Includes pedigree.

MOORE, D.T. 'The descendants of John Lawrence Moore (1779?-1854) of Bristol: carver, gilder and picture frame maker', *J.B.A.* **17**, 1979, 5-9.

THOMAS, NEIL. *The Moores of Hartley Vale.* Belair, South Australia: the author, 1995. Primarily concerned with the family in South Australia, but originally of Aveton Gifford; includes pedigree of Hamlyn of Ringmore, 19th c.

'Pedigree of the family of De La Moor or Moore de Moorhays in the parish of Cullompton in the county of Devon', *M.G.H.* N.S., **4**, 1884, 413-6.

See also Greendale

Morgan

BROWN, F. 'Morgan', *M.G.H.* 2nd series **2**, 1888, 134-5. Dorset; pedigree, 16-17th c.

Morice

ACRES, W. MARSTON. 'The Morice family of Werrington', *Notes and queries* **192**, 1947, 178-80. See also 240.

BRACKEN, C.W. 'Sir William Morice, knight, and the three succeeding Morice baronets', *D.C.N.Q.* **21**, 1940-41, 351-7. See also **22**, 1942-6, 34-5 & 71-2.

ROBBINS, ALFRED W. 'The three Humphrey Morices', *W.A.* **11**(1), 1891-2, 5-9. See also 167-8. 17-18th c.

MORRIS, G.T.W. 'Welsh ancestry of the Morices of Werrington', *W.A.* **3**, 1884, 218-9.

Morrell

MORRELL, KEN. 'My seafaring Morrells', *J.B.A.* **86**, 1996, 23-5. Of Bristol, late 19th c.

Morres

ADDISON, W.G. 'Three Wiltshire parsons', *Theology* **54**, 1951, 329-35. Robert Morres, R.H. Hill and A.P. Morres, vicars of Britford.

Morris

MORRIS, REGINALD B. *The Morris family of South Molton, Devon.* Guildford: privately printed, 1908.

See also Litelcote

Morse

SADLER, J. 'Morse, of Rodbourne Cheney, etc.', W.N.Q. **6**, 1908-10, 361-4, 503-7 & 562-5. See also **7**, 1911-13, 46-7. 16-18th c.

Mortimer

BAUMAN, JOHN ANDREW, et al. *The ancestry and descendants of James Mortimer (1842-1917) of Logan, Cache County, Utah, including descendants of the Jordan, Green, Mortimer and Sheppard families of Great Faringdon, Berkshire, and Liddington, Wiltshire, England.* Bismarck, North Dakota: Beth Bauman, 1986. 17-20th c.

PLAYFORD, ROSEMARY. *From Somerset to the promised land: a story of Alfred and Fanny Mortimer and their family.* alstonville, N.S.W.: R. & M. Playford, [1993?]

Morton

TENISON, C.M. 'A London citizen's diary', *M.G.H.* 3rd series **4**, 1902, 176-8. Pedigrees, etc., of Morton and Farrington families, of Devon and London, 17-18th c.

Moule

LEWIS, R.W.M. *The family of Moule of Melksham, Fordington, and Melbourne.* [ ]: privately printed, 1938. 18-20th c.

Mounce

RISDON, PETER. 'Mounce family bible', *D.F.H.* **78**, 1996, 4-5. Of Bideford and Newport, Monmouthshire, 19th c.

Mowlem

MOWLEM, JOHN. *Moulham: a Dorset place and surname.* Fleet: E. Dwelly, 1934.

Moyle

DYER, A. STEPHENS. 'Moyle of Bake, St.Germans', *Notes & queries* 12th series **1**, 1916, 242-3. Medieval.

DYER, A. STEPHENS. 'Pedigree of Moyle', *M.G.H.* 4th series **3**, 1910, 232-3. 18th c.

DYER, A. STEPHENS. 'Pedigree of Moyle of Bake, St.Germans, Cornwall', *M.G.H.* 5th series **9**, 1935-7, 344-56. 14-20th c.

DYER, A. STEPHENS. 'Pedigree of Moyle of Kent, from Bodmin, Cornwall', *M.G.H.* 5th series **4**, 1920-2, 229-34. 15-17th c.

MOYLE, W.J.T. 'Researching the Moyle family tree', *C.F.H.S.J.* **1**, 1976, 7-9. Includes pedigree, 19-20th c.

Moysey

MOYSEY, F.L. 'Pedigree', *D.C.N.Q.* **12**, 1922, 13.

Muchgros

HOUGHTON, F.T.S. 'Family of Muchgros', *Birmingham Archaeological Society transactions* **47**, 1921, 8-34. 11-13th c; of Gloucestershire, Somerset, and various other counties.

Mudge

FLINT, STAMFORD RAFFLES, ed. *Mudge memoirs, being a record of Zachariah Mudge, and some members of his family, together with a genealogical list of the same ...* Truro: Netherton & Worth, 1883.

Mudgley

See Modesley

Mugford

COLE, J.A. 'Out of bounds', *D.F.H.* **25**, 1983, 11. Bradford on Avon parish register entry re marriage of William Mugford of Bideford, 1792.

Mullins

MULLINS, THOMAS MITCHELL. *The Mullins family of Somerset: a personal history.* Johannesburg: [ ], 1988. Includes pedigree, 18-20th c.

Mundy

M., D. 'Mundy of co. Devon', *Notes and queries* **158**, 1930, 255-6. See also 303 & 318.

Musgrave

BARTLETT, R.G. 'Family of Musgrave', *N.Q.S.D.* **6**, 1899, 66-9. 16-17th c.

CHANTER, J.F. 'Dr. William Musgrave', *D.C.N.Q.* **11**, 1920-21, 264-5. Includes pedigree, 17-18th c.

Muttlebury

See Montagu

Naish

SLATTER, DOREEN, ed. *The diary of Thomas Naish.* W.R.S. **20**. 1965. Includes short account of the Naish family, 18th c.

Nancarrow

JEFFERY, C.C. 'The Nancarrows: a forgotten Cornish engineering family', *Old Cornwall* 9(10), 1984, 493-6; 10(1), 1985, 31-5. 18-19th c.

Nankivel

WILLIAMS, ANNE. *Nankivel: a family affair.* Miram, Vic.: the author, 1986. Of Cornwall and Australia; includes pedigrees, 18-20th c.

Napier
'Ancestry of Dorset peasants, Napier',
N.Q.S.D. **8**, 1903, 157-60. 17-19th c.

Napper
RAWLINS, S.W. 'Napper of Tintinhull', *N.Q.S.D.*
27, 1961, 277-85. Includes 16-18th c.
pedigree.

Narramore
See Goddard

Nashe
NORRIS, H. 'James Nashe', *N.Q.S.D.* **3**, 1893,
179. Includes 17th c. pedigree.

Nethercott
NETHERCOTT, ARNOLD WARREN. *From the
lower cottage: some Nethercotts of North
Devon & new world.* London, Ontario:
Lower Cottage Press, 1986. 18-20th c.,
of Devon, the United States and
Canada.

Neville
HICKS, M.A. 'The Neville Earldom of Salisbury,
1429-71', *W.A.M.* **72/3**, 1980, 141-7.

Newcombe
BODDINGTON, REGINALD STEWART. 'Newcombe
pedigree', *M.G.H.* 2nd series **2**, 1888, 90-91.
18-19th c.

NEWCOMBE, M.O.L. *Newcombes of Chard,
Drewsteignton, Exeter and Starcross,* ed.
Jud Burgoyne-Newcombe. [Newport,
Gwent]: the author, 1996. Medieval-19th c.;
includes pedigrees.

NEWCOMBE, M.O.L. *The Newcombes of
Inwardleigh (Okehampton).* ed. Jud
Burgoyne-Newcombe. Newport, Gwent: the
author, 1995. Medieval-19th c., includes
pedigree.

NEWCOMBE, PETER R. *The Newcombe family of
Devonshire.* Exeter: the author, 1994. 14-
20th c.

Newcomen
WATKIN, HUGH R. 'Thomas Newcomen',
D.C.N.Q. **15**, 1928-9, 337-47. Includes 17-
18th c. extracts from Dartmouth parish
register, monumental inscriptions, etc.

Newman
'The family of Newman', *Somerset year book*
28, 1929, 88-9. 17-18th c.
See also Holdsworth

Nicholas
KITE, E., ed. 'Judge Nicholas: his parentage and
birthplace', *W.N.Q.* **3**, 505-10 & 539-46.
Includes pedigree, 15-17th c.

K[ITE], E., & S[CHOMBERG], A. 'Nicholas and
Knight', *W.N.Q.* **8**, 1914-16, 374-8. Marriage
settlement, 1670.

SCHOMBERG, A. 'Judge Nicholas'. *W.N.Q.* **5**,
385-91. Includes marriage settlement and
probate inventory, 17th c.

*Genealogical memoranda relating to the
family of Nicholas.* Hounslow: J. Gotelee,
1874. Medieval-19th c.

Nicholls
MOYLE, TERRY. 'The family of Sir George
Nicholls (1781-1865)', *C.F.H.S.J.* **61**, 1991, 30-
31. Includes pedigree, 18-19th c.

Nind
SKELTON, HENRY ROUGHTON. 'The name of
Nind', *Cockney ancestor* **70**, 1996, 8-9. Of
London, Gloucestershire, *etc.*

Noad
See Westall

Norman
FRENCH, ELIZABETH. 'Genealogical research in
England: Norman', *N.E.H.G.R.* **68**, 1914,
62-3. Will of Hugh Norman of Orchard
Portman, 1623, with extracts from parish
register.

Norris
DANIEL-TYSSEN, J.R. 'Norris pedigree', *M.G.H.*
N.S., **1**, 1874, 101-3. Of Somerset, London,
etc. 16-19th c.

North
M., J.H. 'North family marriage licences,
Devonshire and Cornwall, 1532 to 1762',
D.C.N.Q. **23**, 1947-9, 49-50.

Northcote
JONES, W. 'The early Northcote pedigree',
N.G.D.C. **4**, 1891, 133-43. See also
172-3.

JONES, W. 'The Northcotes and Coleridges',
N.G.D.C. **1**, 1888, 4.

MULES, R.J. 'Northcote, Wotton and Prouz',
D.C.N.Q. **22(1)**, 1942, 102-3.

WORTHY, CHARLES. *The life of the late Right
Honourable the Earl of Iddisleigh ... and a
complete history of the Northcott family.*
Hamilton, Adams & Co., 1887.

'The family of Northcote', *Devonian year
book* **1911**, 33-5.
See also Clarke and Pitman

Northleigh
See Hippisley

78

Norton
See Buck

Norwood
COKAYNE, G.E. 'Norwood', *M.G.H.* N.S., **2**, 1877, 43. Of Gloucestershire; 16-17 c.

Notcutt
NOTCUTT, MICHAEL EDWARD, & SARTIN, MARIAN PHYLLIS. *The Notcutt family history, 1515-1989.* Chatham: Backman & Turner, 1989. Somerset, Essex & Suffolk.

Notley
PEARSON, EUSTACE H. *Do not lie! The Notleys of Somerset & Dorset.* Cardiff: the author, 1991. Includes pedigree of Notley, 17-20th c., and Chick, 18-19th c., with many extracts from original sources.

Nott
'Pedigree of Nott of London and Braydon, Wilts', *M.G.H.* N.S. **3**, 1880, 233-5.

Noyes
W., J. 'Noyes', *W.A.M.* **3**(9), 1857, 380. Brief note, 16-17th c.
'John Noyes of Calne', *W.N.Q.* **4**, 1902-4, 365-71, 420-24 & 461-4. Includes 17th c. pedigree.

Nuntley
See Galpin

Nutcombe
MONDAY, A.J. 'Clayhanger, in the county of Devon, and Raddington, in the county of Somerset', *W.A.* **3**, 1884, 98-9. Descent of Nutcombe family.

Nutt
BHANJI, SADRU. 'The Nutts of Lympstone, brothers in piracy', *D.A.Tr.* **128**, 1996, 51-63. 17th c.

Oaten
OATEN, EDWARD F. 'Longevity in a Pitminster family', *N.Q.S.D.* **28**, 1968, 110-12.

Odgers
HEARN, J. RUDLAND. 'Leading seaman William Odgers, V.C.', *D.C.N.Q.* **30**, 1965-7, 143. Includes genealogical information, 19th c.

Oke
SKINNER, A.J. 'Marriage of John Edye', *D.C.N.Q.* **9**, 1916-17, 47-8. Oke and Walrond families, 17-18th c.
TEMPLETON, JOHN F. 'Dorset origins of the Oke family in Newfoundland', *G.T.* **9**(4), 1984, 118-9. 17-19th c.
See also Spooner and Walrond

Oldisworth
WADLEY, THOMAS 'Oldisworth family', *G.N.Q.* **4**, 1890, 556-7. Extracts from Bourton-on-the-Hill parish register, 1606-78.

Oldmixon
COWARD, HAROLD. 'John Oldmixon and his family: more facts and conjectures', *N.Q.S.D.* **33**(335), 1992, 105-10. Of Bridgwater and Hutton, 17th c.
ROGERS, 'Two notes on John Oldmixon and his family', *Notes & queries* **215**; N.S. 17(8), 1970, 293-300. 17-18th c., includes pedigree.

Oliver
GILES, PATRICIA. *The Oliver family of Great Trethew in the parish of Menheniot, Cornwall.* Braunton: Merlin, 1987. 15-20th c.
OLIVER, V.L. 'The Oliver family', *G.N.Q.* **5**, 1894, 155-60. See also 322-5. 18th c. pedigree.
OLIVER, W.H. *The Oliver family of Lankelly, County Cornwall: an account of a West Country family from earliest times.* Galashiels: the author, 1985. Medieval-20th c., includes pedigrees.
also Hungerford

Olivier
See Conybeare

Orchard
VIVIAN-NEAL, A. W. 'Materials for the history of Orchard Portman', *S.A.N.H.S.* **89**, 1943, 35-53. Includes pedigree of Orchard, 12-15th c.
also Pollard

Osborne
KENT, ALAN. 'Coincidences', *C.F.H.S.J.* **7**, 1988, 8-9. Concerns the Osborne, Kent and Crawshaw families; includes pedigree, 17-19th c.
LINGEN-WATSON, A. 'Fathers-in-law: the Osbornes and Seagers, Bristol solicitors', *J.B.A.* **15**, 1979, 9-10. 18th c.

Ourry
WAGNER, HENRY. 'Huguenot family of Ourry', *M.G.H.* 3rd series **5**, 1904, 12-16. 18-19th c.

Overbury
MARSHALL, G.W. 'The Overbury family', *Genealogist* **1**, 1877, 267-70. See also **2**, 1878, 364-5. Includes will of Sir Nicholas Overbury of Bourton-on-the-Hill, 1640, with extracts from London parish registers, 16-17th c.

'Pedigree of Overbury', *Genealogist* **1**, 1877, 271-6. Of Gloucestershire and Warwickshire, 16-17th c.

Pabenham
See Engayne

Packer
PACKER, DONNA SMITH. *On footings from the past: the Packers in England.* U.S.A.: [the author], 1988. Of Gloucestershire, Westminster, Wiltshire and U.S.A.; 15-18th c. Includes a good bibliography.

Painel
'The Painels of Bampton', *N.Q.S.D.* **17**, 1923, 201-4, 246-7 & 287-90.

Painter
C. 'Name Painter in and near North Wilts', *W.N.Q.* **4**, 1902-4, 80-88 & 121-4. 16-18th c.

Palamountain
See Ridington

Paleologus
H., W.S.B. 'The family of Theodore Paleologus', *D.C.N.Q.* **12**, 1922-3, 177-9. See also 217-9. 17th c.

Palgrave
PALGRAVE, D.A. 'The Palgraves of Somerset', *Palgrave chronicle* 1(9), 1985, 79-80. Medieval.

Palk
See Pitman

Palling
See Little

Palmer
COLBY, F.T. *Pedigree of the Palmer family, formerly of South Molton and Great Torrington, Devon.* Exeter: Privately printed, 1892.
'An old Devonshire house and family', *D.C.N.Q.* **19**, 1936-7, 300-3. Palmer of Great Torrington, 18-19th c.
'A Stafford family in Great Somerford', *W.F.H.S.* **57**, 1995, 19-21. Palmer family, late 17th c.
See also Colby

Paradise
KITE, EDWARD, & SCHOMBERG, ARTHUR. 'Family of Paradise', *Genealogist* N.S. **37**, 1921, 74-84 & 151-4. 16-18th c., includes wills.
'Paradise family', *W.N.Q.* **7**, 1914-16, 49-58. Includes pedigree, 16-18th c., monumental inscriptions, parish register extracts. etc.

Pardee
JACOBS, DONALD LINES, ed. *The Pardee genealogy.* New Haven: New Haven Colony Historical Society, 1927. Of Somerset and New Haven; includes extracts from parish registers, wills, etc.

Parker
FLETCHER, RONALD. *The Parkers of Saltram, 1769-89: everyday life in an eighteenth-century house.* British Broadcasting Corporation, 1970.
PARKER, EDWARD MILWARD SEEDE. *Genealogical memoranda relating to the family of Parker, of Upton House, Upton Cheyney Manor, Bitton, Gloucestershire, and Welford House, Keynsham, Somerset, of Henbury, Clifton, Bristol, London and elsewhere, from 1543 to 1898.* Bristol: Lavars & Co., 1899.
SMITH, BARRY. 'Rosewarne, the Parkers and the Lewises: insanity, imbecility and inter-relationships in a Victorian family', *C.F.H.S.J.* **56**, 1990, 28-30. 19th c., also concerns Hartley family.
'Genealogical memoranda relating to the family of Parker of Upton Cheyney Manor, Bitton, Gloucestershire', *M.G.H.* 3rd series **1**, 1896, 14-15. From family bible, 17-18th c.
See also Paulet & Poulet(t)

Parkyn
See Martin

Parr
PARR, JOHN FRANK. 'Parr family of Chudleigh, Alphington, Powderham, Shillingford and Exeter', *W.A.* **3**, 1884, 47-8.
PARR, JOHN FRANK. 'Parr family of Chudleigh and Exminster', *W.A.* **3**, 1884, 19-20.
PARR, JOHN FRANK. 'Parr family of Devonshire', *W.A.* **3**, 1884, 72-4.
PARR, JOHN FRANK. 'Parr family of Exeter', *W.A.* **3**, 1884, 61-2. Includes parish register extracts.
PARR, JOHN FRANK. 'Parr family of Exminster, near Exeter', *W.A.* **2**, 1882, 77-8. Includes parish register extracts, 17-19th c.

Parry
See Hillier, Knight and Westall

Parsons
PARSONS, WILLIS S. 'Jeffrey Parsons of Loddiswell, Devonshire, and Gloucester, Massachusetts', *N.E.H.G.R.* **142**, 1988, 245-9. 17th c.

PARSONS, GERALD JAMES. 'Were Joseph and Benjamin Parsons and David Wilton, of Beaminster, Dorset, England, the New England colonists?', *N.E.H.G.R.* **143**, 1989, 101-19. See also **146**, 1992, 297-8. 17th c., also includes notes on Wilton and Hoskins families.
See also Knight

Partridge
PARTRIDGE, C. HAROLD. *Pedigree and notes of the Partridge family, with some account of Wishanger Manor House, in Gloucestershire, which was for 250 years the family seat.* Edgbaston: the author, 1903.
See also Clarke

Pascoe
KLUE, KATHRYN. 'Copper in Cornwall, gold in Georgia - a Pascoe adventure', *C.F.H.S.J.* **41**, 1986, 15-16. 19th c.
PASCOE, W.H. 'The Cornish name Pascoe', *C.F.H.S.J.* **44**, 1987, 19-20. 16th c.
PASCOE, W.H. 'Erasmus Pascoe of Phillack, Cornwall (1654-1723)', *D.C.N.Q.* **33**, 1974-7, 165-7.
PASCOE, W.H. 'Is your name Pascoe?', *C.F.H.S.J.* **32**, 1984, 23-4. Mainly medieval.
PASCOE, W. HARRY. *Pascoes all over the world.* Truro: Cornwall Family History Society, 1994. Originally of Cornwall; includes pedigrees.
PASCOE, W.H. 'The origin of the name Pascoe', *D.C.N.Q.* **32**, 1971-3, 173-5. Medieval-16th c.
WATSON, IAN M. 'The Pascoes in America', *C.F.H.S.J.* **36**, 1985, 24. 17-19th c.

Pasmore
FICE, JOHN. The Pasmore family and the Goodleigh militia in Armada year 1588', *Family history* **14**(120); N.S., **96**, 1989, 482-93. Includes pedigree, 16-17th c., of Devon.

Passemer
See Duke

Passmore
BERNAU, CHAS. A. *The pedigree of the Passmores of Passmore Hayes, Devon.* [ ]: Alfred E. Passmore, 1929. 12-20th c.

Paston
LANGSTON, J.N. 'The Pastons of Horton', *B.G.A.S.T.* **77**, 1958, 97-126. Includes pedigree, 15-19th c.

Patch
FRENCH, ELIZABETH. 'Genealogical research in England: Patch', *N.E.H.G.R.* **71**, 1917, 166-70. Includes extracts from South Petherton parish register, 16-17th c.

Patey
HARVEY, CHRISTOPHER. *The naval history of the Patey family.* [ ]: the author, [1909?] Includes folded pedigree, 19-20th c.

Paul
HYETT, FRANCIS, SIR. 'Sir George Onesiphorus Paul', *B.G.A.S.T.* **51**, 1929, 143-68. Includes pedigree, 17-19th c.

Paulet
FRANKLYN, CHARLES A.H. *A genealogical history of the families of Paulet (or Pawlett), Berewe (or Barrow) Lawrence and Parker ...* Bedford: Foundry Press, 1963. Paulet of Somerset and Gloucestershire, Barrow of Gloucestershire, Lawrence of Lancashire and Gloucestershire, Parker of Glamorganshire and Monmouthshire.
'Paulet', *M.G.H.* 5th series **9**, 1935-7, 142-7. Of Somerset, *etc.*, pedigree, 14-16th c.
'Pedigree of Constance Paulet', *M.G.H.* 5th series **9**, 1935-7, 88-90. Of Somerset, 14-15th c.

Paull
PAUL, HENRY N. *Joseph Paull of Ilminster, Somerset, and some of his descendants who have resided in Philadelphia, Penns.* Philadelphia: the author, 1932.

Pauncefote
DIGHTON, CONWAY. 'The Pauncefote family', *G.N.Q.* **5**, 1894, 268-9. Extracts from Ashelworth parish register.
LANGSTON, J.N. 'Old Catholic families of Gloucestershire I: The Pauncefotes of Hasfield', *B.G.A.S.T.* **71**, 1952, 122-44. See also **73**, 1954, 235-6.

Paveley
See Botreaux

Payne
FRY, E.A. 'Payne family', *N.Q.S.D.* **9**, 1905, 172-4. Includes pedigree, 14-15th c.

Paynter
HOSKING, J.M. 'Boskenna and the Paynters', *Cornwall Association of Local Historians journal* **27**, 1994, 11-14. 17-20th c.
PAYNTER, T.C. 'Camborne alias Paynter: skeleton pedigree of five generations', *D.C.N.Q.* **1971-3**, 154. 17-18th c.

PAYNTER, T.C. 'Francis Paynter', *D.C.N.Q.* **32,**
1971-3, 85-93. Includes genealogical notes,
17-18th c.

Pearce

EDGCUMBE, EDWARD ROBERT PEARCE, SIR. *Family
records relating to the families of Pearce
of Holsworthy, Edgcumbe of Laneast, Eliot
of Lostwithiel, Livingstone of Calendar,
Reynolds of Exeter, Gayer of Liskeard,
and others.* Exeter: Wm. Pollard & Co.,
1895.

HILL, RONALD A. 'Pearce/Pearse I.G.I. entries',
C.F.H.S.J. **82,** 1996, 14-15.

WHETTER, J.C.A. 'John and William Pearce of
St.Ives: men with problems during the
Commonwealth period', *Old Cornwall* **7,**
1967-72, 424-9 & 460-5.

Pearn

PEARN, JOHN HEMSLEY, & PEARN, VENA BEATRICE.
*New horizons: the biographies of Jonathan
Pearn, and of William Henry Pearn,
Cornishmen, and their families.* 3rd ed.
Brisbane: Amphion Press, 1992. Of New
Zealand.

Pedler

PEDLER, F., SIR. *A Pedler family history.*
Chichester: Phillimore, 1984.

PEDLER, FREDERICK, SIR. *A wider Pedler family
history.* Chichester: Phillimore, 1989.
Medieval-20th c. Includes many pedigrees.
Mainly concerned with the Pedlers of
Withiel and their descendants.

Pelling

'Pelling family', *W.N.Q.* **6,** 1908-10, 459-63.
16-17th c.

Pellowe

PELLOWE, E.F. *The Pellowes of Penryn: a
family history.* Caversham: Quality
Printers, 1965. Medieval-20th c.

Penhale

PENHALE, GLEN. 'The Gwinnear connection',
C.F.H.S.J. **38,** 1985, 24-5. Penhale family,
17-19th c.

Penhallow

SARGENT, WILLIAM M. 'The Penhallows of
Cornwall and New Hampshire', *W.A.* **8,**
1888-9, 108-11. Includes pedigree, 17-19th c.

Peniston

COWAN, MICHAEL. 'The Penistons: a Salisbury
family of Catholic architects and yeomen,
1770-1911', *W.A.M.* **80,** 1986, 184-91.
Includes pedigree.

Penn

COLEMAN, JAMES. *Pedigree and genealogical
notes from wills, registers and deeds of
the highly distinguished family of Penn,
of England and America.* [ ]: J. Coleman,
1871. 16-18th c.

HOGG, O.F.G. 'Pedigree of Penn of Co. Wilts
and of Bristol', *W.A.M.* **60,** 1965, 130(f).
Folded; 16-17th c.

HOGG, OLIVER F.G. *Further light on the
ancestry of William Penn.* Society of
Genealogists, 1964. Of Buckinghamshire,
Hertfordshire, Shropshire, Wiltshire and
Gloucestershire; includes pedigrees, 12-18th c.
'Penn of Rodbourne', *W.N.Q.* **7,** 1911-13, 158-60.
17th c.

Pennington

BRUSHFIELD, T.N. 'Pennington family, bell
founders', *W.A.* **7**(11), 1888, 249-51.

Penny

EURE. 'Penny family', *N.Q.S.D.* **3,** 1893, 288.

PENNY, FRANK. 'Penny family of Yeovil and
Weymouth', *N.Q.S.D.* **15,** 1917, 61-3.
17-19th c.

PENNY, FRANK. 'Penne of East Coker,
Somerset, and Toller Whelme, Dorset',
N.Q.S.D. **10,** 1907, 12-17 & 53-9. 14-18th c.
also Huntley

Penrose

PENROSE, CHARLES. *Penrose family of Helston,
Cornwall, and Wheldrake, Yorkshire, and
Co.Wicklow, Ireland, and other ancestors
of James Brinton Penrose ...* Potsdam, N.Y.:
Penrose, 1975.

HENDRA, PETER. 'He that is soon angry, dealeth
foolishly: Thomas Penrose (1627-1669) and
the stresses of command', *C.F.H.S.J.* **62,**
1991, 18-20. Includes pedigrees, 17th c.

Penruddock

NOBLE, ARTHUR. *The Penruddock family: the
genealogical & historical account of the
Penruddock families of Cumberland and
Wiltshire, with a pedigree of 17
generations from about 1400 to present
day.* [ ]: A.H. Noble, 1968. Duplicated
typescript.

Pentreath

HOBLYN, W. TREFFRY. 'The probable parentage
of Dorothy Pentreath', *Old Cornwall* 2(11),
1936, 7-11. 18th c., includes a note by R.M.
Nance on Dolly Pentreath, reputedly the
last native speaker of Cornish.

Pepperrell

BROWNE-WILKINSON, VIRGINIA. *Pepperrell posterity.* Florence: The Author, 1982. Descendents of William Pepperrell of Revelstoke, who emigrated to New England.

Peppin

PUGSLEY, STEVEN. *The sturdy breed: the story of the Peppins of Dulverton and the development of the merino sheep.* Zeal, Somerset: Hawkridge Press, 1988. Australian pioneer family from Dulverton.

Percy

BARROW, GEOFFREY. 'The marriages of the Lady Constance, I: Percy of Great Chalfield, Wiltshire', *North West Kent family history* 3(3), 1983, 93-5. Includes pedigree, 12-14th c.

Perham

MAYO, C.H. 'The Perhams of Beaminster and Stoke Abbas, Dorset', *N.Q.S.D.* 11, 1909, 118-24. Includes deed abstracts.

Perne

ROBINSON, C.J. 'Gillingham, Dorset', *N.Q.S.D.* 3, 1893, 72-3. Includes pedigree showing descent of lands in Gillingham through Perne, Tyse, Goddard, Helyar and Pitcher.

Perrett

PERRETT, GEORGE E. *In search of the Perretts.* Bath: the author, 1983. Dorset family.

PERRETT, GEORGE EDWARD. *In search of the Perrets: a family history and genealogical survey.* Crowborough, Sussex: the author, [1983]. 16-19th c.

The Perrett Society journal. 1984-

Perry

PRICE, JACOB M. *Perry of London: a family and a firm on the seaborne frontier, 1615-1753.* Cambridge: Harvard University Press, 1992. Includes pedigrees; originally of Devon.

Peter(s)

TAPLEY-SOPER, H. 'Chapter in the history of the Peter or Petre family of Devon', *D.A.Tr.* 50, 1918, 417-30. 16th-17th c.

'Some account of the Peters family', *N.E.H.G.R.* 2, 1848, 50-64. 16-17th c.

Petre

See Tucker

Pett

REA, C.F. 'Phineas Pett, vicar of Totnes, 1669-1674', *D.C.N.Q.* 14, 1926, 122. See also 167-8.

Pever

See Botreaux

Peverell

JAMES, F.B. 'The Peverells of Dorset', *N.Q.S.D.* 1, 1890, 86-8 & 102-4.

Phelips

PHELIPS, J. H. C. 'Phelips of Montacute: two early representatives', *N.Q.S.D.* 31, 1980-85, 85-95. 15-16th c.

Phelps

PHELPS, RON. 'Phelps brides and their grooms', *G.T.* 12(3), 1987, 82-3. Lists men marrying Phelps brides, with parishes and dates.

PHELPS, RON. 'Phelps brides and grooms', *J.G.F.H.S.* 52, 1992, 18-20; 53, 1992, 18-20.

TANN, JENNIFER. 'Some account books of the Phelps family of Dursley', *B.G.A.S.T.* 86, 1967, 107-17. General discussion with list of 18th c. clothiers.

'Phelps grooms and their brides', *G.T.* 15(3), 1990, 100-101.

Phillipps

MUNBY, A.N.L. *The family affairs of Sir Thomas Phillipps.* Phillipps studies 2. Cambridge: C.U.P., 1952.

P[HILLIPS], T. *Collectanea de familiis diversis, quibus nomen est Phillipps, praesertim vero de illis apud Wanborough in Com. Wilton, et quid Broadway in Com. Wigorn.* [Middle Hill]: Typis Medio Montanis, [1840?]. Includes many wills, deeds, pedigrees, etc.; medieval-19th c.

SKINNER, A.J.P. 'Humphrey Phillipps', *N.Q.S.D.* 12, 1911, 224-7. Lists descendants, 17-19th c., including England and How families.

Phillipson

PHILLIPSON, WAYNE. 'The Phillipson family in Bristol', *J.B.A.* 73, 1993, 22-3. 19th c.

Phripp

PHRIPP, FRANK. 'The Phripps found at Kilmington', *J.D.F.H.S* 4(3), 1991, 105-7. Parish register extracts, 19-20th c.

Pidgeon

ATHERTON, RALPH S. 'Pidgeons of Winchcombe: did they fly to Shropshire?', *J.G.F.H.S.* 55, 1992, 15. Early 19th c.

Pigott

See Smyth-Pigott

Pillinger

LINDEGAARD, PATRICIA. 'Extracts from the visiting book of the Rev. Charles Parkin, curate of Brislington, 1827', *J.B.A.* **8**, 1977, 5-6. Notes on various Pillinger families.

LINDEGAARD, PATRICIA. 'Wiltshire wanderings', *W.F.H.S.* **1**, 1981, 24-6. Pillinger family, 17-18th c.

Pine

See Rowe

Pinney

UDAL, J.S. 'The Bettiscombe skull: Pinney family', *N.Q.S.D.* **8**, 1903, 308-14. See also 315-23, 350-4, & 363. Includes pedigree, 17-18th c.

Pinsent

PINSENT, R.F.J.H. 'A surname and a source', *Devon historian* **10**, 1975, 32-5. Pinsent family.

Piper

SOPER, H.T. 'Piper family', *D.C.N.Q.* **9**, 1916, 31.

Pitcher

See Perne

Pitman

PITMAN, CHARLES E. *History and pedigree of the family of Pitman of Dunchideock, Exeter, and their collaterals, and of the Pitmans of Alphington, Norfolk, and of Edinburgh, with part pedigrees and accounts of families connected by marriage: Andrew, Sanders, Barnes, Kitson, Astley, Keats, Northcote, Gordon, Walrond, Bulteel, Stapleton, Harris, Senhouse, Coker, Manley, Palk, and Williams, with biographies of individuals ... and with extracts from wills and parish registers, and list of Dunchideock title deeds and other family papers.* Mitchell, Hughes & Clarke, 1920. Includes folded pedigree. 16-19th c.

PITMAN, H.A. 'Pitman of Quarley and North Tidworth', *M.G.H.* 5th series **6**, 1926-8, 72-8. Quarley, Hampshire.

See Lavor

Pitt

ALMACK, A.C. 'The Pitt family of Blandford S. Mary', *D.N.* **31**, 1910, 165-75. 17-18th c.

BOYCE, CHARLES. 'A 17th century manorial rent roll', *N.Q.S.D.* **19**, 1929, 228-33. Tenants not named, but includes a pedigree of Pitt, 16-19th c.

See also Dackombe

Player

NEWTON, A. J. P. 'The Player family of Cleeve', *Yatton yesterdays* **8**, 1991, 27-8. 19th c.

Plumley

CURTIS, C. D. 'Monmouth rebellion: the Plumleys of Locking and Locking manor', *N.Q.S.D.* **29**, 1974, 269-72. See also **30**, 1980, 290-2.

Pointz

REYNOLDS, HY. FITZGERALD. 'Pointz family', *D.C.N.Q.* **13**, 1924-5, 281-8. 16-18th c.

Pole

VIVIAN, J.L. *Pedigree of the Pole-Carew family of Devon, reprinted from the visitation of the county of Devon, with additions and corrections.* Exeter: W. Pollard, 1892.

See also Bonville, Carew, Courtenay and St. Barbe

Polglase

D'ARCY, LORRAINE. *The Polglase family history from 1239 A.D.* Geelong: the author, 1992. Of Cornwall and Australia; includes pedigrees.

Polkinghorne

PASCOE, W.H. 'A pool of Polks', *C.F.H.S.J.* **82**, 1996, 27. Polkinghorne family; brief note.

Pollard

LINEHAN, C.D. 'Pollard and Forde Abbey', *D.C.N.Q.* **29**(9), 1964, 252. See also **29**(11), 1964, 302-4.

POLLARD, W.B. 'William Pollard of Devon and the West Indies and some of his descendants', *Barbados Museum journal* **25**(2), 1958, 54-74.

ROBERTS, JOHN. 'Pollard and Forde Abbey', *D.C.N.Q.* **29**, 1962-4, 252. See also 302-4. 16-17th c.

ROWE, J.V. 'Pollard, Martin, Orchard', *D.C.N.Q.* **30**, 1965-7, 185-95.

See Fox

Polmear

SEED, R. 'Polmear of Zennor', *C.F.H.S.J.* **40**, 1986, 23. 17-18th c.

Polrudden

BATCHELOR, K.M. 'A forgotten family: the Polruddens of Pentewan', *Old Cornwall* **6**, 1961-7, 30-31. Medieval.

Pomeroy

BENSON, JOHN. 'Pomeroy', *D.C.N.Q.* **24**, 1950-51, 9-10.

BOND, THOMAS. *Pedigree of the family of Pomeroy of Berry Pomeroy in Devonshire, with its branches.* Exeter: William Pollard, 1891. Reprinted from *Visitations of Devon,* 12-18th c.

POMEROY, ALBERT. *A history and genealogy of the Pomeroy family, comprising the ancestors and descendants of Eltweed Pomeroy from Beaminster, County Dorset, England, 1630.* 2 vols. Toledo, Ohio: the author, 1912-22.

POWLEY, E. *The house of De La Pomerai: the annals of the family, which was, from the conquest to 1548, seated at Beri (Berry Pomeroy), in Devonshire, and, from c.1620 to 1719, resident at Sandridge in Stoke Gabriel, in that county: the status of the lords of Beri: their castle home, together with many notices of scions of the house and of other bearers of the De La Pomerai (Pomeroy) name.* Liverpool: Liverpool University Press, 1944.

SCANES, J. 'The Pomeroys of Berry Pomeroy', *D.A.Tr.* **64**, 1932, 257-71.

WORTHY, CHARLES. 'Berry castle and its ancient lords', *D.A.Tr.* **15**, 1883, 163-79. Pomeroy family, including a pedigree to the 17th c.

See also Cheevers

Pontius
See Allin

Poole
DUNLOP, J. RENTON. 'Pedigree of the Pooles of Sapperton and Coates, Gloucestershire, and of Poole, and Chelworth, Wiltshire', *M.G.H.* 5th series **3**, 1918-19, 205-11. 16-17th c.

'Pedigree of the Pooles of Coates, Gloucestershire', *M.G.H.* 5th series **3**, 1918-19, 216-7. 16-18th c.

'Pedigree of the Pooles of Poole, Chelworth, Oaksey and Kemble, Wiltshire', *M.G.H.* 5th series **3**, 1918-19, 212-5. 16-18th c.

'Wiltshire members of the Long Parliament', *W.N.Q.* **1**, 1893-5, 329-34. Despite the title, concerns the Poole family of Oaksey, 16-17th c.

Poore
JONES, W.H. 'On the surname Poore: its origin and meaning', *W.A.M.* **19**(56), 1881, 232-4. Medieval.

Pope
HALL, IVY. 'Whitson Court Sugar House, Bristol', *B.G.A.S.T.* **65**, 1944, 1-97. Pope family, includes pedigree, 17-19th c.

POPE, A. *A book of remembrance, being a short summary of the service and sacrifice rendered to the Empire during the Great War by one of the many patriotic families of Wessex: the Popes of Wrackleford, Co. Dorset.* Chiswick Press, 1919.

POPE, CHARLES HENRY. *A history of the Dorchester Pope family, 1634-1888, with sketches of other Pope families in England and America, and notes upon several intermarrying families.* Boston: the author, 1888.

POPE, F.J. 'The Pope family of Sterthill, Dorset, and Massachusetts', *N.Q.S.D.* **15**, 1917, 54-6. 16-17th c.

Popham
POPHAM, FREDERICK W. *A West Country family: the Pophams from 1150.* Sevenoaks: The Author, 1976. Somerset, Devon and Hampshire.

See also Calston

Portal
PORTAL, WILLIAM WYNDHAM, SIR. *Abraham Portal, born 1726, died 1809, and his descendants.* Winchester: Warren & Son, 1925. Includes pedigree 17-20th c.

PORTAL, WILLIAM, SIR. *The story of Portals Ltd., of Laverstock, makers of good paper for over 200 years, 1719-1925.* [ ], 1925. Brief.

Porter
PORTER, ELEANOR, & ABBOTT, MARY. *Yeomen of the Cotswolds: a journey of discovery which traces the history of a Cotswold farming family back to the 14th century.* Upton upon Severn: Images Publishing (Malvern), 1995. Porter family of Oxfordshire and Gloucestershire. Includes pedigree, 15-20th c.

'Early history of the Cornish family, Porter of Trematon', *M.G.H.* 4th series **5**, 1914, 189-93. Includes pedigree, medieval-16th c., with *inquisitions post mortem.*

Portman
HAWKINS, M. J. 'Wardship, royalist delinquency and too many children: the Portmans in the seventeenth century', *Southern history* **4**, 1982, 55-89.

MAYBERRY, T.W. *Orchard and the Portmans.* Taunton: the author, 1986. Includes pedigrees, medieval-20th c.

PORTMAN, MARJORIE. *Bryanston: picture of a family.* Sherborne: Dorset Pubs., 1987.

Pote

HARVEY, H.H. 'Pote family', *D.C.N.Q.* 20(4), 1938, 173-6.
See also Rudman

Poulet(t)

FRANKLYN, CHARLES A.H. *A genealogical history of the families of Paulet (Pawlett), Bereure (Barrow), Lawrence and Parker ... from circa 750 ... to 1963.* Bedford: Foundry Press, 1963. A supplement was published Hassocks, Sussex: the author, 1968. Dorset family.

WINN, COLIN G. *The Pouletts of Hinton St. George: the story of a Somerset village and its first family.* 2nd ed. Stroud: Alan Sutton, 1995, Includes pedigree, 13-20th c.

Powell

POWELL, EDWARD. *The pedigree of the family of Powell, sometime resident at Mildenhall, Barton Mills, and Hawstead in Co. Suffolk, and afterwards at Homerton and Clapton, Co. Middlesex, and elsewhere, from Henry VII to Victoria, to which are added pedigrees of Thistlethwaite of Co. Wilts.* The author, 1891.

CONNER, PHILLIP S.P. 'Somerset knighthood compositions', *N.Q.S.D.* 4, 1895, 181. See also 5, 1897-8, 273-4 & 317-8. Powell family.

Pownall

DYER, ARTHUR STEPHENS. 'The Pownall family', *M.G.H.* 4th series 3, 1910, 45-6. Pedigree, 17-18th c.

Powys

FAIRMAN, M. F. D. 'The Powys family', *Dorset year book* 1974-75, 19-21.
POWYS, LITTLETON C. *The Powys family.* New York: Haskell House, 1974.

Poyntz

MACLEAN, JOHN, SIR. *Historical and genealogical memoirs of the family of Poyntz, or, eight centuries of an English house.* Exeter: William Pollard, 1886. Includes pedigrees, medieval-19th c., of Cory Malet, Somerset, North Ockendon, Essex, Iron Acton, Gloucestershire, Reigate, Surrey, Benefield, Northamptonshire, *etc.,* etc.

THOMPSON, H.L. 'The Poyntz family', *B.G.A.S.T.* 4, 1879-80, 73-85.

Prater

PRATER, JOHN WILLIAM. *Praters in Wiltshire, 1480-1670 volume 1.* Hendersonville, N.S.: [the author?], 1987. Includes pedigrees, and many extracts from parish registers, wills, deeds, etc. Volume 2 deals with the American branch of the family.

Pratt

PRATT, R.M. 'Pratt-Sydenham', *D.C.N.Q.* 17, 1932-3, 228-31. Pratt family, 16-17th c.

Preece

PREECE, JIM. 'From Jim Preece', *F.F.* 9, 1992, 16-17. Preece family, 19th c.

Prestwood

See Prowse

Prettejohn

COWELL, PETER. 'Prettejohn', *Stokenham occasional papers* 3, 1981, 60-64. Includes pedigree, 17-20th c.

Prideaux

ALEXANDER, J.J. 'Prideaux of Orcherton and Adeston', *D.C.N.Q.* 21(6), 1941, 257-60. 13-16th c.

FEATHERS, CLIFFORD PRIDEAUX. *Prideaux families.* Merlo Park, California: [?], 1952.

FINBERG, H.R. 'Prideaux of Tavistock and Altarnun', *D.C.N.Q.* 21(8), 1941, 337-45. 16-19th c.

HUTCHINSON, O. 'Arms of the Prideaux family', *W.A.* 10, 1891, 138-40. See also 9, 1890, 161 & 203. Includes pedigree, 15-18th c.

MACLEAN, JOHN, SIR. *A brief memoir of the families of Prideaux of Devon and Cornwall, and of Brune of Hants and Dorset.* Exeter: William Pollard, 1874. Reprinted from his *History of Trigg-Minor.* Includes pedigree, medieval-19th c.

PRIDEAUX, R. 'Descending lines and the search for connections in an expanding population', *Local population studies* 36, 1986, 8-18.

PRIDEAUX, R.M. *Prideaux: A Westcountry clan.* Chichester: Phillimore, 1989. Medieval-20th c., includes many pedigrees.

PRIDEAUX, T. ENGLEDUE. *Pedigree of the family of Prideaux of Luson in Ermington, Devon.* Exeter: W. Pollard, 1889. Medieval-18th c., also of Cornwall.

THOMAS, MARGARET A. 'The Prideaux family and their patronage of Padstow church', *Cornwall Association of Local Historians journal* 31, 1996, 15-19. 16-20th c.

'Entries on fly-leaves of the holy bible ... belonging to C.G. Prideaux Brune, esq., of Prideaux Place', *M.G.H.* N.S. **1**, 1874, 195-6. Prideaux family of Padstow, 18-19th c.

Prince
JONES, WINSLOW. 'The author of the worthies of Devon and the Prince family', *D.A.Tr.* **25**, 1893, 382-7.
WATKIN, HUGH R. 'John Prince's genealogy', *D.C.N.Q.* **14**, 1926-7, 180-3. See also 202-3.

Pring
PRING, JAMES H. 'The Prings of Awliscombe, Devonshire, Eng', *N.E.H.G.R.* **41**, 1887, 86-8. 16-17th c. extracts from the parish register.

Prout
LEA, J. HENRY. 'Genealogical gleanings among the English archives', *N.E.H.G.R.* **55**, 1901, 95-106. Prout family of Devon and Cornwall; includes wills, extracts from parish registers, and Chancery proceedings, with folded pedigree, 16-18th c.
R., J.H. 'Ancestry of Samuel Prout', *D.C.N.Q.* **12**, 1922-3, 59. See also 137-8. Mostly 18-19th c.
PROUT, CHARLES H., & DOWNES, JEAN E. PROUT. *Prout family history: Cornwall, England/Cleveland, U.S.A.* 2nd ed. Milwaukee: C.H. Prout, c.1974.

Prouz
See Cood and Prowse

Provis
WARRICK, A.B. 'Provis family of Warminster', *W.F.H.S.* **49**, 1993, 22-3. 18-19th c.

Prowse
BENSON, J. 'The ancestors of Prouz of Chagford', *D.A.Tr.* **72**, 1940, 179-84.
BENSON, J. 'The heritage of Prouz', *D.A.Tr.* **73**, 1941, 139-51. Connections with De Moelys, Daumarle, Wibbery, Wotton, Durnford and Gorges families.
BENSON, J. 'Prowse of Prowse', *D.C.N.Q.* **26**, 1954-5, 140-3.
COLBY, F.T. 'Deed of gift from Sir William Le Pruz to his brother William Le Pruz', *Genealogist* N.S., **6**, 1890, 171-2. Concerns lands in North Devon, 13th c.
EVANS, H.R. 'Broadhempston: The background of an unfilled official form', *D.C.N.Q.* **26**(6), 1955, 177-83. Prowse, Prestwood and Tozer families.

PROWSE, IRWIN. *From Cornwall to the colonies: a Prowse chronicle, 1760-1990.* [Merimbula]: I.Prowse, 1992.
WADE, E. F. 'Notes on the family of Prowse, of Compton Bishop, Co. Somerset', *M.G.H.* N.S., **3**, 1880, 162-3 & 165-9. Monumental inscriptions, extracts from parish registers, and pedigree, 17-19th c.
See also Gye and Northcote

Prudum
LEGA-WEEKES, ETHEL. 'Prudum, Produm, etc., of Exeter, and the first city seal', *D.A.Tr.* **47**, 1915, 248-56. 13th c.

Puddicombe
See Halfyard

Pugsley
PUGSLEY, ROBERT JAMES. *The Pugsley story: celebrating 100 years in Australia, 1891-1991.* Moe: the author, 1991. Originally of Devon; includes pedigrees, 18-20th c.
PUGSLEY, A., SIR,. 'The Pugsley family', *D.C.N.Q.* **32**(7), 1973, 203-10.

Pulvertoft
'The Pulvertofts of Dorset', *Pulvertoft papers* **1**(7), 1984, 50-53 & 56. Includes pedigree, 16th c.

Punchard
PUNCHARD, E.G. *Punchards of Heanton-Punchardon: records of an unfortunate family.* [ ]: Privately printed, 1894. Also of various other counties. Includes pedigrees, medieval-19th c., wills, etc.
PUNCHARD, E.G. 'Punchard of Heanton-Punchard', *D.A.Tr.* **25**, 1893, 382-7.

Purnell
NEWBURY, PAUL A.R. 'The Purnells of Bristol: their origins and descendants', *J.B.A.* **84**, 1996, 32-5. 19th c.
See also Bush

Pye
MINNITT, JOHN. 'Scandal at the Vicarage', *Family tree magazine* **12**(12), 1996, 21-2. Pye *als* Woolcock of Blisland, Cornwall; 19th c.

Pyles
PRATT, R.M. 'The Pyles of Talaton', *D.C.N.Q.* **18**, 1934-5, 70-72. Extracts from Talaton parish registers, 16-17th c.

Pym
'An unpublished pedigree of Pym, from the original parchment roll', *Genealogical magazine* **2**, 1898-9, 361-4.

CROUCH, W. 'Notes on the pedigree of Pym of Brymore, 1643', *Genealogical magazine* **2**, 1898-9, 475-7.

Pyne

BENSON, J. 'The Pyne family', *D.C.N.Q.* **22**(3), 1942, 103-8.

DODDERIDGE, SIDNEY E. 'Pyne of Edington, Co. Somerset', *N.Q.S.D.* **16**, 1920, 229-31. See also **23**, 1942, 240-2 & 252-3.

DODDERIDGE, SIDNEY E. 'Pyne of Stawell', *N.Q.S.D.* **17**, 1923, 248-9.

PYNE, FREDERICK WALLACE. *The John Pyne family in America, being the comprehensive genealogical record of the descendants of John Pyne (1766-1813) of Charleston, South Carolina.* Baltimore: Gateway Press, 1992. Originally (pre-18th c.) of Devon; includes pedigrees, medieval-20th c.

P[YNE], M.T. 'The family of Pyne', *D.C.N.Q.* **7**, 1912-13, 134-8. See also 155-6 & 233-6.

PYNE, M. TAYLOR. *Descendants of Galeran De Pinos in Spain, France, England and America.* New York: Tobias A. Wright, 1915.

SKINNER, A.J. 'Pyne, of Hay, in the parish of Axmouth, Devon', *N.Q.S.D.* **12**, 1911, 304-9. Pedigree, 16-18th c; includes will of Hercules Pyne of Axmouth, 1610.

Pynsent

See St. Barbe

Pyper

KING, EDWARD. 'Pyper, of Launceston and Tresmarrow, Cornwall', *Genealogist* **6**, 1882, 57-60. Includes parish register extracts and monumental inscriptions, 16-18th c.

Radford

RADFORD, C.D. 'Radfordiana Devoniensis', *D.C.N.Q.* **28**, 1959-61, 16-23, 42-6, 82-4, 112-6, 137-41, 176-82, & 288-90. 16-18th c.

RADFORD, C.D. 'The royal descent from Edward I, of the Radford families', *D.C.N.Q.* **27**, 1956-8, 209-12.

WILKIN, W.H. 'Radford of Lapford', *D.A.Tr.* **64**, 1932, 505-8. 18-19th c.

Rafarel

SNETZLER, MARJORIE F. 'The elopement', *D.F.H.* **76**, 1995, 3-8. Rafarel family of Exeter, Barnstaple, *etc.,* includes pedigree, 19th c.

Rale(i)gh

B[RUSHFIELD], T.N. 'Ralegh family', *D.N.Q.* **1**, 1900-1, 63-4. Tombstone in Cyprus.

BRUSHFIELD, T.N. 'Notes on the Ralegh family', *D.A.Tr.* **15**, 1883, 163-79.

BRUSHFIELD, T.N. 'Raleghana', *D.A.Tr.* **28**, 1896, 272-312. 17th c.

BRUSHFIELD, T.N. 'Raleghana, part iii: remarks on the ancestry of Sir Walter Ralegh', *D.A.Tr.* **32**, 1900, 308-40.

BRUSHFIELD, T.N. 'Raleghana, pt. iv: Sir Henry De Ralegh, knight', *D.A.Tr.* **34**, 1902, 455-81.

A number of other essays in this 'Raleghana' series appear in *D.A.Tr.* but they are primarily biographical essays concerning Sir Walter Raleigh, and are therefore not included here.

BRUSHFIELD, T.N. 'Sir W. Ralegh: a plea for a surname', *D.A.Tr.* **18**, 1886, 450-61. On the spelling of the name.

COXWELL-ROGERS, R.R. 'Raleigh pedigree', *M.G.H.* **2**, 1876, 155-7. 17th c.

COXWELL-ROGERS, R.R. *Raleigh pedigree: extracted from the records of the College of Arms.* Privately printed, 1869. 17-18th c.

D., S.G. 'Memoir of Sir Walter Ralegh, born 1552, beheaded, 18 Oct 1618', *N.E.H.G.R.* **16**, 1862, 105-18. Includes Ralegh pedigree, 15-17th c.

H[AMMOND], J.J. 'Raleigh of Downton, Wilts', *W.N.Q.* **7**, 1911-13, 332-3. Heraldry.

PINK, W.D. 'Raleigh of Downton', *W.N.Q.* **2**, 1896-8, 90-91. See also **5**, 1905-7, 574-5.

ROBERTS, J. 'The second marriage of Walter Rawley', *D.C.N.Q.* **34**(1), 1978, 11-12.

STANFORD, J.G. 'The Raleghs take to the sea', *Mariners' mirror* **48**, 1962, 18-35. *See also* Gilbert and Trevelyan

Ralph

RALPH, EUNICE, & RALPH, THOBURN. *The Ralphs of Saint Ives and beyond.* Wauwatosa, Wisconsin: the authors, 1973. Of St.Ives and the United States.

Randall

RUNDELL, W.W. *Notes relating to the family surnames Randall, Rendell and Rundell, and to persons who have borne these names.* Chiswick Press, 1891. Medieval-18th c., includes pedigrees.

Rashleigh

HONY, T.L. 'The Rashleigh family', *Royal Cornwall Polytechnic Society report* **106**, N.S. 9(3), 1940 (for 1939), 26. 16-17th c.

See also Ridington

Rawle

RAWLE, EDWIN JOHN. *Records of the Rawle family, collected from national archives, parish registers, wills and other sources.* Taunton: Barnicott & Pearse, Athenaeum Press, 1898. Of Somerset, Devon, Cornwall, etc., 15-19th c. Includes parish register extracts, will abstracts, monumental inscriptions, etc.

Rawlins

RAWLINS, COSMO W. H. *Family quartette: the families of Rawlins of Stoke Courcy (Somerset); Hooper of Devonport and Maidstone; Smith-Wyndham of E. Yorks, and Russell (Dukes of Bedford).* Yeovil: the author, 1962. 19-20th c

Rawlinson

See Wainwright

Raymond

RAYMOND, JOHN MARSHALL. *Raymond, Abbot, Jackson and allied families.* Palo Alto: Runnymede Press, 1962. Primarily American, but includes pedigree of Raymond of Somerset and Dorset, 16-17th c.

Rede

ROWLAND, ROBERT. 'The Rede family of Wembury', *D.F.H.* **1**, 1977, 18-20.

Redman

O'GRADY, CLODAGH. *The Redmans of Halfway House.* Ramsbury: the author, 1978. Includes pedigrees, 18-20th c.

Redvers

G., H.F. 'The Whitchurch fee', *D.N.Q.* **1**, 1900-1, 63. See also 77-9. Redvers and Giffard families, 11th-12th c.

ROSE-TROUP, F. 'The hereditary sheriffs of Devon', *D.A.Tr.* **64**, 1932, 397-413. Descendants of Baldwin the sheriff and Richard de Redvers, 12th c.

WHITEHEAD, J.L. 'Notes on the early de Redvers', *D.C.N.Q.* **11**, 1920, 445-6. *See also* Brionne and Hamlyn

Redway

REDWAY, LAURENCE ALVA. *The Redway family: a genealogical study of the family Redway, showing family trees and name registers of known Redways.* Auckland: the author 1975. Mainly 18-20th c. Includes folded pedigrees.

Reed

REED, S.D., ed. *Our Cornish heritage, genealogies of Reed, Rowe, Ebbott and related families, immigrants to Jefferson County, Wisconsin.* Rockford, Illinois: [ ], 1979.

Reeks

REEKS, LINDSAY S. *Ancestors of Reeks and Rogers, Christchurch, Dorset.* Baltimore: Gateway Press, 1989.

Reeve

REEVES, JAY, et al. *From Dorset farm to Ohio factory: a history of the family of Albert George and Martha Reeves.* [ ]: J. M. Reeves, 1992. Supplement 1994. Reeve of Motcombe and Gillingham.

Reeves

See Whitaker

Rendall/Rendel(l)

DAVIES, I. R. 'Charles Rendall, blacksmith', *G.T.* 13(2 & 3), 1988, 49 & 79. Crewkerne area.

HALL, R. de Z. 'Rendells of West Coker', *N.Q.S.D.* **28**, 1968, 265-7. 17-20th c.

LANE, MICHAEL. *The Rendel connection: a dynasty of engineers.* Quiller Press, 1989. 19-20th c., of London; originally of Devon.

REYNOLDS, CHRIS F. *The Rendell family of South Devon.* Tring: Codil Language Systems, 1988. 17-19th c., computer generated listing.
See also Randall

Retter

RETTER, FRANK. *An East Devon farm and its village.* Exeter: Obelisk Publications, 1985. Includes pedigrees of Retter and Walrond.

STANES, R. 'Retter: the making of a surname', *D.C.N.Q.* 33(4), 1975, 124-5. Of East Devon and West Somerset, 18th c.

Revel

See Reynell

Reynell

GIBSON, BARBARA. *The story of West Ogwell House.* West Ogwell: [Community of the Companions of Jesus the Good Shepherd], 1970. Includes pedigree of Reynell, 14-19th c.

UPHAM, R. 'Reynell of Exeter Castle', *D.N.Q.* **2**, 1902-3, 110-12. 12th-13th c.

HUMPHERY-SMITH, CECIL. *Hugh Revel: master of the Hospital of St. John of Jerusalem, 1258-1277.* Phillimore, 1994. Reynell family.

UPHAM, R. 'Reynell of Parker's Well', *D.N.Q.* **2**, 1902-3, 137-8. Includes part of will of Robert Prudom of Exeter, 1792.

UPHAM, W.R. 'Reynell, Steede, Easterbrooke, Sainthill', *D.N.Q.* **1**, 1900-1, 111-2.

Reynolds

CRONIN, WILLIAM VINE. *A history of the works of Sir Joshua Reynolds.* Includes pedigree of Reynolds of Exeter, 17-19th c.

EDGCUMBE, ROBERT, SIR. *The parentage and kinsfolk of Sir Joshua Reynolds.* Chiswick Press, 1901.

R., C.B. 'Reynolds family', *N.Q.S.D.* **11**, 1909, 23-4. 17-18th c.

REYNOLDS, ROBERT W. *Thomas and Ann Reynolds of Cornwall and their descendants.* Livonia: R.W. Williams, 1979. 19-20th c., includes pedigrees.

The Reynolds family: their association with Pinhoe. [Exeter: Devon & Exeter Daily Gazette], 1911. Reprinted from the *Gazette.*

See also Colby and Pearce

Reyny

LYTE, H. MAXWELL. 'The heirs of Sir William de Reyny', *N.Q.S.D.* **19**, 1929, 52-4. 13-14th c.

Richards

GLANVILLE-RICHARDS, W.S. 'Richards of Kentisbury, Devon: extracts from the registers of that parish', *M.G.H.* N.S., **4**, 1884, 17 & 29-30.

MOORE-SMITH, G.C. 'Richards of Kentisbury, Co. Devon', *Genealogist* N.S., **27**, 1911, 78-84.

SYKES, E.R. 'John Richards of Warmwell: his family, diary (1697-1701), and day-book', *D.N.* **65**, 1943, 112-22. Includes parish register extracts, 17-18th c.

See also Ridington

Rickard

RICKARD, R.J. 'The hunting of poor Henry', *D.F.H.* **25**, 1983, 22-5.

Richmond

RICHMOND, HENRY I. *Richmond family records.* 3 vols. Adlard & Sons, 1933-38. v. 1. Maryland, Virginia, New England, Ireland and Somerset. v.2. The Richmonds *alias* Webb of Wiltshire. v.3. The Richmonds of Wiltshire. 15-20th c.

'Pedigree of Richmond *alias* Webb, of Draycott Folliot, Wilts', *M.G.H.* 5th series **7**, 1929-31, 41-9. 17-19th c.

Ridington

CLINK, WILLIAM L. *Ridington: the genealogy of the Thomas Ridington family from its inception in 1790 and its spread from Cornwall into areas of England and North America. Connected Cornish families include Bottrall, Chynowith, Ennor, Gidley, Huthnance, Julian, Matthews, Palamountain, Richards, Rashleigh, Scoborgo, Symons, Tallack, Tonkin, Tregoning, Williams, Wright.* Willowdale, Ontario: W.L. Clink, 1989.

Rigaud

See Dutill

Rillstone

'The Rillstone family', *D.C.N.Q.* **8**, 1914-15, 85-6. 16-17th c.

Ring

PRICE, ROGER, et al. *The Ring family of Bristol, clay tobacco pipe manufacturers.* Bristol: the authors, 1982. 19th c.

Riou

WAGNER, HENRY. 'Pedigree of Riou', *M.G.H.* 3rd series **4**, 1902, 190-191. Of Frome, Somerset, and London; 18-19th c.

Risdon

JORDAN, MARY HALL. 'Leaves from the notebook of John Risdon of Netherton Manor and West Teignmouth', *D.A.Tr.* **40**, 1908, 138-47. Includes pedigree of Risdon of Bableigh, 15-18th c., together with monumental inscriptions, etc.

Rivers

See Savage

Robartes

ROWE, J. HAMBLEY. 'Robartes family of Lanhydrock', *Royal Cornwall Polytechnic Society annual reports* **98**, N.S. **7**, 1932, 131-4. 17-19th c.

Robins

ROBBINS, MILLS R. *Gleanings of the Robins or Robbins family of England ...* 2nd ed. Devizes: C.H. Woodward, 1908. 13-20th c., includes pedigrees.

G., J. 'The Robin family: Gloucestershire', *G.N.Q.* **4**, 1890, 159-62. 16-18th c.

Robinson

DARWIN, BERNARD. *Robinsons of Bristol, 1844-1944.* Bristol: E. S. & A. Robinson, 1945.

Roche

PAYNE, H.M.C. 'A mystery of Roche', *Royal Cornwall Polytechnic Society report* **112**, N.S. 9(4, section 2), 1945, 7-12. Roche family (later Tregarrick), medieval.

Rocke

ROBINSON, C.J. 'Rocke family', *N.Q.S.D.* **3**, 1893, 164-5.

Rockwell

ROCKWELL, FRANCIS WILLIAMS. *The Rockwell family in one line of descent.* Pittfield, Mass: [.], 1924.

Rodda

See Berryman

Rodney

RODNEY, EDWARD, SIR. 'The genealogy of the family of Rodney of Rodney Stoke', *Genealogist* N.S., **16**, 1900, 207-14; **17**, 1901, 6-12 & 100-106.
See also Fitzroger

Rogers

ROGERS, W.H. HAMILTON. 'Rogers-Courtenay-Huddesfield of Bradford-on-Avon, Wilts, Cannington, Somerset, and Shillingford, Devon', in his *Archaeological papers relating to the counties of Somerset, Wilts, Hants and Devon.* [ ]: the author, 1902.

ROGERS, W.H.H. 'Rogers-Courtenay-Huddesfield of Bradford-on-Avon, Wilts, Cannington, Somerset, and Shillingford, Devon', *W.N.Q.* **3**, 1899-1901, 337-45. 16th c.

R[OGERS], W.H.H. 'Rogers of Brianston, Dorset, and Barwick, Somerset', *N.Q.S.D.* **8**, 1903, 290-4 & 337-42. See also **9**, 1905, 61.

'Rogers genealogy', *M.G.H.* **1**, 1868, 258-65. Of Dorset and Gloucestershire. 15-19th c.

'The Lady Mary Harington's pedigree (nee Rogers of Cannington, Somerset)', *M.G.H.* N.S., **3**, 1880, 219-20. 16-17th c. descent from Sidenham.
See also Harington, Reeks and St. Barbe

Rohaut

See Fitzalan

Rolf

FORSYTH, C.L. *John Rolf and his descendants.* Melbourne: the author, 1984. Of Wiltshire and Australia; 18-20th c.
See also Dyer

Rolfe

FRENCH, ELIZABETH. 'Genealogical research in England', *N.E.H.G.R.* **66**, 1912, 244-52. Rolfe family of Downton, Wiltshire and Andover, Hampshire, 16-17th c., includes pedigree, wills and extracts from parish registers.

Rolls

'Rolls family', *N.Q.S.D.* **3**, 1893, 129-30. See also 184.

Rooke

WAGNER, HENRY. 'Pedigree of Rooke, of Co's Kent and Gloucestershire', *Genealogist* **4**, 1880, 195-208. 16-19th c., includes wills, extracts from parish registers, and monumental inscriptions.

Rose

CLENCH, H. 'Dorset's pioneering seven: a family among the first thirteen 'free settlers' of Australia', *Dorset year book* 1918-19, 109-11. Rose family of Sturminster Newton.

Rosewarne

ROSEWARNE, PEARCE VICTOR, & ROSEWARNE, WINNIFRED. *The family history of Thomas B. Rosewarne of Cornwall, England and Muskoka, Canada, his ancestors and descendants, 1716-1968.* Ottawa: [?], 1968.

ROSEWARNE, GILLIAN. *The romance of the Rosewarnes: an ancient and modern history of the Rosewarne family of Kadina, South Australia.* West Beach, S.A.: Eureka Press, [1982?]. Also of Rosewarne; includes pedigrees, 16-20th c.

Rosewell

JAMES, FRANCES B. 'Sir Henry Rosewell: a Devon worthy: his ancestry and history', *D.A.Tr.* **20**, 1888, 113-22. Includes pedigree.

LONGDEN, H.I. 'Rosewell family', *N.Q.S.D.* **3**, 1893, 185. Includes will of William Rosewell of Dunkerton, 1565-6.

Rosier

See Waymouth

Rosse

DENARIUS. 'Rosse of Shepton Beauchamp, Co. Somerset', *Genealogist* N.S., **17**, 1901, 72. Pedigree, 18th c.

Rossiter

ROSSITER, W.J.C. 'The origin of the surname Rossiter', *D.C.N.Q.* **36**(7), 1990, 249-54. Medieval.

Rosuggan

HUGO, FRANCIS H.M. 'Notes of the surname Rosuggan', *D.C.N.Q.* **24**, 1950-51, 88-92. 15-19th c.

Rouse

CARBONELL, B.M.H. 'The Rouse or Royal Goblet', *D.C.N.Q.* **18**, 1934-5, 290-94. Includes notes on the Rouse family of Devon and Cornwall, mainly 16-19th c.
See also Harington

Rousmaniere

See Eyre

Rowe

DRAKE-BROCKMAN, E.D. 'Rowes of Kingston in Staverton', *D.C.N.Q.* **19**, 1936, 156-7.

FURNEAUX, H. 'Supplemental notes: pedigree of Rawe or Rowe (as bearing on that of Furneaux) of Cutlinworth, Landrake, Cornwall, also of other places in Landrake, and of Markwell, St.Erney', *M.G.H.* N.S. **2**, 1877, 252-6. 16-19th c., includes deed abstracts, etc.

ROWE, J.Y. 'Descent of John Rowe, serjeant-at-law, Staverton', *D.C.N.Q.* **28**, 1959-61, 59-60. 15-16th c.

ROWE, J.L. 'Rowe family and El Cid', *D.C.N.Q.* **30**, 1965-7, 314-6.

ROWE, J.Y. 'Rowe family', *D.C.N.Q.* **27**, 1956-8, 314-7; **28**, 1959-61, 266-9; **29**, 1962-4, 65-7 & 116-8.

ROWE, J.Y. 'Rowe, Methuen, Howard families and Holcombe Court', *D.C.N.Q.* **30**(5), 1966, 136-8.

ROWE, J.Y. 'Some Rowe-Pine-Coffin connections', *D.C.N.Q.* **30**(1), 1965, 15-18. Of Cheshire, Leicestershire and Devon; mainly medieval.

ROWE, J.Y. 'Spicer family', *D.C.N.Q.* **30**, 1965-7, 173-4. 17-18th c. Despite the title, mainly concerned with the Rowe family, 18th c.

ROWE, KENNETH ALLYN. *Research in Rowe* search. Danvers, Mass: V. Rowe, 1980.

Rowland(s)

ROWLAND, A.B. *The Rowland journal: a pilgrimage through some references to the surname, with particular reference to those originating in Bradninch within the county of Devonshire.* Dawlish: the author, 1996. 17-20th c.

ROWLANDS, ELISABETH. *John and Annie Rowlands and their family.* Cheltenham: the author, 1985. Gloucestershire family.
See also Reed

Rudder

PHILLIMORE, W.P.W. 'The Rudder family', *G.N.Q.* **2**, 1884, 80-82. 17-18th c.

Ruddock

COTTON, W. 'A family story from the register of Broadwoodkelly', *N.G.D.C.* **1**, 1888, 3-4.

Rudman

MELVILLE, JANET. *Rudman register and related families: Erasmus, Pole, Kirch.* Port Elizabeth, Western Australia: the author, 1980. 19-20th c. Of Wiltshire and Australia, etc.

Rundle

CROW, RICHARD. 'The Hole Story: the history of a Cornish house', *Old Cornwall* **10**(9), 1989, 446-57; **10**(10), 481-6. Descent of property; includes pedigrees of Rundle, 16-19th c., and Bawden, 16-17th c., also will of James Rundle, 1637.

HUGO, FRANCIS H.M. 'Rundle, Arundel', *D.C.N.Q.* **24**, 1950-51, 158-61. See also 196-7 & **25**, 1952-3, 79-80.

RUNDLE, DONALD WORTH. *The book: Rundle, 1796-1947.* [?]: Rundle, [1974?]. Of Cornwall and the United States, 18-20th c.
See also Randall

Rush

see Bush

Russ

CURNOW, E. 'Russ of Kingsbury', *G.T.* **12**(3), 1987, 86. New Zealand migrants.

LINDSAY, KAY L. 'Russ of Tintinhull, Martock and Stoke Sub Hamden', *G.T.* **9**(2), 1984, 54-6. Includes pedigree, 17-20th c.

Russell

CRESSWELL, B.F. 'Cowick Barton', *D.C.N.Q.* **18**(6), 1935, 242-6. Russell and Baron families.

THOMSON, G.S. 'Exeter and the Russell Earls of Bedford', *D.C.N.Q.* **17**, 1932, 13-30.

THOMSON, GLADYS SCOTT. *Family background.* Jonathan Cape, 1949. Russell family in Dorset, Cambridgeshire and Bedfordshire.

THOMSON, GLADYS SCOTT. *Two centuries of family history: a study in social development.* Longmans Green & Co., 1930. Of Swyre.

TRATEBAS, GLADYS N. 'Russell and Coates family of Cheltenham and London', *J.G.F.H.S.* **38**, 1988, 22-3. Includes pedigree, 19th c.

TRENT, CHRISTOPHER. *The Russells.* Frederick Muller, 1966.

WIFFEN, J.H. *Historical memoirs of the house of Russell, from the time of the Norman Conquest.* 2 vols. Longman, Rees, Orme, Brown, Green, & Longman, 1833. *See also* Banger, Hooper, Rawlins and Spicer

Rydon

RYDON, JOAN. *The Rydon family, Somerset to Australia.* [Kew, Victoria]: John Soper, 1994. Includes pedigrees, 16-20th c.

Ryve

CHILDS, J.R. *Reliques of the Rives (Ryves) ... being historical and genealogical notes of the ancient family of Ryves of County Dorset and of the Rives of Virginia ...* Lynchbury, Virginia: J. P. Bell Co., 1929. See also *supplement,* 1954.
'Ryve of Dorset', *G.T.* **13**(3), 1988, 97. Compiled solely from *Alumni Oxoniensis.*

Sadler

EVERETT, C.R. 'Notes on the prebendal mansion of Sherborne Monastery, commonly known as the King's House, in the Close of Sarum', *W.A.M.* **47**(164), 1936, 398-405. Includes notes on Sadler and Beach families.
'Wroughton registers: Sadler', *W.N.Q.* **5**, 1905-7, 570-73. 17-18th c. births and baptisms.

St.Aubyn

HARTLEY, DIANA. *The St.Aubyns of Cornwall, 1200-1977.* Chesham: Barracuda Books, 1977. Includes pedigrees.

St.Barbe

URQUHART, MARGARET. *Sir John St. Barbe, Bt., of Broadlands.* Southampton: Paul Cave Publications, 1983. Includes pedigrees of St. Barbe, Pynsent, Fiennes, Chernocke, Pole, Sydenham and Rogers. 16-18th c.

St.Clair

WILLIAMS, C.L. SINCLAIR. 'The manor of Stapleton in Martock and the St. Clairs', *S.A.N.H.S.* **131**, 1986/7, 171-80. 11-14th c.

Sainthill

RADFORD, A.L. 'Portraits of the Sainthill family formerly in Bradninch manor house', *D.A.Tr.* **50**, 1918, 405-10.
ST. HILL, AMMABEL. *The history of the Sainthill family.* Mitchell Hughes and Clarke, 1938. Includes pedigrees, 13-19th c.
ST. HILL, A. 'Sainthill family of Bradninch', *D.C.N.Q.* **10**, 1918, 90. Quarterings.

TROUP, FRANCES B. 'The Sainthills of Bradninch, Devon: being a pedigree of the family, with notes thereon, and copies of documents relating to the family history', *D.A.Tr.* **21**, 1889, 383-94. *See also* Reynell

Saint Lee

See Botreaux

St. Maur

'Chelvey Court', *Somerset Archaeological and Natural History Society, Proceedings of the Bath and District Branch,* 1909-13, 101-4. Descent; especially St. Maur and Tynte families, includes the will of Edmund de St. Maur, 1421.
SAYER, M.J. 'Pedigrees of county families', *Genealogists' magazine* **20**(9), 1982, 306.
See also Botreaux

Salisbury

See Neville

Salter

SALTER, S.J.A. 'Armorials of the Salter family', *N.Q.S.D.* **2**, 1891, 209-16.
See Bartlett

Samborne

SANBORNE, V.S. 'A possible Samborne ancestry', *Ancestor* **1**, 1904, 61-70. Somerset, Wiltshire, and Berkshire.
SANBORN, V.C. *Genealogy of the family of Samborne or Sanborn in England and America, 1194-1898.* 2 pts. Concord: privately printed, 1899. Of Wiltshire, Berkshire, Hampshire, Somerset and America. Includes pedigrees.
SANBORNE, V.C. 'The Samborne ancestry', *Genealogist* N.S. **13**, 1897, 145-52. See also **14**, 1898, 72, & **15**, 1899, 264. Medieval.
SANBORNE, V.C. 'The Sambornes of England and America', *N.E.H.G.R.* **39**, 1885, 245-55. Of Somerset, Oxfordshire and Berkshire; includes pedigrees, 11-17th c.
S[ANBORNE], V.C. 'Samborne family', *N.Q.S.D.* **3**, 1893, 274-5.
'Samborne family', *W.N.Q.* **1**, 1893-5, 373-4. See also 564-5, and **2**, 1896-8, 43-5 & 92-3. 13-14th c.
'Pedigree of Samborne, from visitation of London, 1687', *Genealogist* **1**, 1877, 218-9. Of Somerset and London; 16-18th c.

Sampson

SAMPSON, ALBERT LEONARD. *The family tree of John and Ann Sampson.* Hilton, Western Australia: the author, [1984]. Of Cornwall and Australia, 17-20th c.
See also Haskett

Sandercock

THOMAS, NEIL. *1740-1981 Branching out: the family history of Richard and Elizabeth Sandercock and their descendants.* Naracoorte, South Australia: Naracoorte Herald, 1981. Of Cornwall and South Australia.

Sanders

See Pitman

Sanderson

See Merryweather

Sanxay

SANXAY, THEODORE F. *The Sanxay family, and descendants of Rev. Jacques Sanxay, Huguenot refugee to England in sixteen hundred and eighty-five.* New York: Privately Printed, 1907. Of Devon, Surrey, Sussex, etc.

Sargent

SARGEAUNT, W.T. 'Sargent of Gloucester, U.S.A.', *B.G.A.S.T.* **85**, 1966, 224-6. 17th c.

SARGEAUNT, W.T. 'The family of Sargeaunt of Hart Barn, Longhope', *B.G.A.S.T.* **78**, 1959, 110-17. Includes pedigree, 16-20th c., with will of William Sargent, 1568/9.

Saunder

KELLAND, W.H. 'Saunder of Chittlehampton', *W.A.* **4**, 1885, 175-7.
See also Clarke

Saunders

EVANS, G.E. *Pastoral pedigree.* Privately published, 1977. Saunders family, 18-20th c.

Savage

HORTON-SMITH, L.G.H. 'The family of Savage of Burbage Savage, Co. Wilts', *Notes & queries* **188**, 1945, 233-4. 13-16th c.

HORTON-SMITH, L. GRAHAM H. *The family of Savage of Co. Wilts, with a passing note on the dormant Earldom of Rivers.* Devizes: C.H. Woodward, 1944.

SALTER, JAMES. 'On armorials of the Savage family in Bloxworth church, Dorset', *D.N.* **10**, 1889, 153-61.

Savery

CURIOSUS II. 'Savery memorials', *D.C.N.Q.* **9**, 1916, 31.

Memoir of the Saverys of Devon. S. & J. Bentley, Wilson and Fley, [1934?]. Includes pedigrees (one folded) 16-19th c.
See also Cotton

Scammell

SCAMMELL, A.J. 'Ancient family rediscovered', *G.T.* **7**(2), 1982, 35-6. Scamell family of Tisbury.

Schneider

'Schneider of North Wraxhall', *W.N.Q.* **5**, 1905-7, 384. Pedigree, 18-19th c.

Schuyler

REDWOOD, URSULA. *The Schuyler family of Flushing, Cornwall.* Flushing: the author, 1988. Includes pedigree, 18-19th c.

Scoborgo

See Ridington

Scrope

See Hooke

Scrupes

CLAY, C.T. 'The family of Scrupes or Crupes of Whittington, Gloucestershire', *B.G.A.S.T.* **65**, 1944, 129-40.

Seagar

See Osborne

Seaborough

See Golde

Sealy

DAVIS, WALTER GOODWIN. 'The Sealy brothers of the Isles of Shoals', *N.E.H.G.R.* **85**, 1931, 74-79. Of Stokeinteignhead, 16-17th c., includes wills and parish register extracts.

Seaman

JEBOULT, EDWARD. *An epitome of the history of the Seaman family of Shiplette manor, Somerset.* Taunton: the author, 1891. Also includes information on Hippisley family.
See also Hippisley

Seavey

SEAVEY, JAMES I. *The ancestry of Elisha Porter Seavey, 1838-1913.* Ann Arbor, Michigan: Edwards Bros., 1958. Of Stokeinteignhead and the United States, medieval-19th c.

Seavier

See Haskett

Seccombe
JUDDERY, J.Z., TURTON, S.D., & WEDDELL, J. *Roadford Reservoir Project: The Seccombe family documents*. Exeter: Exeter Museum's Archaeological Field Unit, 1988. Transcript of 36 deeds, 15-17th c., relating to the Seccombe family.

Seede
'Genealogical notes and memoranda relating to the family of Seede, collected from title deeds, county histories, wills and other data', *M.G.H.* 2nd series **4**, 1892, 28-31, 42-3 & 52-4. Of Gloucestershire, 16-18th c.
'Seede of Tetbury, Upton Cheyney, Bitton, Bisley, Rodborough, Stroud and Bristol, Gloucestershire, and of Castlecombe, Wiltshire', *M.G.H.* 3rd series **4**, 1892, 7-11. 16-18th c.

Selhurst
See Maynard

Selleck
SELLECK, A.D. 'The Selleck family and the clay industry', *D.F.H.* **36**, 1985, 10-19.

Selfe
HEATHCOTE, T.G.J. 'Place House, Melksham with some account of the Selfe family', *W.N.Q.* **4**, 1902-4, 193-201. 17th c., includes monumental inscriptions.
HEATHCOTE, T.G.J. 'Thomas Selfe, of Cadley, in Melksham', *W.N.Q.* **4**, 1902-4, 349-56. Includes will of Isaac Selfe of Melksham, 1741.

Selwyn
BAZELEY, WILLIAM. 'Some records of Motson in the County of Gloucester, and of the Selwyns', *B.G.A.S.T.* **2**, 1877/8, 241-84. Includes pedigrees of Selwyn of Sussex and Gloucestershire, 15-19th c.
SWYNNERTON, CHARLES. 'Some early Selwyns', *B.G.A.S.T.* **47**, 1925, 205-9. Medieval.

Senhouse
See Pitman

Sevier
See Haskett

Seward
SQUIBB, G.D. 'Seward family of Yeovil', *N.Q.S.D.* **25**, 1950, 234-7. 17th c.

Sewster
ANDREWS, HERBERT C. 'The Sewster family of Godmanchester, Hunts., Steeple Morden, Cambs., and Ashwell, Herts., with notes on

the Dodington family of Wilts and Herts.', *M.G.H.* 5th series **7**, 1929-31, 333-48. Includes pedigrees, medieval-17th c.

Seymer
FRY, GEO. S. 'John Seymer of Stoke Wake, Dorset', *N.Q.S.D.* **7**, 1901, 262-3. 17th c., includes genealogical notes.

Seymour
BARTLETT, R.G. 'Seymour in Rollestone registers', *W.N.Q.* **2**, 1896-8, 533. See also 586-9.
JACKSON, J.E. *Wulfhall and the Seymours, with an appendix of original documents discovered at Longleat.* [ ]: privately printed, 1874. Reprinted from *W.A.M.* **15**(44), 1875, 140-207. 16-17th c., includes appendix calendaring 26 documents, which give many names of household members.
LOCKE, A. AUDREY. *The Seymour family: history and romance.* Constable, 1911. 16-19th c.
ST. MAUR, H. *Annals of the Seymours, being a history of the Seymour family from early times to within a few years of the present.* Kegan Paul, Trench, Trubner & Co., 1902. Devon and Somerset.
'Genealogical account of the most noble family of Seymour', *Universal magazine* March 1765, 128-32. Medieval-18th c.

Seyntclere
HANHAM, H.J. 'The Seyntcleres of Tidwell: the rise and fall of a Budleigh family', *D.A.Tr.* **99**, 1967, 139-46.

Shapcote
SHAPCOTE, DOROTHY. 'Shapcote or Shapcott family of Knowstone', *D.C.N.Q.* **14**, 1928-9, 98-9 & 162-3; **15**, 1928, 30-37. 18th c.

Shapleigh
SARGENT, W.M. 'The Shapleighs of Devonshire', *W.A.* **5**(10), 1886, 221-7.

Sharington
VERNON, THELMA E. 'Inventory of Sir Henry Sharington: contents of Lacock House, 1575', *W.A.M.* **62**, 1967, 72-82. Includes notes on family; not a probate inventory.

Sharpe
SCHOMBERG, A. 'Sharpe family', *N.Q.S.D.* **3**, 1893, 105-7. Memoranda book giving dates of birth.

Sheate
'Connections', *G.T.* 10(3), 1985, 107. List of families connected with Sheate of Baltonsborough and New Zealand, 18-20th c.

Shebbeare
SHEBBEARE, C.E. 'Abbotsham Court in bygone days', *D.C.N.Q.* 11, 1920-21, 289-95. Includes account of the Shebbeare family.

Shepherd
SKINNER, A.J. 'Shepherd of Watton Court, Honiton, and Lawell', *D.C.N.Q.* 11, 1921, 315-20. Includes 18th c. pedigree, and wills of James Shepherd, 1733, and Sir James Shepherd, 1730.

SOPER, M.W.S. *Thrice three times told tales.* Winchester, Tennessee: Franklin, 1979. Shepherd family.

Sheppard
[BODDINGTON, R.S.] *Pedigree of the family of Sheppard.* Mitchell and Hughes, 1883. 17-19th c.

GILL, D.J. *The Sheppards and eighteenth century Frome.* Frome: Frome Society for Local Study, 1982.

SHEPPARD, WILLIAM ALBERT. *A brief history of the Sheppard family, formerly seated at the manors of Avening, Minchinhampton, and Colesbourne, in the county of Gloucestershire, England, with pedigrees of the elder and junior branches of these ancient families ...* Calcutta: Thos. C.Smith, 1891. Includes folded pedigree, 17-19th c.
See also Mortimer

Sherborne
See Dutton

Sherman
HUTCHINSON, O. 'The families of Cooke and Carwithen', *W.A.* 10, 1891, 12-14. Despite the title, this article primarily deals with the Sherman family.
See also Bonville

Sherrill
SHERRILL, W.A. 'The Sherwill/Sherrill family of Devon', *D.F.H.* 10, 1979, 7.

Sherwill
See Tuckett

Shilstone
ALEXANDER, J.J. 'The Shilstones', *D.C.N.Q.* 21(1), 1940, 25-30.

Shipp
See Spooner

Shipway
HAINES, ROBERT J. 'The Shipway pedigree fraud, or, Regina v. Davies, 1897', *Gloucestershire history* 4, 1990, 5-6.

PHILLIMORE, W.P.W. *The 'principal genealogical specialist', or, Regina v. Davies and the Shipway genealogy, being the story of a remarkable pedigree fraud.* Phillimore & Co., 1899.

Shore
See Bater

Shumack
SHUMACK, JOHN. *The Shumack family.* Wisbech: Ye Olde Prynt Shoppe, 1982. Somerset family.

Shute
HYLTON, LORD. 'Kilmersdon manor-house', *S.A.N.H.S.* 75, 1929, 42-5. Shute family; 17-19th c.

Sidenham
See Rogers

Siderfin
SANDERS, JAMES. *History of the Siderfin family of West Somerset.* Exeter: W. J. Southwood & Co., 1912.

Sidmouth
See Addington

Silverthorn
REED, FRANK FREMONT. *History of the Silverthorn family.* Chicago: Silverthorn(e) Family Association, 1982. Continued in *Silverthorn(e) family newsletter,* 1984- . Steeple Ashton and U.S.A., 16-20th c. Includes many transcripts of original sources.

Sirr
See Mate

Sikes
SYKES, JOHN. 'Sikes of Dartmouth', *W.A.* 4, 1885, 200. Pedigree, 17-18th c.

Skeffington
WERE, F. 'Drake and Skeffington', *D.C.N.Q.* 9, 1917, 143-4.

Skrine
WALKER, E.W. AINLEY. *Skrine of Warleigh in the county of Somerset, with pedigrees, being some materials for a genealogical history of the family of Skrine.* Taunton: Wessex Press, 1936.

Skues

SKUES, KEITH. *Cornish heritage.* Werner Shaw, 1983. Includes numerous extracts from, and abstracts of, original sources, medieval-20th c.

Skutt

POYNTON, F.J. 'Skutt notes', *N.Q.S.D.* **2**, 1891, 17-18. Includes 16th c. pedigree.

Slade

See Wallis

Slanning

JONES, WINSLOW. 'The Slannings of Leye, Bickleigh, and Maristow', *D.A.Tr.* **19**, 1887, 451-66. Includes pedigree, 16th-18th c.

Slaughter

'The Slaughter family', *G.N.Q.* **2**, 1884, 64-8. See also 17.

Sleeman

HARDY, GLYNN. *The Sleeman family tree.* 2nd ed. [ ]: Brent L. Hardy, 1990. Of Boyton and New Zealand, etc., 19-20th c. Includes pedigrees.

Sleep

SLEEP, RICHARD PETER. *The Sleep connection.* [ ]: the author, 1992. 18-20th c.

Slocum

MORIARTY, G. ANDREWS. 'Parentage of Giles Slocum of Portsmouth, R.I.', *N.E.H.G.R.* **70**, 1916, 283-4. See also **78**, 1924, 395-6. Of Old Cleeve; includes notes on 17th c. wills etc.

Smallbone

GEORGE, BRIAN. 'Genealogical agony', *W.F.H.S.* **7**, 1982, 4-6. Smallbone family, 19-20th c.

GEORGE, BRIAN. 'The Smallbones discovered, or, if at first you don't succeed ...', *W.F.H.S.* **20**, 1985, 13-15. 19-20th c.

GEORGE, BRIAN. 'More Smallbones discovered', *W.F.H.S.* **35**, 1989, 27-8. Berkshire, Hampshire and Wiltshire, 17-19th c.

Smerdon

BROWN, MIKE. *Buckland who's who 1600-1900. Vol. 1 The Smerdons.* Dartmoor archive researchers transcripts and guides 5. Plymouth: Dartmoor Press, 1995. Biographical dictionary of an extensive family.

Smerdon newsletter. Plymouth: Dartmoor Press, 1996- .

Smith

BRYANT, EDITH. 'Smith of Devon and Somerset; Smith of Cornwall', *D.C.N.Q.* **16**, 1930-31, 250-3. 16-17th c.

BRYANT, EDITH. 'Smith of Thornecombe, Devon', *D.C.N.Q.* **15**, 1928-99, 275-82. See also 357-62; **16**, 1930-31, 55-63. 151-3 & 253-5.

BRYANT, EDITH. 'Smith of Thornecombe, Devon; Smith of Cawood, Nr. Selby, Yorks', *D.C.N.Q.* **16**, 1930-31, 296-8.

PHILLIMORE, W.P.W. *Some account of the family of Smith anciently of Shute in Devonshire.* Phillimore & Co., 1900. 17-19th c., includes parish register extracts.

P., T. 'Smith family', *W.N.Q.* **1**, 1893-5, 374-5. See also 425-6. 17th c.

SMITH, ARTHUR M. *Some account of the Smiths of Exeter.* Exeter: William Pollard & Co., 1896.

SMITH, EDWARD FLOYER NOEL. *The pedigree of Smith, (sometimes Smyth, Smythe and Smithe), now Smith-Marriott, of Sydling and the Down House, Dorset, Baronet (formerly of Exeter, Madford and Larkbeare, Devon); also of Suttons, Essex, Baronet.* Harrison and Sons, 1878. Includes folded pedigree, 14-19th c.

WELCH, C.E. 'A Hampshire sailor in Devonport', *D.C.N.Q.* **29**(4), 1963, 113-5.

'Two informative bibles', *W.F.H.S.* **31**, 1988, 31. Births, marriages and deaths of Smith of Salisbury, and Ellison. 19-20th c.

See also Henbury and Montagu

Smith-Marriott

See Smith

Smith-Wyndham

See Hooper and Rawlins

Smyth

BANTOCK, ANTON. *The earlier Smyths of Ashton Court from their letters, 1545-1741.* Bristol: Malago Society, 1982. Includes pedigree.

BANTOCK, ANTON. *The inside story of the Smyths of Ashton Court.* Bristol: Malago Archives Committee, 1977.

BANTOCK, ANTON. *The later Smyths of Ashton Court from their letters, 1741-1802.* Bristol: Malago Society, 1984.

BANTOCK, ANTON. *The last Smyths of Ashton Court, Pt.1. 1802-1860.* Bristol: Malago Society, 1980.

BETTEY, J.H. *The rise of a gentry family: the Smyths of Ashton Court, c.1500-1642.* Bristol: Historical Association, 1978.

BETTEY, J.H. *Calendar of the correspondence of the Smyth family of Ashton Court, 1548-1642.* Bristol Record Society **35**. Bristol: the Society, 1982.

PINK, W.D. 'The Smyths of Nibley', *G.N.Q.* **5**, 1894, 420-22. American branch of the family.

WAY, LEWIS UPTON. 'The Smyths of Ashton Court', *B.G.A.S.T.* **31**, 1908, 244-60. Includes list of Bristol merchants, 16th c.

See also Smith

Smyth-Pigott

Portraits of the Smyth-Pigott family: a catalogue of the oil paintings and busts in Woodspring Museum, Weston Super Mare. [Weston Super Mare]: Woodspring District Council, [198-?] Includes pedigree, 17-19th c., and biographical notes.

Smythies

'Pedigree of the Smythies family', *M.G.H.* 4th series **4**, 1912, 170-82, 193-200, 276-86, 306-19 & 354-63. Of Somerset, Essex and Suffolk; 16-20th c

Snell

HOPKINS, GLENDA. *The life and times of Captain Edwin Snell, master mariner of Brixham, Devon 1825-1882.* Brentwood: the author, 1995. Includes pedigree, 19-20th c.

Snigg

'Snigg', *W.N.Q.* **5**, 1905-7, 145-8. See also 330. Includes will of Sir George Snygge, 1617.

JEWERS, A.J. 'Snigg family', *N.Q.S.D.* **5**, 1897-8, 276-7. 17-18th c.

Soady

MORRIS, G.T. WINDYER. 'Soady or Sowdon family', *D.C.N.Q.* **6**, 1910-11, 251-3. Mainly 16-17th c.

Soltau

See Symons

Somers

POPE, F.J. 'Sir George Somers and his family', *D.N.* **32**, 1911, 26-32. 16-17th c. Dorset family.

See also Harington

Somerwill

SUMMERWILL, JOHN S. *Somerwill: a Devon family.* Bangor: the author, 1990. 17-20th c; includes pedigrees, parish register and census extracts, wills, memorial inscriptions, etc.

South

H., J.J. 'Thomas South, of Bossington Hall, Hants', *W.N.Q.* **6**, 1908-10, 381-4. See also 326. Includes brief pedigree of South of Salisbury, 16th c.

S[TORY]-M[ASKELYNE], A.ST.J. 'The family of South', *W.N.Q.* **7**, 1911-13, 9-15, 51-7 & 214-17. 15-16th c., includes pedigrees.

Southcomb

BENSON, J. 'Southcombe and Tristram', *D.C.N.Q.* **26**, 1954-5, 6-71.

WILKIN, W.H. 'Southcomb of Rose Ash', *D.A.Tr.* **57**, 1925, 289-306; **62**, 1930, 341-6. Rectors from 1675 until 1854.

Southcott

SKINNER, A.J. 'Southcott of Dulcishayes, Kilmington: an extension of the pedigree as given by Vivian', *D.A.Tr.* **48**, 1916, 290-301.

Southey

SOUTHEY, H.W. *Family notes.* Hereford: [ ], 1913. Southey family of Wellington, Somerset, 16-19th c.

Sowdon

See Soady

Sparkes

See Hippisley

Spargo

SPARGO, JOHN. *Notes on the name and family of Spargo, of Mabe parish in Cornwall.* [ ]: [ ], 1945.

Speccott

POYNTON, F.J. 'Pedigree of Speccott of North Devon', *M.G.H.* N.S., **4**, 1884, 86-9. See also 112-4, 132, & 145-6. Not continued. Includes will abstracts.

Speke

ALEXANDER, J.J. 'The early Spekes', *D.C.N.Q.* **21**(4), 1940, 151-7. 12-16th c.

MURDOCH, SOPHIA. *Record of the Speke family (Jordans, Somerset).* Reading: H. T. Morley, [1900]. Of Somerset, Devon, Yorkshire, Lancashire, Wiltshire and Berkshire.

PINE-COFFIN, MATILDA. *The Speke family.* Exeter: Godfrey & Bartlett, 1914.

SNELL, F.J. 'A family of politicians', in his *Memorials of old Somerset.* Bemrose & Sons, 1906, 218-38. Speke family, 17- 18th c.

SPEAKE, JOHN. 'The Speke families of Hazelbury Manor, Box, Wiltshire, and of Whitelackington, Somerset', *Catholic ancestor* **6**(1), 1996, 14-19. Includes pedigrees, 16-17th c.

Spicer

RAWLINS, C.W.H. 'The recollections of a nonagenarian: Charlotte Russell, 1808-', *D.C.N.Q.* **25**(5), 1953, 133-9. Nee Spicer.

SPICER, D.R. 'Spicer family', *D.C.N.Q.* **30**, 1965-7, 121. See also 173-4.

WOOD, A.W. *The Spicers of Devon.* Chiswick Press, [1854?]

See also Rowe and Roland

Spooner

SPOONER, E.T.C. *The Spooners of Sherborne and Blandford Forum: an amateur essay in local history.* Colyford: M.G. Bremridge, 1993. 18-20th c., includes pedigrees of Oke, Casswell, Bradley and Shipp as well as Spooner.

Spry

O'TOOLE, LAURENCE. *Place and the Sprys.* St.Anthony in Roseland: Place, 1980. 16-20th c. Includes pedigree.

Squibb

LONDON, H.S., & SQUIBB, G.D. 'A Dorset King of Arms: Arthur Squibb, Clarenceaux, 1646-1650', *D.N.* **68**, 1946, 54-65. Includes pedigree, 15-17th c.

SQUIBB, G. T. 'Squibb family of Swyre', *N.Q.S.D.* **22**, 1938, 49-50. 16-17th c. pedigree.

Stabb

See Ellis

Stafford

JEFFCOAT, R. 'Arms and badges of Edward Stafford, third Duke of Buckingham', *B.G.A.S.T.* **54**, 1932, 133-6.

KITE, EDWARD. 'John Stafford, Archbishop of Canterbury, and his Wiltshire parentage', *W.N.Q.* **2**, 1896-8, 218-22 & 255-61. See also 298-301, 438-9 & 488-91. Includes folded pedigree, 15th c., with monumental inscription.

LANGSTON, J.N. 'Old Catholic families of Gloucestershire, II: the Staffords and Howards of Thornbury,' *B.G.A.S.T.* **72**, 1953, 79-104. Includes pedigree. 14-18th c.

PINK, W.D. 'Stafford of Southwick, Grafton and Blatherwick', *Genealogist* N.S. **31**, 1915, 173-8. Southwick, Wiltshire; Grafton, Worcestershire; Blatherwick, Northamptonshire. 14-15th c.

ROGERS, W.H.H. 'Stafford family of Suthwyke in North Bradley, Wilts., and Hoke, Dorset', *W.N.Q.* **3**, 1899-1901, 193-202. See also **4**,

1902-4, 45. Reprinted in his *Archaeological papers relating to the counties of Somerset, Wilts, Hants and Devon.* [ ]: the author, 1902. Includes pedigree, 14-15th c.

See also Botreaux

Stanbury

THOMAS, NEIL. 'My Stanbury family: Australian and Devon connections', *D.F.H.* **80**, 1996, 7-10. 19th c.

Stapleton

See Pitman

Standerwick

See Heal

Stawell

STAWELL, GEORGE DODSWORTH, ed. *A Quantock family: the Stawells of Cothelstone and their descendants, the Barons Stawell of Somerton, and the Stawells of Devonshire and the County Cork.* Taunton: Barnicott & Pearce, Wessex Press, 1910.

Staynings

WILLIAMS, M. 'Staynings family', *M.G.H.* N.S., **3**, 1880, 20-2. Includes the will of Charles Staynings of Holnycote, Somerset, 1693.

Steede

See Reynell

Stephens

DAVIES, W.H. SILVESTER. 'Notes on Chavenage and the Stephens family', *B.G.A.S.T.* **22**, 1899, 128-37. Includes pedigree. 16-19th c.

DYER, ARTHUR STEPHENS. 'Stephens family', *M.G.H.* 4th series. **3**, 1910, 139-40. 18-19th c.

SKINNER, A.J. 'Stephens family', *D.C.N.Q.* **10**, 1918-19, 89-90.

WARD-JACKSON, C.H. *Stephens of Fowey: a portrait of a Cornish merchant fleet, 1867-1939.* Maritime monographs and reports **43**. National Maritime Museum, 1980. Includes Stephens family pedigree, 19-20th c.

See Clarke

Stevens

BENSON, JOHN. 'Ms. history of the Stevens family of Plymouth, by Major G. K. S. Hamilton-Edwards', *D.C.N.Q.* **24**, 1950-51, 133-4. Review.

HAMILTON-EDWARDS, GERALD. *The Stevens family of Plymouth: a record of their achievements.* Plymouth: the author, 1949.

Pedigree of the family of Stevens, of Vielstone, Cross and Winscott. Exeter: William Pollard & Co., 1891. 17-19th c.

'John Stevens', *W.N.Q.* **8**, 1914-16, 236-7. See also 192. Lists many Stevens baptisms at Manningford Bruce, 16th c.

Stewart
STEWART, R.H.M. 'Stewarts in Cornwall', {D.C.N.Q. **29**, 1962-4, 60. 18th c.

Stibb(s)
MORIARTY, G. ANDREWS. 'Genealogical research in England: records relating to the Stibb family, *N.E.H.G.R.* **84**, 1930, 435-6. Brief notes on miscellaneous records, 16-17th c. Of Somerset.

MORIARTY, G. ANDREWS. 'Genealogical research in England: the Stibbs family', *N.E.H.G.R.* **92**, 1938, 67-71. Of Henstridge, Somerset, 16-17th c.; includes extracts from chancery proceedings, *etc.*

Stiff
PHILLIMORE, W.P.W. 'The Stiff family', *G.N.Q.* **2**, 1884, 614-22. 16-19th c.

'Medieval Stiffs of Hawkesbury', *G.N.Q.* **5**, 1894, 273-83 & 463-76. Includes pedigree.

'On the origin of the surname of Stiff', *G.N.Q.* **5**, 1894, 113-22, 178-85 & 249-51.

Still
See Goldesborough

Stoate
POINTON, A. 'West Somerset Circuit: Watchet Methodist Church and the Stoate family', *Methodist Historical Society of the Plymouth and Exeter District proceedings* 5(1), 1978, 4-5. 19th c.

STOATE, THOMAS L., & STOATE, GEOFFREY L. *Records of the Stoate family*. Bristol: Stonebridge Press, 1965. 17-19th c.

Stocker
See Sydenham

Stockhay
See also Arbalister

Stoke
S[KINNER], A.J. 'Captain John Stoke', *D.C.N.Q.* **10**, 1919, 167-8. Stoke family of Colyton.

Stokes
SCHOMBERG, ARTHUR. *Some notes of the Stokes family, (Cos. Wilts & Glos.)* Devizes: Gazette Printing Works, 1909. Reprinted from *W.N.Q.*

SCHOMBERG, A. 'Stokes of Seend', *W.N.Q.* **5**, 1902-5, 193-8, 240-48, 289-95, 348-53, 391-6, 458-62, 503-10 & 552-61; **6**, 1908-10, 4-9,

495-7, 99-107, 171-6, 193-7, 244-8 & 289-302. See also 404-5. Includes monumental inscriptions, extracts from family bible, inquisitions post mortem, wills, Chancery proceedings, pedigree, 14-17th c., etc.

S[CHOMBERG], A. 'Stokes', *M.G.H.* N.S. **3**. 1880, 309. Extracts from family bible, 17-18th c.

Stone
COOKE, ROBERT. 'Stone of Wedmore: a lost gentry family?', *G.T.* **4**(2), 1979, 15-16.

MEAD, L. G. 'Stones of Wiveliscombe', *G.T.* **13**(1), 1988, 11.

Stothard
X. 'The tombstone of Charles Alfred Stothard in Beer-Ferrers churchyard', *N.G.D.C.* **1**, 1888, 110-11.

Stourton
MOWBRAY, LORD. *The history of the noble house of Stourton, of Stourton in the county of Wilts ...* 2 vols. Elliot Stock, 1899. Medieval-19th c.

WERE, F. 'Stourton pedigree', *N.Q.S.D.* **90**, 1905, 125-9. Dorset family.

Stowford
SHEPPARD, WALTER LEE. 'Descent of the manor of Wollacombe through Stowford to Brightley to Cobley to Gifford', *D.C.N.Q.* **32**, 1971-3, 148-52. See also 179-82. Medieval.

Strangway
WERE, F. 'Col. George Strangway's shield of arms', *N.Q.S.D.* **12**, 1911, 170-2. See also 97-8.

'Not so strange', *G.T.* **13**(2), 1988, 46. Strangways at Oxford University, 1509-1706.

Stratton
STRATTON, RICHARD FLOWER. *A history of the Wiltshire Strattons.* Castle Cary: Castle Cary Press, 1987. 19-20th c. This supersedes STRATTON, JAMES. *A history of the Wiltshire Strattons.* Winchester: Fred Smith, 1902.

See also Brown

Strechleigh
See Golde

Street
LEA, J. HENRY. 'Parentage of Rev. Nicholas Street, of New Haven, Ct.', *N.E.H.G.R.* **46**, 1892, 256-67. Includes pedigree of Street, 16-17th c., together with extracts from parish registers, court rolls and wills from Taunton, Pitminster, Bridgwater, Over Stowey, etc.

STREET, TED. *The Street family of North Dorset and their descendents.* Lyme Regis: the author, 1993. Includes pedigree. Brief.

Strelley
CLUER, B.R. 'George Strelley, Mayor of Plymouth', *D.C.N.Q.* **33**(2), 1974, 44-6. Genealogical notes.

Stride
JONES, MICHAEL. 'The Strides of Odd Down, Bath: three generations of brewer publicans', *Brewery history: the journal of the Brewery History Society* **71**, 1993, 18-19. 19-20th c.

Strode
BATEN, JOHN. 'Additional note on Barrington and the Strodes', *S.A.N.H.S.* **37**(2), 1891, 40-43.

BROWN, FREDK. 'Pedigrees of the Strode family', *S.A.N.H.S.* **30**(2), 1884, 66-73. 16-18th c.

CRISP, F.A. 'Strode family', *Fragmenta genealogica* **8**, 1902, 77-150 & 160-1. Includes wills and many pedigrees, mainly of Dorset and Somerset.

DYER, A. S. 'Strode of Somerset', *Notes & queries* **187**, 1944, 80 & 166-7; **188**, 1945, 19-20. 16-18th c.

HURD, A.S. 'An ancient commoner family', *Genealogical magazine* **1**, 1897-8, 195-200.

SEREL, T. 'On the Strodes of Somerset', *S.A.N.H.S.* **13**(2), 1865-6, 6-20.

SOMASTER, SAM. 'An account of some noble families in Devonshire, and Members of Parliament in the year 1640', *W.A.* **1**, 1881, 56-7, 66-7, 69, 80, 82, 96-7, & 108-9. See also 162. Strode, Chudleigh, Drake, and various other 'county' families.

See also Fox

Strong
'Strong family of Somerset', *N.Q.S.D.* **2**, 1891, 51-2.

Stuckey
SKINNER, A.J.P. 'Descent of the Tytherleigh estate', *N.Q.S.D.* **14**, 1915, 307-10. See also **15**, 1917, 287-8. Stuckey family, 17-18th c; includes pedigree and wills.

Stukeley
HUNT, JOHN G. 'The Stukeley-Wood connection', *D.C.N.Q.* **28**, 1959-61, 60-61. 15-16th c.

STUCLEY, DENNIS, SIR. 'A Devon parish lost, a new home discovered', *D.A.Tr.* **108**, 1976, 1-11. Stucley family.

Stumpe
J., J.G. 'Memorials of the family of Stumpe of Malmesbury', *Collectanea topographica et genealogica* **7**, 1841, 81-4. Pedigree, 16-17th c.

LEWIS, GORDON. 'A family tree ... Stump', *W.F.H.S.* **32**, 1989. 10-12. 16-20th c.

'A Stump pedigree'. *W.N.Q.* **8**, 1914-16, 369-72. See also 427. 17-19th c.

'William Stumpe of Malmesbury, his descendants and relatives', *W.N.Q.* **8**, 1914-16, 385-95, 444-54, 482-7 & 531-7. See also 552. 15-17th c. Includes wills, *inquisitions post mortem*.

Sturge
GOODBODY, MARGARET. *Five daughters in search of learning: the Sturge family, 1820-1944.* Bristol: M. Goodbody, 1986.

STURGE, ELIZABETH. *Reminiscences of my life, and some account of the children of William and Charlotte Sturge and of the Sturge family of Bristol.* Privately published, 1928. Includes folded pedigrees of Sturge, Young, Player and Stephens families, 16-20th c.

See also Clarke

Sturges
STURGES, G.W. *Child of Turgis: an account of the Sturges-Turgis family of Dorset and of Sherborne in particular.* Clacton-on-Sea: Windrush Press, 1978.

Sudeley
SUDELEY, LORD, & WINKLESS, D. 'Medieval Sudeley', *Family history* **10**(61/2), N.S., 37/8, 1977, 9-39. Sudeley and Boteler families of Gloucestershire.

Sutton
MUMFORD, ALFRED A. 'The Suttons: a Dorset race of scholars', *N.Q.S.D.* **10**, 1907, 201-5. See also 305-6. 17-18th c.

Swete
HOOPPELL, J.L.E. 'Old Traine in Modbury: the house and its owners', *D.A.Tr.* **59**, 1927, 265-70. Swete family, 17th c.

Swinnerton
MARTIN, E. H. 'Swinnerton-Dyer family', *N.Q.S.D.* **10**, 1907, 309-27 & 341-52; **11**, 1909, 24-35. See also **11**, 1909, 75-7. 17-19th c.

See also Dyer

Sydenham

HEAD, H.S. 'Sydenham of Brympton', *M.G.H.* 2nd series **3**, 1890, 323-36 & 349-51. Pedigree, medieval-17th c.

JEWERS, ARTHUR J. 'Sydenham pedigree', *N.Q.S.D.* **8**, 1903, 315-21. See also **9**, 1905, 38.

MARSHALL, J. C. 'Sydenham heraldry', *N.Q.S.D.* **16**, 1920, 19-23.

STOCKER, CHARLES J.S. 'Sydenham and Stocker families', *N.Q.S.D.* **18**, 1926, 25-6. See also **17**, 1923, 290.

SYDENHAM, G.F. *The history of the Sydenham family, collected from family documents, pedigrees, deeds, and copious memoranda,* ed. A. T. Cameron. East Molesey, Surrey: E. Dwelly, 1928. Includes monumental inscriptions, extensive list of wills, many pedigrees, etc., etc.

See also Pratt and St. Barbe

Symcoke

POYNTON, F.J. 'Symcoke and Jessop', *N.Q.S.D.* **3**, 1893, 152-3. Stray from Butleigh, marrying at Worksop, Nottinghamshire.

Symes

See Bond

Symonds

MORIARTY, G. ANDREWS. 'Genealogical research in England: Symonds-Femell', *N.E.H.G.R.* **80**, 1926, 343-69. 16-17th c., includes wills, parish register extracts, Chancery proceedings, etc.

SYMONDS, HENRY. *A memoir of the family of Symonds in Somerset and Dorset, with some account of their connexions by marriage.* Taunton: Wessex Press, 1933. Includes wills, parish register extracts, Chancery proceedings, etc.

SYMONDS, JOHN L. *Which Francis Symonds? Cornish Oak or Australian Eucalypt. A history of the Symonds family in Cornwall and Australia, 1675 to 1992.* Cronulla, N.S.W.: J.L. Symonds, 1993. 17-20th c.; includes extensive pedigrees.

'Symonds' shield of arms, Chardstock church', *N.Q.S.D.* **13**, 1913, 127-30. Includes pedigree of Symonds, 16th c., and D'Ewes, 16-17th c.

Tabart

EVANS, K. JANE. *Tabart of Fonthill: from England to Van Diemen's Land.* Weston Super Mare: privately published, 1991. Includes pedigrees, 16-20th c.

Talbot

BENSON, J. 'Talbot, Hamley and Champernowne', *D.C.N.Q.* **19**, 1936-7, 26-9. See also 265-70. Medieval.

Tallack

See Ridington

Tame

HOLT, HENRY F. 'The Tames of Fairford', *Journal of the British Archaeological Association* **27**, 1871, 110-48. Includes pedigree, 15-16th c.

See also Greville

Tangye

PARKER, J.F. *Some notes on the Tangye family.* Evesham: Journal Press, 1972.

Tanner

WILKIN, W.H. 'Tanner: A clerical family', *D.C.N.Q.* **16**, 1930-31, 214-5. 17-19th c.

WILKIN, W.H. 'Tanner of Witheridge', *D.C.N.Q.* **21**, 1940-41, 260-7. See also **22**, 1942-6, 37. 16-19th c.

Tapley

TAPLEY, HARRIET SILVESTER. *Genealogy of the Tapley family.* Danvers, Massachusetts: Endecott Press, 1900. Of Devon and U.S.A.

WILKIN, W.H. 'Genealogy of the Tapley family', *D.C.N.Q.* **21**(2), 1940, 74-7.

Taswell

'Taswell pedigree from the visitation of London, 1664', *M.G.H.* N.S., **1**, 1874, 254-6. Includes parish register extracts from Buckland Newton and Hazelbury Bryan, Dorset, and Limington, Somerset; late 17th c.

Taylor

TAYLOR, EDMUND-DENISON. *The Taylor family of Riseley, Co. Bedford, St. Neots, Co. Huntingdon, City of Oxford, Buckland Brewer, Co. Devon, Loughborough, Co. Leicester.* Leicester: W. Thornley & Sons, 1933. 18-20th c.

See also Acland

Tassell

'Tassell family', *N.Q.S.D.* **28**, 1968, 218-9. 17-18th c.

Teague

ANSTIS, RALPH. *The industrial Teagues and the Forest of Dean.* Gloucester: Alan Sutton, 1990. 18-19th c.

Teape

DAY, JESSE H. *Teape: a genealogy with special reference to those outside the U.S.* Athens, Ohio: the author, 1983.

Templer

CHRISTIE, IAN R. 'The family circle of George Templar (1755-1819) M.P. for Honiton, 1790-1796', *D.A.Tr.* **123**, 1991, 195-201.

TEMPLER, J.F.H. 'Templer family', *D.C.N.Q.* **20**(6), 1939, 280-3.

WATKIN, HUGH R. 'Templer family', *D.C.N.Q.* **13**, 1924-5, 326-30. See also 357-8, & **14**, 1926-7, 18-19. 17-18th c.

Terrill

See Deighton

Tetley

TETLEY, J. GEORGE. *Old times and new.* T. Fisher Unwin, 1904. Tetley family of Devon, *etc.*, 18-19th c.

Thistlethwayte

See Powell

Thomas

ANDERSON, GILBERT JOHN. *The Thomas family of Zennor, Cornwall: some notes on its history, with a pedigree showing eight generations.* Sanderstead: [ ], 1922. Brief, with folded pedigree, 18-20th c., and parish register extracts, 17-18th c.

See also Bater

Thornbrough

SHEWEN, E.T. 'Some notes on the family of Thornborough', *W.A.* **7**(3), 1887, 56-9.

Thorner

See Harington

Thornton

RIZZO, BETTY. 'Thorntons of Sherborne: literary research and local history', *N.Q.S.D.* **30**, 1974-9, 375-9. 17-18th c.

Throckmorton

BIDDLE, DANIEL. 'Some account of the Throckmortons of Tortworth, and a few of their ancestors in other lines', *G.N.Q.* **10**, 1914, 65-72.

MACLEAN, JOHN, SIR. 'Pedigree of Throckmorton of Tortworth and Clowerwall', *B.G.A.S.T.* **7**, 1882-3, 194. 17th c.

Thurleby

H., D. 'Family of Thurleby in Cornwall', *D.C.N.Q.* **6**, 1910-11, 30-31. 17-18th c.

Thurber

See Hicks

Thynne

BURNETT, DAVID. *Longleat: The story of an English country house.* Collins, 1978. Thynne family, 16-20th c. Includes pedigree.

ROUND, I.H. 'The origin of the Thynnes', *Genealogist* N.S. **11**, 1895, 193-5. Includes pedigree, 15-16th c.

WALL, ALISON D. *Two Elizabethan women: correspondence of Joan and Maria Thynne, 1575-1611.* W.R.S. **38**, 1983.

See also De Boteville

Tilly

BROWN, FREDERICK. 'The Tilly family', *W.A.* **4**, 1885, 242-3.

Tippett

'Julia Tippett's family', *J.G.F.H.S.* **7**, 1980, 10. Pedigree, 17-19th c.

Titford

TITFORD, DONALD, et al. *Moonrakers in my family.* Bath: the author, 1995. Wiltshire family; includes pedigrees, 16-17th c.

TITFORD, JOHN, et al. *The Titford family, 1547-1947: come wind, come weather.* Phillimore, 1989. Prize-winning study. Of Wiltshire, Somerset, etc, includes pedigree, 17-20th c.

TITFORD, JOHN. 'The Titford Family: come wind, come weather', *W.F.H.S.* **29**, 1988, 10-13.

Todeni

BROWNE, A.L. 'Robert de Todeni and his heirs', *B.G.A.S.T.* **52**, 1920, 103-11. Medieval.

Tolchard

TOLCHARD, BRIAN. *The Tolchards of Devon: a history of a working-class Devon family, 1332-1991.* Bristol: the author, 1991. Includes pedigrees.

Toller

See Hippisley

Tom(b)es

TOMES, JOHN. 'Pedigree of Tomes, Tombes, Toms, Tommes, Tommys or Thomme of Merston or Marston Sicca als Dry or Long Marston, Co. Gloucester', *M.G.H.* N.S., **3**, 1880, 273-9. 16-19th c.

'The Tombs of the Cotswolds', *J.G.F.H.S.* **38**, 1988, 15. Tombs family, 18-19th c.

'The Tomes family of Marston Sicca', *G.N.Q.* **1**, 1881, 194-5. 14-15th c.

Tomkins

SKINNER, A.J.P. 'Chichester Tomkins,' *D.C.N.Q.* **10**, 1918-19, 148-50. Tomkins family of Axminster, Devon 18th c., includes will of Thomas Tomkins, 1688.

TOMKINS, H.A. COLTHURST. 'Tomkins family of Lostwithiel', *D.C.N.Q.* **10**, 1918-19, 116-7. See also 148. Includes pedigree, 17th c.

Toms

DEACON, J.N. 'Twelve generations', *Genealogists' magazine* **10**(1), 1947, 7-10. Toms family.

See also Tom(b)es

Tonkin

See Ridington

Toope

See Goldesborough

Toriton

ALEXANDER, J.J. 'Early barons of Torrington and Barnstaple', *D.A.Tr.* **73**, 1941, 153-79. De Toriton family, 13th c; De Braose and De Tracy families, 11-13th c.

Torr

PESKETT, H.M. 'The whereabouts of Cecil Torr's papers', *D.C.N.Q.* **32**, 1971-3, 21-2. Primarily concerning the Torr family and Wreyland.

Tothill

See Hippisley

Townsend

WALEY, M.H. 'James Townsend of Great Cheverell, 1654-1730, with some notes on his family in Great Cheverell and Stratford sub Castle, 1653-1748', *W.A.M.* **60**, 1965, 109-19. Includes pedigrees of Townsend and Merewether.

Towse

TOWSE, CLIVE. *An account of an estate in Garton in the East Riding, the property of the Towse family, 1537-1800, with a note on the Somerset branch of the family.* Cardiff: privately printed, 1980. Includes pedigree, 17-18th c.

Toy

ROWE, J.Y. 'Toy(e) family', *D.C.N.Q.* **30**, 1965-7, 282-4. Medieval.

Tozer

CARBONELL, BARBARA M.H. 'Village Smithies', *D.C.N.Q.* **17**, 1932-3, 46-7. Gives names of Tozer family, blacksmiths at Bow, Devon, 1398-1879.

See also Prowse

Tracy

BENSON, J. 'The Tracys', *D.C.N.Q.* **19**, 1937, 194-201. See also 229 & 273-7; **20**, 1938-9, 85-7. Includes medieval pedigree.

DANES, EMANUEL. *Tracy heritage: a three-part genealogical narrative bringing into focus Erasmus Darwin Tracy (1810-1877).* [Jacksonville]: the author, 1983.

TRACY, JOHN. *A short memoir, critically illustrating the histories of the noble families of Tracy and Courtenay, exhibiting likewise, the ancient usage, or variation, of coat armour in that of Tracy.* Canterbury: the author?], 1796.

REICHEL, O.J. 'Tracy and Brewer', *D.N.Q.* **2**, 1902-3, 24-5 & 63. See also 157-8 & 187-9.

SUDELEY, LORD. 'Becket's murderer: William de Tracy', *Family history* **13**(97), 1983, 3-36. Includes notes on the Tracy family of Toddington, Gloucestershire.

SUDELEY, LORD. 'Toddington and the Tracys', *B.G.A.S.T.* **88**, 1969, 127-72. See also **90**, 1971, 216-9. 12-19th c., includes medieval pedigree.

SUDELEY, LORD. 'Toddington and the Tracys', *Local history bulletin* **32**, 1975, 3-5; **33**, 1976, 4-5. Brief notes. 11-20th c.

See also Toriton

Traske

TRASKE, WILLIAM BLAKE. 'The Traske family in England', *N.E.H.G.R.* **54**, 1900, 279-83. Mainly extracts from East Coker, Somerset, parish registers, 16-17th c.

Travers

TRAVERS, S.SMITH. *A pedigree with biographical sketches of the Devonshire family of Travers, descended from Walter Travers of Nottingham, goldsmith.* Dublin: privately printed, 1898. Includes folded pedigrees, 16-19th c.

WAGNER, HENRY. 'Huguenot refugee family of Travers', *M.G.H.* 5th series **2**, 1916-17, 196-7. Of Stonehouse, Gloucestershire, London, *etc.*

Trease

TREASE, G.E. 'The ancestry of a Crediton-born artist', *D.C.N.Q.* **33**(8), 1977, 306-8.

TREASE, G.E. 'Trerys, Treise or Trease family', *D.C.N.Q.* **29**(3), 1962, 87-8. Mainly 15-17th c.

Treat
TREAT, JOHN HARVEY. *The Treat family: a genealogy of Trott, Tratt and Treat for fifteen generations, and four hundred and fifty years, in England and America.* Salem, Mass: Salem Press, 1893.

Trebarfoote
BARFETT, THOMAS. *Trebarfoote: a Cornish family.* [ ]: the author, 1989. Includes pedigrees, 16-20th c.
WALTER, R. 'Trebarfoote of Poundstock, Cornwall', *D.C.N.Q.* **28**, 1959-61, 233. See also 290-91. 17-18th c.

Treffry
RIDEOUT, ADELAIDE. *The Treffry family.* Chichester: Phillimore, 1984. Of Fowey; includes pedigrees, medieval-20th c.
TREFFRY, R. 'Richard Treffry, senior and junior, 1771-1842 and 1804-38', *Wesley Historical Society proceedings* **32**(4), 1960, 66-73.
WHETTER, JAMES. 'The Treffry brothers, William and John', *Old Cornwall* **11**(2), 1992, 89-96; **11**(3), 1992, 130-37. 15th c.

Trefusis
TREFUSIS, NICHOLAS. 'The Trefusis family', *C.F.H.S.J.* **65**, 1992, 30-34. 12-20th c.

Tregaskes
TREGASKES, W.H. *What's in a name? Tregaskes. Tregaskis.* Donhead St.Mary: privately published, 1981. 15-19th c., includes pedigrees.

Tregear
WILLIAMS, ROBERT W. *Tregears around the world.* Livonia, Michigan: the author, c.1982. 17-20th c.

Tregenna
TREGENNA-SMITH, G. 'Tregenna family', *C.F.H.S.J.* **16**, 1980, 6-7. Medieval-18th c.

Tregennow
EDWARDS, A.G. 'Tregennow family', *D.C.N.Q.* **33**, 1974-7, 181. 14-17th c.

Tregian
TAYLOR, T. 'Francis Tregian, his family and possessions', *J.R.I.C.* N.S. **18**(1), 1910, 103-16. Includes folded pedigree, 16th c.

Tregoning
TREGONING, E.A. *Two centuries of a Cornish family.* Leicester: Edgar Backus, 1950. 18-20th c. Includes folded pedigree.
See also Ridington

Trehawke
UPHAM, R. 'Trehawke ms. Armory', *D.N.Q.* **2**, 1902-3, 171-4.

Trelawny
BRYANT, EDITH. 'Trelawney of Bake in Pelynt; Tom (Tome) of Pelynt', *D.C.N.Q.* **16**, 1930-31, 99-100. 17-18th c.
HARVEY, H.H. 'Further notes on the Trelawny family', *D.C.N.Q.* **23**, 1947-9, 357-8 & 383-4; **24**, 1950-51, 10-11. Mainly 17-19th c.
HARVEY, H.H. 'Trelawny family', *D.C.N.Q.* **23**, 1947-9, 256-8 & 292-3. Medieval.

Treloar
TRELOAR, ORSON LEE. *Treloar genealogy: tree of Treloar.* Salt Lake City: Paragon Press, [1962?]. 16-20th c.

Trelour
See Tucker

Tremain
TREMAIN, JOY, & CHAPPLE, MANDY. *The Tremain family history.* Inverell: Tremain Family History Book Committee, 1989. Cornish-Australian family; 16-20th c. Includes pedigrees.

Tremayne
HERRING, IVOR J. 'Heligan and the Tremayne family', *Old Cornwall* **10**(8), 1989, 376-84. 16-20th c.
See Wyse

Tremenheere
TREMENHEERE, SEYMOUR GREIG. *The Tremenheeres.* H.J. Rymans, 1925. Medieval-19th c., includes pedigrees and extracts from various sources.

Trenbath
WESTON, SHEILA R. 'A variety of Trenbaths', *C.F.H.S.J.* **77**, 1975, 24-6. 17-18th c.

Trenchard
FRY, E.A. 'Trenchard', *W.N.Q.* **4**, 1902-4, 472. Pedigree, 16-17th c.
See Herbert

Trengrouse
DODD, GAIL. 'Regarding Henry', *C.F.H.S.J.* **75**, 1995, 26-7. Trengrouse family, 18-20th c.

Trenhaile

SAWYER, F.E. *The Trenhaile family: a genealogy and history of the descendants and ancestry of George Trenhaile (1812-1879) and his wife Mary Ann Stephens (Stevens) (1814-1878) of Cornwall County, England, who immigrated to America, 1847, and settled in Iowa Co., Wisconsin.* 3rd ed. American Falls, Idaho: the author, 1978.

Trenhayle

MILLETT, VINCENT V. 'Trenhayle family', *D.C.N.Q.* **29**, 1962-4, 123-5. See also 182. 16-18th c.

Tresilian

ANDREW, C.K.C. 'Mr. Thomas Tresilian', *D.C.N.Q.* **23**(1), 1947, 30. See also **23**(5), 1948, 158. 17th c.

HUGO, FRANCIS H.M. 'Notes on the surname Tresilian', *D.C.N.Q.* **24**, 1950-51, 77-8.

KENT, ALAN. 'Sir Robert Tresilian and his family', *C.F.H.S.J.* **84**, 1997, 20-23. 14th c.

See also Carne

Trevanion

ROWSE, A.L. *The Byrons and Trevanions.* Weidenfeld and Nicolson, 1978. Byron of Nottinghamshire, Trevanion of Caerhayes; medieval-20th c.

TREVANION, D.A. 'The Trevanions in Devon and East Cornwall', *D.C.N.Q.* **23**(8), 1948, 258-60. See also 265; **24**, 1950-51, 62-4, & **25**, 1952-3, 78-9 & 110. Mainly 18th c.

Trevelyan

BUSH, R.J.E. 'Nettlecombe Court, 1: the Trevelyans and other residents at the Court', *Field studies* **32**, 1970, 275-87. Includes pedigree showing descent of Nettlecombe through Ralegh, Whalesburgh, Trevelyan and Wolseley, 12-20th c.

SIRAUT, MARY, ed. *The Trevelyan letters to 1840.* Somerset Record Society **80**. 1990. Of Nettlecombe, Somerset; includes pedigree, 16-19th c.

S[KINNER], A.J. 'Josias Trevelyan', *D.C.N.Q.* **9**, 1916-17, 54-6. Trevelyan extracts from Wiltshire parish registers, 16-18th c.

Trevena

PEGLER, A.N. 'The Trevena family: from Cornwall to New Zealand via Australia', *C.F.H.S.J.* **75**, 1995, 8-9. 19-20th c.

Trewavas

MITCHELL-FOX, MADELINE. *Trewavas: Tylu Kesunyes.* Penzance: Wordens of Cornwall, 1972. 18-20th c.

Trewithan

See Drew

Trewman

LUGARD, CECIL E. *The family of Trewman of Exeter.* [ ]: the author, 1947. 16-19th c., includes pedigree.

Trigg

GREENWOOD, DAVID. 'The Trigg family', *F.F.* **15**, 1994, 27-9. 18-20th c.

Trist

NORTH, CHRISTINE. 'The Trists of Veryan', *J.R.I.C.* N.S. **8**(3), 1980, 191-223. Includes folded pedigree, 17-19th c.

Tristram

'Pedigree of Tristram', *M.G.H.* 3rd series **1**, 1896, 229-32. 16-19th c.

Trosse

LONG, L.H. 'Trosse family of Exeter', *D.C.N.Q.* **30**(5), 1966, 138-9.

SKINNER, J. 'Rev. Roger Trosse of Rose Ash', *D.C.N.Q.* **15**, 1928-9, 154-5. Genealogical notes, 17th c.

Trotman

TROTMAN, F.H. *The Trotman family, 1086 to 1963.* Nottingham: the author, 1965. Includes pedigrees.

PHILLIMORE, W.P.W. 'The Trotman family', *G.N.Q.* **2**, 1884, 201-12. See also 341-6 & 429. 16-19th c.

'Notes on the Trotman family', *G.N.Q.* **5**, 1894, 14-28, 76-84, 122-5, 195-209, 234-40, 283-300 & 334-44. See also 493. Includes many extracts from Cam, Dursley, Syston, and other parish registers, and from wills, monumental inscriptions, etc.

Trounce

BAKER, JANE. *A Cornish heritage: the Trounce family of Veryan.* Bristol: the author, 1991. Includes pedigree, 19th c.

Trowbridge

MCCLINTOCK, EMORY. 'Thomas Trowbridge and Elizabeth Marshall', *N.E.H.G.R.* **59**, 1905, 291-7. Of Somerset and Devon, 17th c.

TROWBRIDGE, C.W. *The Trowbridge family history, 1690-1990.* Wantage: Wessex Press, 1991. Includes pedigrees and many extracts from parish registers.

Trump

ROUND, E. 'The Trump family: a study in local continuity', *D.C.N.Q.* **34**, 1978-1980, 144-6.

Truscott

JOLLY, L.V. 'The wrestling Truscotts, 1800-1814', *Old Cornwall* **4**, 1943-50, 320-27.

Tucker

HANNAN, NORMAN. *Travels and heartaches of a mining family.* Romford: the author, 1984. Tucker family of Devon and Cornwall, 19-20th c. Also includes notes on Trelour.

TUCKER, ROBERT DENNARD. *The descendants of William Tucker of Throwleigh, Devon.* Spartanburg: Reprint Company, 1991. Of Devon and the United States, 17-20th c.

WICKES, MICHAEL. *The Tucker family of Devon.* Bideford: M. Wickes, 1984.

Tuckett

TUCKETT, JAMES HYLTON. *Tuckett family history: born in a hurry and educated with speed.* Trentham, New Zealand: the author, 1993. Of Devon and Cornwall, Australia, Canada, New Zealand and the United States. Includes pedigree of Tuckett, 17-19th c., and Sherwill 18-19th c.

Tuckey

TAYLOR, W.A. 'Notes and queries on the Tuckey family of Banwell', *Search: journal of the Banwell Society of Archaeology* **12**, 1974, 4-11. See also **14**, 1978, 51-5. Includes pedigree, 18-19th c.

Tugwell

BARNES, F.H. *History of a family: Barnes supplement; no.2.* [ ]: the author, 1972. Includes pedigree of Tugwell, 16-19th c.

Tunkin

BARNETT, GORDON A. *Tunkin, 1740-1988: a family history.* Macquarie, A.C.T: the author, 1989. Of Devon and Australia. Includes pedigrees.

Turbervile

B., R.G. 'The last of the Turbervills', *N.Q.S.D.* **18**, 1926, 53-5. See also 277-80; 19, 1929, 5-8, 36-40, 104-6, 166-8, & 248-9. 18th c.
'Pedigrees from the visitation of Dorset, 1623: Turbervile', *M.G.H.* 2nd. series **2**, 1888, 133-5. Includes Morgan pedigree.

Turner

TURNER, N.P. 'Notes on the Turner, Emery, Law and Cotgrave families', *Search: journal of the Banwell Society of Archaeology* **18**, 1982, 66-8. 17-19th c.

TURNER, SAMUEL BLOIS. *Turner genealogy,* Privately printed, 1884. Of Gloucester, Suffolk, Middlesex, *etc.,* includes pedigrees, 17-19th c.

Tuson

COX, J. S. *The Tuson family of Ilchester.* St. Peter Port: Toucan, 1984.

Tuthill

TUTHILL, P.B. *Pedigree of Tuthill of Peamore, Co. Devon, of Kilmore and of Faha, Co. Limerick, with genealogical notes of the family.* Mitchell Hughes and Clarke, 1908. Reprinted from *M.G.H.* 4th series **3**, 1910, 10-17, 49-53, 115-8, 177-81, 217-21 & 267-72. Includes pedigrees (one folded), 16-19th c.

Twyniho

'The Twyniho family', *N.Q.S.D.* **22**, 1938, 2-3. 14-15th c.

Twining

TWINING, STEPHEN H. *Some account of an early Twining pedigree and of other references to the name in the fourteenth and fifteenth centuries.* McCorquodale & Co., 1927.

Tyler

The family history of Tyler of Gloucestershire and Bristol. Colchester: E.W. Cullingford & Co., 1913.

Tyndale

COOKE, JAMES HERBERT. 'The Tyndales in Gloucestershire', *B.G.A.S.T.* **2**, 1877-8, 29-46. 15-18th c.

GREENFIELD, B.W. 'Notes relating to the family of Tyndale, of Stinchcombe and Nibley in Gloucestershire, the result of an attempt to discover the parentage of William Tyndale alias Hutchyns the martyr', *Genealogist* **2**, 1878, 1-7, 38-43, 123-8, 159-62, 227-30, 319-26, 356-63 & 369-71. See also 68. 15-16th c.

GREENFIELD, B.W. 'Pedigree of the family of Tyndale of Stinchcombe and Nibley, Co. Gloucester', *Genealogist* **2**, 1878, 373-8. 16-19th c.

GREENFIELD, B. WYATT. 'Tyndale: extracts from parish registers, etc.', *M.G.H.* **1**, 1868, 244-5 & 274-5. Of Thornbury and Iron Acton, Gloucestershire. and Kington St. Michael, Wiltshire.

OVERY, CHARLES, & TYNDALE, ARTHUR C. 'The parentage of William Tyndale, *alias* Hutchyns, Translator and Martyr', *B.G.A.S.T.* **73**, 1954, 208-15. 14-16th c.
See also Annesley

Tyrwhitt
ROWE, J. BROOKING. 'Sir Thomas Tyrwhitt and Princetown', *D.A.Tr.* **37**, 1905, 465-81. Includes genealogical notes.

Tyse
SCHOMBERG, ARTHUR. 'Family of Tyse', *W.N.Q.* **7**, 1911-13, 347-53. Probate records, 17th c.
See also Perne

Tytherleigh
SKINNER, A.J.P. 'Tytherleigh or Tiderleigh, of Tytherleigh, in the parish of Chardstock, Dorset', *N.Q.S.D.* **14**, 1915, 272-8. See also 256, & **16**, 1920, 262-3 for wills. 16-19th c; includes wills, parish register extracts, etc.
See also Stuckey

Uddy
UDY, JAMES S. *A pride of Lions: the story of a Cornish family called Uddy.* [ ]: Yarraandoo Life Centre, 1995. Includes pedigrees, 16-20th c.

Udy
FOLKEMA, ANNE E. *Udy: the New Zealand perspective.* Wellington: A. & C. Folkema, 1989. Also of Cornwall; 16-20th c

Upham
UPHAM, F.K. 'The name of Upham in England', *N.E.H.G.R.* **33**, 1879, 40-45. Of Somerset, medieval-17th c.

Upjohn
LIGHT, RICHARD UPJOHN. *Upjohn.* 2 vols. Michigan: privately printed, 1990. v.1. A study in ancestry, covering 14 generations and 450 years. v.2. Two early journals. The life and travels of James Upjohn, 1784. The ocean diary of William Upjohn, 1830. Of Shaftesbury, London, the United States, *etc.,* 17-20th c.

Upton
ROWE, J.B. 'Upton pedigree', *M.G.H.* 2nd Series **2**, 1888, 161-2. Of Puslinch, Devon.
UPTON, W.H. 'Upton pedigree: shewing families descended from Upton of Upton in the parish of Lewannick near Launceston, Cornwall', *M.G.H.* 2nd series **4**, 1892, 21-4, 45-51 & 73-6. Medieval-19th c

'Upton: extracts from parish registers', *M.G.H.* 2nd Series **3**, 1890, 197-202 & 221-6. From registers of Brixham, Newton Ferrers, *et al;* also monumental inscriptions from Brixham.
'Upton pedigree: visitation of Devon, 1620', *M.G.H.* 2nd Series **2**, 1886, 103-4. See also 113-4 & 129.
'Upton pedigrees', *M.G.H.* 2nd series **2**, 1888, 65-8, 102-4, 113-4, 129, 161-5 & 182-4. Of Cornwall and various other counties, medieval-19th c.

Urtiaco
BATES, E. H. 'The family of De Urtiaco', *S.A.N.H.S.* **42**(2), 1896, 26-55. Medieval.

Uvedale
COLBY, DR., & RYLANDS, J.P. 'Pedigrees from the visitation of Dorset, 1623', *M.G.H.* 2nd series **2**, 1888, 345. Includes Uvidall & Sidney.
FRY, E.A. 'The Uvedale family of Dorset', *N.Q.S.D.* **19**, 1929, 54-62. Includes pedigree, 15-16th c.
GOWER, GRANVILLE LEVESON. 'Pedigree of Uvedale of Dorset', *M.G.H.* 2nd series **5**, 1894, 297-8 & 305-7. 15-17th c.
GOWER, G.L. 'Uvedale family: entries from the parish register of Horton, Co. Dorset', *M.G.H.* 2nd series **5**, 1894, 228-9. Also from More Crichell.
UDAL, J.S. 'Heraldic visitation of Dorset, 1623: Uvedale family', *N.Q.S.D.* **1**, 1890, 138-9.

Vagg
VAGG, C. MERVYN. *Somerset Vaggs in Australia: a short history of the Somerset family of Vagg, and their pioneers in early Australia.* Elwood: Vagg Family Reunion Committee, 1960.

Valletort
B[ENSON], J. 'The Valletorts', *D.C.N.Q.* **20**, 1938-9, 145-51. See also 228-31 & 330.
BENSON, J. 'The Valletorts of Clyst St. Lawrence', *D.C.N.Q.* **20**(6), 1939, 247-54. Medieval.
BENSON, J. 'The Valletorts of North Tawton', *D.C.N.Q.* **20**(7), 1939, 289-94. Medieval.
BENSON, J. 'Valletort of Somerset', *D.C.N.Q.* **20**(8), 1939, 355-61.
ROSE-TROUP, F. 'The honour of Harberton', *D.A.Tr.* **67**, 1935, 253-83. Valletort descent, 12-14th c.

Vallibus
ROSE-TROUP, F. 'Vallibus family', *D.C.N.Q.* 22(1), 1942, 36-7.

Vanbrugh
MARSH, A.J. 'The Vanbrughs at Plymouth', *Devon historian* 39, 1989, 3-8.

Vanstone
TOMS, H.N.W. 'The surname Vanstone', *D.C.N.Q.* 33, 1974-7, 24. Medieval.

Varwell
'A history of Varwells of Brixham', *Family history* 7, 1973, 9-13.

Vassall
VASSALL, WILLIAM. 'The Vassall family and the Armada', *W.A.* 8(3), 1888, 45-6.

Vaughan
BRADNEY, JOSEPH A. 'Vaughan and Cecil', *M.G.H.* 5th series 6, 1926-8, 50. Of Bristol; pedigrees, 17-18th c., with will of Herbert Vaughan, 1694.
COLERIDGE, LORD. 'Vaughan of Ottery St. Mary', *D.C.N.Q.* 11, 1920, 40-1.
SKINNER, A.J. 'Vaughan of Ottery St. Mary', *D.C.N.Q.* 10, 1918-19, 98-109.

Veale
VEALE, M.J. 'A Veale history', *C.F.H.S.J.* 30, 1983, 13. Includes pedigree from 1590.

Veitch
HERIZ-SMITH, S. 'The Veitch nurseries of Killerton and Exeter', *Garden history* 16, 1988, 42-57 & 174-88. Veitch family, 18-20th c.

Venn
VENN, JOHN. *Annals of a clerical family, being some account of the family and descendants of William Venn, Vicar of Otterton, Devon, 1600-1621.* Macmillan, 1904.

Venner
VENNER, D. *The Venners of Somerset and Devon.* South Molton: the author, 1980.
WILKIN, W.H. 'Venner of Rose Ash', *D.C.N.Q.* 16, 1930-31, 155-9. Includes extracts from Rose Ash parish register, 17th c.

Verco
CALDICOTT, ARNOLD. *The Verco story: hopes we live by.* Adelaide: Halstead Press, 1970. Of Cornwall and Australia, 18-19th c.

Vilett
'The Society's mss., note 1: the Vilett family', *W.A.M.* 30(91), 1899, 221-9. Includes pedigree, 16-17th c.

Vincent
B[ARTELOT], R.G. 'Vincent family, Co. Dorset; Dewlish parish', *N.Q.S.D.* 23, 1942, 305. Notes from family Bible, 17-19th c.
See Wyeth

Virgo
VIRGO, W.C. 'On the Virgo trail', *C.F.H.S.J.* 36, 1985, 26-7.

Vivash
VIVASH, E.P. 'What's in a name?', *W.F.H.S.* 7, 1982, 22-3. Vivash family, medieval-17th c.

Vivian
COATE, M. 'The Vyvyan family of Trelowarren', *Transactions of the Royal Historical Society* 4th series 32, 1950, 111-9. 14-19th c.
EVANS, SHIRLEY, & HUMPHREYS, JUNE. 'The Vivians of Langton Herring', *J.D.F.H.S.* 8(3), 1995, 111. 18-19th c.
HUGHES, M.V. *Vivians.* Oxford: Oxford University Press, 1935. Reprinted 1980. 19th c.
MARTIN, EDWARD. 'The Vivians of Camborne', *C.F.H.S.J.* 14, 1979, 10-11. 17th c.
MEAD, C.J.H. 'The Vivian family', *D.C.N.Q.* 22, 1942-6, 255-8 & 265-7. 18th c.
MILLETT, VINCENT VIVIAN. 'Cornish connections? Roger Vivian and the master of the *Aleppo Merchant* (E.I.Co.)', *D.C.N.Q.* 29, 1962-4, 264-9. 17th c. Vivian and Millet families.
SAYER, M.J. 'Pedigrees of county families, 7', *Genealogists' magazine* 20(9), 1982, 308.
STEPHENS, WILLIAM J. 'Vivians of Truro and St.Crantock', *D.C.N.Q.* 8, 1914-15, 99-100. See also 9, 1916, 189-90. 16-17th c.
VIVIAN, J.L., ed. *Pedigree of the family of Vivian of Cornwall, reprinted with additions and alterations from the Visitations of Cornwall.* Exeter: William Pollard, 1887. Medieval-19th c.
VIVIAN, J.L. *Pedigree of Vivian, reprinted, with additions, from The Visitations of the County of Devon.* Exeter: William Pollard & Co., 1893. 14-19th c.
VIVIAN, STANLEY. 'Some ancient Vivians: a look into the origins of a Cornish, and now world-wide family', *C.F.H.S.J.* 51, 1989, 12. Medieval.

VIVIAN, STANLEY. *The story of the Vivians: a Cornish family through seven centuries at home and abroad.* Truro: the author, 1989. Includes pedigrees.

Vowell

HOLLOWAY, ESTELLE. *Elinor with the pleading eyes.* Melksham: E. Holloway, 1988. Vowell family, 15-20th c. Devon, Somerset & Norfolk.

'Prior Vowell and his Kinsmen', *N.Q.S.D.* 18, 1926, 10-11. Includes pedigrees 15-16th c.

Wadham

D., W. 'Wadham family', *N.Q.S.D.* 1, 1890, 101-2.

PESKETT, H.M. 'The Wadham family estates', *D.C.N.Q.* 31, 1968-70, 238-45. See also 32, 1971-3, 93-4. 14-18th c; of Wadham and Seaton, Devon, and Merifield, Somerset.

WYNDHAM, WILLIAM. 'The Wadhams and Merifield', *S.A.N.H.S.* 80(2), 1934, 1-10.

Wainwright

MITTON, A.W.D. 'Wainwright and Rawlinson families', *D.C.N.Q.* 32(5), 1972, 155. 18-19th c., of Lostwithiel.

Wake

WAKE, LINA. 'The Wakes of Dorset', *Dorset year book* 1975-76, 100-5. 11-19th c.

Wakeman

FETHERTON, JOHN. 'Wakeman pedigree, from the visitation of Gloucestershire 1583-1623', *M.G.H.* N.S., 2, 1877, 183-4. Medieval-17th c.

Walcot

WALCOT, M.G., & WALCOT, J. *The Walcots of Birmingham and Bristol: an account of a cadet branch of the ancient family of Walcot of Walcot and Bitterley Court, Shropshire.* Sutton Coldfield: the authors, 1975.

'Pedigrees from the visitation of Dorset, 1623: Walcot', *M.G.H.* 2nd series 2, 1888, 120-1.

Walker

'Dalison notes: Walker pedigree from visitation of Somerset, 1623', *M.G.H.* 2nd series 2, 1888, 241. Walker and Dalison families.

Wallis

PALMER, VICKY. 'Wallis/Slade marriages', *J.D.F.H.S.* 4(2), 1991 63. List, 17-19th c.

Wallop

WATNEY, VERNON JAMES. *The Wallop family and their ancestry.* 4 vols. Oxford: John Johnson, 1928. Extensive; includes pedigree of Wallop, medieval-19th c., and of over 1,000 related families.

Walrond

SKINNER, A.J. 'Family of Walrond of Bovey', *D.C.N.Q.* 11, 1920-21, 18-24. Walrond and Oke family extracts from the parish register, 18-19th c.

WALROND, CHARLOTTE. *The Walrond papers.* Arthur L. Humphreys, 1913.

SKINNER, A.J. 'Pedigree of the family of Walrond of Bovey in the parish of Seaton and Beer, County Devon', *D.A.Tr.* 39, 1907, 264.

See also Oke, Pitman, and Retter

Walter(s)

GRILLS, CLIFFORD T. *Bradworthy to the Barrabool Hills: the history of the Walter family.* Geelong: Henwood & Dancy, 1985.

JUDD, J.S. 'A Walter family at Winterslow', *W.A.M.* 53(190), 1949, 63-4. Pedigree, 16-17th c.

WALTERS, FRED. *The family of Walters of Dorset, Hants.* London & County Printing Works, 1907.

WALTERS, HENRY E. 'Additions to the Walters pedigree', *M.G.H.* N.S., 3, 1880, 252. Of Batheaston, Somerset; 19th c.

'Walters pedigree', *M.G.H.* N.S., 3, 1880, 226-7. Of Somerset and Surrey; 17-19th c.

See also Cottell

Walton

'Isaac Walton and his connexion with Wiltshire', *W.V.Q.* 4, 1902-4, 288-94 & 385-93. Includes wills, 17th c.

Wansbrough

DAWSON, FRANK. 'The Wansbroughs of Wiltshire', *W.F.H.S.* 4, 1981, 17-24. See also 24, 1987, 101-4; 25, 1987, 32-7. Includes pedigrees, 17-19th c.

Wansey

MANN, J.L. DE. 'A Wiltshire family of clothiers: George and Hester Wansey, 1683-1714', *Economic history review* 2nd series 9(2), 1956, 241-53.

Wanstrow

See Harding

Wapshat

VINCENT, MARTIN. 'The birth and death of a name', *W.F.H.S.* **9**, 1983, 14-15. Wapshat family, 17-18th c.

Warland

MOSS, O.P. 'The Warlands of Wimborne: emigrants to Australia', *J.D.F.H.S.* 2(1), 1989, 26-7; 2(3), 1989, 87-8. 18-19th c.

Warre

GIBSON, WILLIAM. 'A continuous patrimony: the Warres of Hestercombe & Cheddon Fitzpaine', *S.A.N.H.S.* **132**, 1987/8, 181-2. 14-19th c.

Warren

AMERY, J.S. 'The Warrens of Headborough and their descendants', *D.A.Tr.* **28**, 1896, 494-502.

See also Gundry

Washbourne

DAVENPORT, JAMES. *The Washbourne family of Little Washbourne and Wishenford in the county of Worcester.* Methuen & Co., 1907.

Washer

DAVID, DAVID S.S. *Our Washer forebears: a short history of the Washer family of Over Stowey and Cardiff.* Ottershaw, Surrey: privately published, 1995. Includes pedigree, 16-20th c.

Washington

DALE, T.C. 'The Dorset Washingtons', *N.Q.S.D.* **17**, 1923, 73-4. See also 146, 157-8, 198, & 226-7.

Way

STIRLING, A.M.W. *The Ways of yesterday: being chronicles of the Way family from 1307 to 1885.* T. Butterworth, 1930.

Waymouth

ATTWOOD, J.S. 'Waymouth and Rosier families', *W.A.* 5(12), 1886, 303-4.
WAYMOUTH, DAVID C.R. *The Waymouths: Devon venturers.* [ ], the author, 1996. Includes pedigrees, medieval-19th c.

Wearne

WEARNE-FROST, VALERIE. *Wearne of Cornwall and Australia, 1580-1980.* Sydney: Ballment, 1981. Includes pedigree.
Wearne Family History Society newsletter. Truro: the Society, 1984- .

Webb

HAMMOND, JOHN J. 'Webb of Great Canford, Dorset, and Odstock, Wiltshire', *N.Q.S.D.* **10**, 1907, 209-14.
See also Richmond

Weeds

AVERY, E.M. *Over the years.* Bognor Regis: New Horizon, 1983.

Weekes

WEEKES, ROBT. D. *Genealogy of the family of George Weekes of Dorchester, Mass., part II.* Newark, New Jersey: the author, 1892. Devon and Somerset.

Weights

H., A.W.C. 'The Weights of Clingre', *G.N.Q.* **6**, 1896, 63-5. 17-19th c.

Weld

BERKELEY, JOAN. *Lulworth and the Welds.* Gillingham: Blackmore, 1971. Includes pedigree, 16-19th c.

Wellesley

SEREL, T. 'The origin of the names of Wellesley and the early connection of the family with Wells', *S.A.N.H.S.* 12(2), 1863-4, 177-89. Medieval.

Welsh

See Merryweather

Were

FOX, J.H. *The woollen manufacturers at Wellington, Somerset, compiled from the records of an old family business.* A.L.Humphreys, 1914. Includes pedigrees of Were and Fox families, 17-19th c.

Wescombe

DODDERIDGE, S. E. 'Wescombe of Doddington, Co. Somerset', *M.G.H.* 5th series **1**, 1916, 155-7. 18-20th c.
DODDERIDGE, SIDNEY E. 'Westcombe, *alias* Wescombe, Cos. Somerset and Devon', *N.Q.S.D.* **10**, 1907, 252-9. See also 11, 1909, 329-32. 16-19th c.
'Pedigree of Wescombe of Fiddington, Co. Somerset', *M.G.H.* 5th series **1**, 1916, 276. 17-18th c.

Wesley

DAVIES, GLANVILLE J. 'John Wesly: (c.1636-1670)', *N.Q.S.D.* **30**, 1974-9, 55-60. See also 150-1.
DOVE, JOHN. *A biographical history of the Wesley family, more particularly its earlier branches.* Hamilton Adams & Co., 1840.

NOBLE, MARK. 'Pedigree of the Wesley family', *Reliquary* **8**, 1867-8, 188.

PEARSON, EDITH McCALL. 'The Wesley family and Dorset', *Dorset year book* 1973-4, 8-12.

RIGG, J.H. 'The ancestry of the Wesleys', *London quarterly review* **21**, 1864, 71-117.

STEVENSON, G.J. *Memorials of the Wesley family, including biographical and historical sketches of all the members of the family for two hundred and fifty years, together with a genealogical table of the Wesleys, with historical notes, for more than nine hundred years.* S. W. Partridge & Co., 1876.

West

HARGETION, JULIETTE. 'The Wests of Wiltshire', *W.F.H.S.* **35**, 1989, 16-18. Includes pedigree, 19-20th c

MEAD, C.J.H. 'The West family', *D.C.N.Q.* **22**, 1942-6, 221-3, 233-5 & 244-7. Mainly 18-20th c.

WEST, ARTHUR ANDERSON. *History of our West family: being a record of dates and events in connection therewith, compiled from family papers and public records.* Privately printed, 1893. Of Oxfordshire, Gloucestershire, Warwickshire, etc., includes pedigrees of many related families.

See also Mead

Westall

NOAD, L. MICHAEL. *A short history of Noad and Son, chartered surveyors ... founded 1820.* Chippenham: Noad & Son, 1980. Westall, Parry and Noad families' business

Westcombe

DODDERIDGE, SIDNEY E. 'Westcombe, *alias* Wescombe, cos. Somerset and Devon', *N.Q.S.D.* **10**, 1907, 252-9. 16-19th c.

Westcott

SKINNER, A.J. 'Captain George Blagdon Westcott', *D.C.N.Q.* **11**, 1920-21, 155-6. Westcott pedigree, 17-18th c.

Westover

See Courtenay

Whalesborough

JENNER, HENRY, & TAYLOR, T. 'The legend of the church of the Holy Cross in Cornwall', *J.R.I.C.* N.S. **20**, 1915-21, 295-309. Pilgrimage of Sir Robert Whalesborough, with pedigree of the Whalesborough family, 13-15th c.

See Trevelyan

Whatmore

WHATMORE, A.W. 'Marshwood House, Dinton', *W.N.Q.* **1**, 1893-5, 147-9. Whatmore family; 18th c.

WHATMORE, A.W. 'Whatmore of Wilton', *M.G.H.* 2nd series **4**, 1892, 193-4. Pedigree, 18-19th c., with wills.

WHATMORE, GEORGE. 'The Whatmores of Wilton', *W.F.H.S.* **13**, 1984, 4-7.

Whatton

WHATTON, HENRY WATKINSON, et al. *The family of Whatton: a record of nine centuries.* Sylvan Press, 1930. Reprinted from the *Gentleman's magazine* with additions.

Whetter

WHETTER, J.C.A. 'Five Cornish families in the 17th century', *Old Cornwall* **7**, 1967-72, 81-90. Whetter family.

Whight

B[ENSON], J. 'Whight: an adventure in pedigree construction', *D.C.N.Q.* **26**, 1954-5, 198-203. 16-19th c. pedigree.

Whipple

See Dearing

Whitaker

REEVES, MARJORIE. *Sheep bell and plough share: the story of two village families.* Bradford on Avon: Moonraker Press, 1978. Reprinted Granada, 1980. Whitaker and Reeves families of Bratton; includes pedigrees, 16-20th c.

REEVES, MARJORIE. 'A Wiltshire ancestry', *W.F.H.S.* **19**, 1985, 6-9. Whittaker family, 16-19th c.

Whitby

BURT, SAMUEL. 'Mudford and the Whitby Family,' *Somerset year book* **33**, 1934, 85-6. 16-19th c.

White

STARR, SYLVIA. 'Yatton carriers: the White family', *Yatton yesterdays* **5**, 1988, 30-33. 19-20th c.

WHITE, F. 'The Whites at Fittleford, Dorset', *G.T.* **5**(1), 18-19. Includes pedigree 16-18th c.

WHITE, GLADYS M. *The White family of Cornwall=Tykly Gwyn a Kernow.* Quinnesec, Mich.: the author, 1985.

See also Harington and Little

Whitefield

HUDLESTON, C. ROY. 'George Whitefield's ancestry', *B.G.A.S.T.* **59**, 1937, 221-42. Includes pedigrees of Whitefield and Dymer, 17-18th c., with will abstracts.

Whitford

POOLE, HARRY. 'The Cornish – and other – Whitfords', *C.F.H.S.J.* **36**, 1985, 27. Distribution of the surname, 1837-41.

POOLE, HARRY. 'Did Cornish Whitfords come from Flintshire?', *C.F.H.S.J.* **43**, 1987, 13.

Whitfield

'Genealogical notes of the families of Whitfield and Garland who were successively owners of the manor of Whitfield, in the parish of Marwood, Co. Devon, from the reign of King John down to 1710', in DRAKE, WILLIAM RICHARD, SIR. *Devonshire notes and notelets ...* Privately printed, 188-, 71-9. Includes folded pedigree, 15-18th c.

Whitlock

WHITLOCK, RALPH. *A family and a village.* John Baker, 1969. Whitlock family of Pitton 19-20th c.

Whitmore

WHITE, ELIZABETH. 'The Whitmores and the manor of Keynsham', *S.A.N.H.S.* **129**, 1984/5, 155-60. 17-18th c.

Whitson

LATIMER, JOHN. 'The alleged arms of John Whitson', *Proceedings of the Clifton Antiquarian Club* **5**, 1900-3, 268-76.

Whittier

FRENCH, ELIZABETH. 'Genealogical research in England: Whittier', *N.E.H.G.R.* **66**, 1912, 252-61. Whittier family of Wiltshire; includes wills, extracts from parish registers etc., 16-17th c.

Whittington

BUSH, THOS. S. 'Whittington of Cold Ashton', *G.N.Q.* **6**, 1896, 121-5. Parish register extracts.

MCGREGOR, MARGARET. 'A case history', *F.F.* **2**, 1990-91, 12-13. Whittington of Newland, Gloucestershire, 17th c.

WHITTINGTON, MICHAEL. *The Whittington story: from the three counties to the City.* Cirencester: the author, c.1988. Of Herefordshire, Gloucestershire, Worcestershire and London. Includes pedigree.

Whitworth

THOULD, TONY. 'Five generations of Whitworths in one general practice', *Cornwall Association of Local Historians journal* **26**, 1993, 8-13. 19-20th c.

Wibbery

See Prowse

Willcox

WILLCOX, HELEN RUTHERFORD. *The Willcox family: a family history ...* Ontario: Helen and Tod Willcox, 1993. 18-20th c., of Somerset, etc. Includes pedigrees.

Wille(t)ts

'The Willet family and Banwell Mill', *Search: journal of the Banwell Society of Archaeology* **15**, 1979, 54-62. Includes pedigree, 18-20th c.

'The Willets, or Willett, family', *G.N.Q.* **2**, 1884, 558-61. 16-18th c.

Williams

CHICK, E. 'Williams of Marnhull, Co. Dorset', *N.Q.S.D.* **22**, 1938, 194-8.

PALEY, GEOFFREY, ROWE, MARGERY M., & WYLIE, JOHN A.H. 'The Williams family, gold and silver-smiths of Bristol, and their association with the Exeter Assay Office', *D.C.N.Q.* **36**(1), 1987, 20-26. See also **36**(2), 1987, 69.

THOMAS, VIOLET A. 'The Williams family of Kamarooka: a sequel', *C.F.H.S.J.* **9**, 1978, 9-11. Kamarooka, Australia; originally of Sancreed and St.Just in Penwith. 17-19th c.

WILLIAMS, GEORGE W.F. *A short history of a Williams family: from the sixteenth century in Cornwall to the twentieth century in Australia.* Ulverstone, Tasmania: Jan Litchfield, 1990.

WILLIAMS, H. FULFORD. 'Three centuries in an Exeter family', *D.C.N.Q.* **29**, 1964, 149-52. Williams family.

'The family of Williams of Wotton-Under-Edge', *G.N.Q.* **5**, 1884, 92-6.

See also Berryman, Pitman and Ridington.

Willis

CHURCH, E. M. 'Willis-Drury', *N.Q.S.D.* **3**, 1893, 101. See also 133, 176-8, & 220-1.

Willougby

BODDINGTON, REGINALD STUART. 'Pedigree of the family of Willoughby', *Genealogist* **2**, 1878, 91-4. Of London and Wiltshire; 17th c.

PRIDEAUX, F.B. 'The descendants of Robert, 2nd Lord Willoughby de Broke', *D.C.N.Q.* **18**(1), 1934, 7-11. 16-19th c.

WILLOUGHBY, J.L. 'From Wilbie (Willbye, Willby, etc) to Willoughby in Cornwall', *D.C.N.Q.* **29**, 1962-4, 297. See also **30**, 1965-7, 199.

Wills

TILL, ROGER. *Wills of Bristol.* [ ]: [Imperial Tobacco Co.], [19--]. W.D. & H.O. Wills Co. Ltd., includes pedigree of family, 18-20th c. 'Narrow Combe documents', *D.C.N.Q.* **24**, 1950-51, 28-31, 70-72, 103-4 & 231-2; **25**, 1952-3, 56 & 84. 26 15-17th c. deeds, etc., relating to the Wills family, including the will of William Miller of Lustleigh, 1671.

Wilton

WILTON, ROBERT. *The Wiltons of Cornwall.* Chichester: Phillimore, 1989. Includes pedigrees, 16-20th c., list of marriages in Cornwall and Devon.

WILTON, R. 'The interchange of Wilton/ Wilkin/Wilkey surnames in Cornwall', *D.C.N.Q.* **33**, 1974-7, 211-6. 15-18th c.

WILTON, R. 'The origins of the Wilton surname in Cornwall', *D.C.N.Q.* **35**, 1982-6, 26-33. Medieval.

See also Parsons

Windham

CHALK, E.S., ed. 'Wyndham deeds', *D.C.N.Q.* 18(8), 1935, 383-4.

Windsor

LANE-POOL, RICHARD, SIR. 'The De Windsors of Broadwindsor', *N.Q.S.D.* **27**, 1961, 149-52.

Winsor

KNOWLING, E. 'The Winsors: a case in point', *D.F.H.* **63**, 1992, 9-12. 18-19th c.

Winstanley

See Carkeek

Wise

W., J. '[Wise]', *W.A.* **1**, 1881, 60-61. See also 85.

Withipoll

DUNLOP, J.R. 'Pedigree of the Withipoll family of Somersetshire, Shropshire, Essex, and Suffolk', *M.G.H.* 5th series **5**, 1923-25, 378-86. 15-17th c.

Withy

LEE, F.G. *Pedigrees of the family of Withie, Co. Devon, together with that of Fourdrinier in alliance with Grolleau.* Mitchell and Hughes, 1880. 17-19th c.

LEE, D. 'Pedigree of Withie, Co. Devon', *M.G.H.* N.S., **3**, 1880, 361-2. 15-17th c.

LEE, F.G. 'Pedigree of Withy of Berry Norbert and Westminster', *M.G.H.* N.S., **3**, 1880, 373-9. 17-19th c. Includes extracts from family bible.

Wolcot

EVA, WALTER H. 'Dr. John Wolcot (Peter Pindar)', *D.C.N.Q.* **24**, 1950-51, 21-2. See also **23**, 1947-9, 361-2, & **24**, 1950-51, 192-5. 18th c. genealogical notes.

Wolseley

See Trevelyan

Wood

FALCONER, J.P.E. 'Family of John Wood of Bath', *Notes & queries* **193**, 1948, 403-8. Includes pedigree, 18th c., monumental inscriptions, and will of John Wood of Walcot, 1753.

ROBINSON, C.J. 'Dr. Gerard Wood, Archdeacon of Wells', *N.Q.S.D.* **3**, 1893, 341. Genealogical information from the civil war proceedings of the Committee for Compounding with Delinquents.

'Wood of Harestone', *M.G.H.* 2nd series **3**, 1890, 206. Medieval-19th c., includes grant of arms, 1532.

See also Stukeley

Woodcock

WOODCOCK, TONY. 'The Woodcocks return', *Hampshire family historian* 15(4), 1989, 244-5. Of the Isles of Scilly; includes pedigree 18-20th c.

Woodforde

WOODFORDE, DOROTHY HEIGHES, ed. *Woodforde papers and diaries.* Peter Davies, 1932. Includes folded pedigree, 16-19th c.

Woodman

MORIARTY, G.ANDREWS. 'Genealogical research in England: the Woodman family', *N.E.H.G.R.* **97**, 1943, 281-6. Of Corsham, 16-18th c., includes wills and parish register extracts.

Woodroffe/Woodruffe

'Pedigree of Woodruffe of Plusterwine, Co. Gloucester', *M.G.H.* **2**, 1876, 378-83. See also 5th series **5**, 1923-5, 312. 15-19th c.

Pedigree of Woodroffe of Plusterwine, Co. Gloucester. Mitchell & Hughes, 1876. 15-19th c.

Woolcock

See Pye

Woolfe

JENKINS, R. 'A Cornish engineer: Arthur Woolfe, 1766-1837', *Newcomen Society transactions* **13**, 1934 (for 1932-33), 55-73.

Worth

M., J.H. 'Worth family', *D.C.N.Q.* **23**, 1947-9, 90-91 & 120-2. Marriage licences, 17-18th c.

Wotton

See Prowse

Wreford

WREFORD, GEORGE. *Pedigree and sketch of the Wreford family of Clannaborough and Morchard Bishop, Devonshire*. Vincent Brooks, Day and Son, 1888. Includes folded pedigrees, 17-19th c.

WREFORD, GEORGE. *Records and pedigree of the Wreford family of Devonshire*. 2nd ed. Doherty & Co., 1909. Includes pedigrees, 16-20th c.

Wrey

BENSON, J. 'Wrey of Trebigh', *D.C.N.Q.* **25**, 1952-3, 149-50. 16-17th c.

Wright

See Ridington

Wyatt

ROBERTS, JOHN. 'A note on the family of Wyatt of Braunton', *D.C.N.Q.* **29**, 1962-4, 282-5. 16th c.

BLOOM, J.H. 'Wyatt family', *M.G.H.* 6th series **8**, 1932-4, 49-53. Includes extracts from the parish register and manor court rolls of Priston, Somerset, together with wills.

Wyeth

'Wyeth and Vincent family bible', *M.G.H.* 5th series **8**, 1932-4, 331-2. 18th c., also includes entries for Cragg.

Wyke(s)

DEAS, NICHOLAS. 'The owners of the manor of Wyke Yatton, c. 1330-1356', *Yatton yesterdays* **8**, 1991, 23-6. See also **9**, 1992, 29-32. Includes medieval pedigrees of Wyke.

LEGA-WEEKES, ETHEL. 'William Wykes, 'First recorder of Exeter (14th. cent.) and Wykes, sheriff of Devon', *D.A.Tr.* **44**, 1912, 561-7.

WYKES-FINCH, W. 'The ancient family of Wyke of North Wyke, Co. Devon', *D.A.Tr.* **35**, 1903, 360-425.

See also Cocktree

Wyndham

HARVEY, W.J. 'Memoranda relating to the family of Wyndham of Norrington, of Salisbury and of Dinton, Co. Wilts., of Hawkchurch, Co. Dorset, of Eversley, Co. Hants., etc., 1609-1753', *M.G.H.* 2nd. series **4**, 1892, 36-8, 54-6, & 77-80.

WYNDHAM, AILWARD. 'Kentsford, Watchet and the Wyndham family', *N.Q.S.D.* **23**, 1942, 299-305.

WYNDHAM, H.A. *A family history, 1410-1688: the Wyndhams of Norfolk and Somerset*. Oxford University Press, 1939.

WYNDHAM, H.A. *A family history, 1688-1837: the Wyndhams of Somerset, Sussex and Wiltshire*. Oxford University Press, 1950.

'Memoranda relating to the family of Wyndham of Norrington, of Salisbury, and of Dinton, Co. Wilts., of Hawkchurch, Co. Dorset, of Eversley, Co. Hants, etc., 1609-1753', *M.G.H.* 2nd series **4**, 1892, 36-8, 54-6 & 77-80. From a diary.

See also Rawlins

Wynter

RENDELL, BRYAN, [ed.] *The Wynter family: (a collective research)*. Lydney: Whitecross School, 1988. 16-19th c.

RENDELL, B. *Wyntours of the White Cross: an extended family history*. White Cross: White Cross School, 1987.

Wyrall

HILL, MAY C. 'Wyrall lands and deeds', *B.G.A.S.T.* **63**, 1942, 190-206. Wyrall family, 17-19th c.

Wyse

RADFORD, G.H. 'The Wyses and Tremaynes of Sydenham', *D.A.Tr.* **41**, 1909, 131-51. 17-18th c.

Yarde

MORGAN, VAUGHAN. 'The Yardes of Whiteway', *D.F.H.* **2**, 1977, 12-14.

See also Bussel

Yea

MONDAY, ALFRED JAMES. *The history of the family of Yea ...* Taunton: G. Vincent, 1885. Of Somerset, Devon and Dorset.

Yeatman

YEATMAN, DENNIS. 'The Yeatman family of Stour Provost', *J.D.F.H.S.* **7**(2), 1994, 77; **7**(3), 1994, 117-18. 18-19th c.

Yeend

W., H. 'Yeend family', *G.N.Q.* **8**, 1900, 15-17. See also 33. Pedigree, 18th c.

Yeo

DEVONIA CORNWALL. 'Booksellers and printers in Devon and Cornwall', *D.C.N.Q.* 11, 1920-21, 156-8. Chiefly parish register extracts concerning the Yeo family of Exeter.

WALTER, R., & TOMS, H.N.W. 'An Exeter merchant in Spain', *D.C.N.Q.* **30**, 1965-7, 241-6. Yeo of Stratton, Cornwall, Totnes and Exeter, Devon.
See also Fox and Harington

Yeoman
See Harding

Yescombe

YESCOMBE, E.R. 'The Yescombe family', *J.B.A.* **37**, 1984, 15-19. 18th c.
'The Yescombe family: Yescombes of Blackford', *G.T.* **8**(2), 54-5. 16-18th c.

Young

MACLEAN, JOHN, SIR. 'Notes on the family of Yonge, or Young, of Bristol, and on the Red Lodge', *B.G.A.S.T.* **15**, 1890-12, 27-45. Includes pedigree, 14-17th c.
YOUNG, W.E.V. 'Notes on the Young family of Ebbesbourne Wake', *W.A.M.* **62**, 1967, 110-14. 16-20th c.
YOUNG, WALTER JORGENSEN. *The Young family of Bristol.* Fredericksburg, Virginia: Charles A. Carmichael, 1937. Also of the United States, 15-20th c.
See also Hooke

Author Index

118

119

121

Place Name Index

124

125

126